AGING EDUCATION

Teaching and Practice Strategies

Edited by
Nieli Langer
Terry Tirrito

University Press of America,® Inc.
Dallas · Lanham · Boulder · New York · Oxford

Copyright © 2004 by
University Press of America,® Inc.
4501 Forbes Boulevard
Suite 200
Lanham, Maryland 20706
UPA Acquisitions Department (301) 459-3366

PO Box 317
Oxford
OX2 9RU, UK

Library of Congress Control Number: 2003115464
ISBN 0-7618-2762-5 (paperback : alk. ppr.)

CONTENTS

FOREWORD

We are pleased to introduce you to *Aging Education: Teaching and Practice Strategies* because both the content and approach are ones we feel will help meet the needs of a growing aging population and their families. As it is inferred in the authors' preface, "the best way to learn is through teaching that fosters experiential learning." With the Baby Boom generation approaching older middle age and with the advances in health care extending the average life span, the U.S. population includes a rapidly increasing number of adults older than 65 and an unprecedented number of the oldest old (85 and older). The need and demand for professional health, mental health, and social service personnel with aging competence is growing. At the same time too few professional education programs provide specialized gerontology curriculum to their students or infuse aging content into their foundation courses for all students. There is also a limited amount of opportunity for continuing education in aging. Many of these professionals, even those working primarily with older adults, have had little formal education related to aging. Clearly, there is need for easily used, outcome based, and practical educational resources in gerontology for the educator and trainer.

Langer and Tirrito have done an excellent job in addressing a variety of critical practice issues for both academics and trainers of practitioners, and they do so in a thoughtful and comprehensive fashion. Our experience tells us that gerontology content often exposes students and practitioners to new, different, and sometimes difficult subject matter and this text takes an approach that addresses many of the thorny issues for effective professional education. That is, by using adult education theory, it makes use of learning strategies that encourage active, practical, and critical learning. The framework for each chapter provides teaching strategies, hands-on approaches or use of actual assessment forms and protocols. Instructors can adapt the chapter content to a variety of courses, projects and work settings. In fact, material in this text can be adapted to non-aging specific courses in order to help all students gain competency in aging that is needed by all health, mental health, and social service practitioners.

This text has been edited and written by a number of highly skilled people who bring a new, and a very useful resource to professional training and education.

Anita Rosen
Catherine Tompkins

PREFACE

*A*ging *Education: Teaching and Practice Strategies* is a text that attempts to meet the challenge of providing a teaching tool for the adult educator who teaches and trains students and care providers of the aging population in all the various instructional programs (gerontology/geriatrics degrees) and non-credit workshops currently offered in different settings (hospitals, nursing homes, professional associations, inservice training, etc.). Instruction is the best means for bringing about changes in the way we improve provision and distribution of services to the elderly. Educators need to clearly specify the outcomes or objectives they intend their instruction to accomplish and select and arrange learning experiences that will enhance realization of these objectives. Gerontology instructors and trainers can adapt the methodologies and learning experiences provided in the text to revise stereotypical attitudes, update skills, and gain current information about specific topics in the field of aging studies.

The discussion of what to teach and the rationale for its inclusion in a curriculum or training manual cannot be separated from exploration of how to teach it, especially for adult learners. In an article entitled Whither College Lectures? *New York Times*, 14 August 2002, William Honan described a speech presented by Hamilton Holt, President of Rollins College in Florida in 1931. President Holt astonished his colleagues with the statement that the lectures delivered by his professors and those by professors almost everywhere were examples of ... "probably the worst scheme ever devised for imparting knowledge." He then ridiculed the academic lecture as "that mysterious process by means of which the contents of the professor's notebooks are transferred by means of the fountain pen to the pages of the student's notebook without passing through the mind of either." Mr. Holt theorized that learning takes place when students are empowered to make personal discoveries alone, or with other students rather than when they are overwhelmed with facts and called upon to remember them at exam time. As an educational theorist with an institution where he could test his ideas, he was influential in positively altering the teaching/learning environments at the University of Chicago, Antioch, Bennington, and elsewhere.

This interest in reform teaching had its precedents in ancient Greece where Socrates believed in education by interrogating rather than by propounding. Although during the Middle Ages teachers were sole authorities on their disciplines, the interest in student-centered education was revived by Rousseau who argued that students learn best by doing rather than just listening. Rousseau predicted that the lecture format was destined to be displaced by readings, reports, and discussions with the teacher as facilitator offering guidance with questions, references, and other sources.

In the same article, Mr. Honan addressed remarks made by Dr. Judith Rodin, President of the University of Pennsylvania. Dr. Rodin anticipates a new generation of educators: "In the next 10 years, there will be much more flexibility in teaching modalities. The standard college lecture will be pretty much a thing of the past. The teacher of the future will be more of a mentor and less of a didactic lecturer."

Adult educators need to understand that just *hearing* is the least effective way of learning. Hearing, and *seeing* is better. And hearing and seeing and *doing* is best of all. *Thinking* about the underlying theory, *experimenting* to test out the explanation, *experiencing* what is actually taking place during the action and *reflecting* upon what took place and assessing its meaning enhances learning for the adult learner (Rosenblum 1985).

Since learners bring their unique developmental histories to the classroom, this necessitates the instructor's incorporation of multiple modes of learning. In addition, instructor's knowledge of why learners are engaged in the educational setting will make a difference in both the educational processes and outcomes. College students and gerontological case managers have different motivational reasons for participation. Because motivation for participation increases when learning involves issues relevant to learners, educators need to be alert to class members' reasons for participation. The environment in which teaching/learning occurs requires matching the program design with program goals and adjusting for participants' experience, learning styles, and needs.

The differences between the various teaching strategies are real and significant since each strategy implies a different emphasis on what is important in teaching. The transmission perspective is characterized by lecturing or transmitting facts, skills, and values, often associated with rote learning. In this educational perspective, the educator takes the lead role in information transmission. However, even if this is the most judicious method in a large classroom, participants may be physically present but cognitively absent. Since students are not actively involved, the transmission may not necessarily equate with learning for all students. Overhead transparencies are helpful for taking notes on complex information and the use of printed handouts that may include outlines help to see as well as hear the information especially when providing information on the specific policies and programs that have been established for the elderly.

Unlike the passive listeners in the transmission perspective, students are active participants in dialogue with the teacher in the transaction teaching strategy. The transaction perspective extends beyond the acquisition of skills and abilities. It allows learners to generalize their knowledge to other settings and the application of concepts in the field is easily accomplished. Using teaching activities generated from this educational perspective, facilitators and learners teach each other and both are responsible for the educational process. In addition, this perspective encourages a multicultural perspective since all participants and opinions are valued. Students who are unaccustomed to group participation or refuse to accept learning from peers may be uncomfortable with this learning environment. It is the educator's role to create a learning environment that encourages experimentation without fear of failure or reprisal. Teaching strategies that help develop cognitive skills while encouraging problem-solving include small and large group analyses of case studies. Family history assignments open the possibility that learners will see the value of sharing information between generations and help prepare them for the interviewing and counseling process they will be engaged in when working with elders, their families, and their social support networks.

The transformative learning perspective facilitates personal and social change (Miller and Seller 1990). In the learning strategies used in the classroom, students examine assumptions or challenge the validity of their beliefs and interpretations. This process encourages action learning. The activities applied in this process provide opportunities for learners to discuss dilemmas with others. Since the process provides a safe environment for learners to question their basic belief systems, it facilitates change and empowers learners. It challenges participants to scrutinize themselves, consider alternatives, and take action. Simulation exercises create a realistic context allowing learners to experience first hand the effects of aging. Reflection on the process may lead participants to new action and consequently new beliefs. In this andragogical model, the gerontology educator is a catalyst who provides structured activities that involve the student in learning while using a collaborative teaching model that acknowledges the adult learner as adjunct faculty with personal experience that can be applied to the topics in the curriculum.

The transformative perspective facilitates social and personal change; it is invaluable to the learning process and to its application with aging clients. Gerontology educators who incorporate this process in their teaching strategies anticipate learners will examine their beliefs (i.e., client's abilities), discern how their actions (i.e., proposed case management) are not working in specific situations, and formulate the decision to change (i.e., creative problem solving that makes the client an equal partner in his management).

While the behaviorist may seek to stress skills, the cognitive psychologist stresses the acquisition of information. Instructors who use an inquiry approach emphasize the reasoning process while those educators who favor using groups are more aware of the affective dimensions of learning. Regardless of the strategy used, all of the methodologies require clear objectives stated in precise behavioral terms. The objectives indicate what content and skills will be emphasized in the learning materials so learners can focus on what is important. In order to be effective as educational tools, the strategies require precision in communication. Each strategy requires that the instructor and adult learner have a clear sense of what is being undertaken, why it is being undertaken, and what the outcomes will be.

Each teacher will make the determination of which strategy to use based on: personal preference (an educational philosophy coupled with personal needs); the needs of the students (recognition that people learn in different ways); or the goals of the course or lesson (each strategy achieves slightly different goals). Matching the teaching strategy with the educational goals and students'/practitioners' needs are essential to maximizing participant learning. Not selecting a strategy is not an option! The effective teacher's approach to instruction is informed by how students learn since teaching is not talking and learning is not listening. Regardless of the rationale for the choice of the strategy, each teacher or trainer will always need to consider: 'Which students will learn 'what things with 'this strategy?

Adult learning theory is ideally suited to act as a vehicle for acquiring practice skills and knowledge, and thi s experiential learning process provides students with a paradigm for working with older clients. Michael Galbraith (1991) described the adult learning process as one of collaboration, support, respect, critical analysis, and challenge. In such a process the learners are empowered to make learning choices. These principles accurately describe an effective therapeutic alliance between care provider and older client where the client is involved in a collaborative relationship with the practitioner. Gerontological social work education has identified a need for learner-centered classroom environments that will impact the practice field. A curriculum that utilizes adult learning principles may be one vehicle for achieving this goal, producing practitioners who are capable of developing client-centered relationships with an older population.

Each chapter in the text addresses a specific topic relevant to the study of the aging population. Each provides state-of-the-art content and resources for instructors in addition to educational strategies applicable to the topic. Most of the educational modalities are easily adapted to use with other topics. Each of the chapters is followed by a commentary by the editors who have offered their own professional interpretation of the topic and/or experiential learning experiences.

References

Galbraith, M. 1991. *Facilitating adult learning.* Malabar, Florida: Krieger Publishing.
Miller, J.P. and Seller, W. 1990. *Curriculum perspectives and practice.* New York: Longman.
Rosenblum, S.H. 1985. *Involving adults in the educational process.* San Francisco: Jossey-Bass.

Chapter Summaries

Programs and Services for Older Adults: A National and Internaitonal Focus by Terry Tirrito: Home health and community care services are important components of a comprehensive long-term care system. Social workers, geriatric nurses, geriatricians, geropsychiatrists, case managers, and nutritionists are some of the professional practitioners who serve older adults by utilizing the informal and formal support networks to help many older people remain in their own homes and communities. The activities and strategies described in this chapter will support the efforts of educators and practitioners to develop and enhance skills and attitudes that meet the needs of individuals for personal freedom and self-expression while balancing the goals of informal and formal institutions to provide care.

Strategies for Teaching Aging Social Welfare Problems and Policies by Julie Miller-Cribbs: This chapter explores some of the major problems faced by older persons in the areas of finance, health care, and independent living, and describes policies that address these areas. The multiple teaching strategies are applicable to various sites and levels of service and address the composition and needs of a culturally diverse older population.

Teaching the Adult Learner about 'Mental Health Issues in Aging by Vicki Murdock: The chapter focuses on training professionals to recognize and help older adults to come to terms with and incorporate age-related changes into how they view themselves and their roles in the world. It provides a discussion of the implications of those mental health problems requiring comprehensive assessment to determine the older person's service needs. Students will learn to be proficient in the use and value of different assessment tools. Placing students in the client's role may sensitize them to the discomfort elders may feel when they are the focus of the interview. This format is effective in building competent interview skills and learning appropriate ways of asking questions in different cultural settings. The chapter provides numerous strategies that can be revised to accommodate many levels and learning needs.

Families and Aging: Alzheimer's Disease Spousal Caregiver Support Group by Gil Choi: Although changes have occurred in the American family, the family is the basic support system for most older Americans. The type of family support an older person receives depends to a great extent on his/her family situation—whether married, widowed, separated, divorced, never married, has living children, is living alone, living with adult children, or living with other relatives. The chapter explores the physical and emotional challenges faced by spouses who provide care to their partners suffering from Alzheimer's disease. An educational intervention model is presented that provides for the behavioral and emotional needs of care providers.

An Approach to Teaching Spirituality for Practice with the Older Adult by Larry P. Ortiz and Melissa B. Littlefield: Spiritual well-being is the affirmation of life in a relationship with God, self, community, and environment that nurtures and celebrates wholeness. From this perspective people can be spiritual without being religious. The spiritual dimensions of health have been examined and some practitioners view spiritual well-being as very important to an older person's physical and mental health. As an increasing number of older adults live longer lives, there has been increased interest in including spirituality in the bio-psycho-social model of assessment and treatment of the problems they encounter. This chapter reviews terms relating to the concept of spirituality and offers a spirituality mini-assessment protocol that may be used by social service and health care providers who work with older adult clients. This type of assessment protocol can be used to help older adults identify their individual sources of spirituality that empower them to provide meaningful interpretations of their lives.

Education about Dying, Death, Grief and Loss: Principles and Strategies by Kenneth J. Doka: As human beings we grieve our own personal losses. As professionals working in social service/health care positions, we encounter terminally ill patients and their families experiencing a variety of emotions and feelings during the progression of an illness and impending loss. The chapter provides sensitively designed educational strategies designed to help students and practitioners reach a conscious awareness of thoughts, feelings, attitudes, and values associated with dying, death, grief, and loss.

Act III: Maximizing Choices in Retirement by Nieli Langer: The concept of retirement as we've known it is obsolete. Across the nation, millions of older active Americans are retiring old notions of what it means to be retired. The combined effect of the senior boom and the birth dearth in America is creating a senior population of retirees who, with the gift of longevity and the added years it brings, are rethinking and revitalizing their lives. They are reinventing retirement—trying new careers, launching new businesses, volunteering, and returning to school while simultaneously taking stock of their social, financial, and health care needs. This chapter is primarily concerned with how the retirement counselor can address the major concerns facing older adults in stages of pre-retirement and retirement.

Senior Volunteers: Staying Connected with the Community by Nina Dubler Katz: Retired elders are often discussed as a great sea of untapped volunteers. Studies have shown that older volunteers can be counted on to perform well on an ongoing basis. However, how to motivate volunteers who sincerely wish to commit to either rigid or flexible schedules of volunteer activities will require the types of adult learning strategies that are described in this chapter.

Elder Abuse: Policy and Training For Law Enforcement Personnel by Nieli Langer and Tan Kirby Davis: Law enforcement and criminal justice professionals need to be key players in every community's effort to prevent and address elder abuse, neglect, and exploitation. But in order for law enforcement and criminal justice professionals to coordinate their efforts, the elder abuse network needs to partner with them to develop appropriate training and technical assistance. This chapter provides resources and strategies that are currently in place to maximize law enforcement participation in these efforts.

Gericare Specialist©: An Educational Response to the Elder Home Care Crisis by Jane M. Cardea, Jane F. McGarrahan and Bernice C. Brennan: This chapter describes the strategies for training marginally employable individuals, p articularly disenfranchised homemakers and minority or economically disadvantaged women, as providers of professional, in-home care of medically-frail or physically/mentally challenged elder clients unable to manage independent living activities. Competencies in communication, assessment, observation, personal care, and management skills enable these individuals to function as both a companion and a caregiver to an older person living at home. The systematic creation of a new paraprofessional health care provider will infuse the current inadequate cadre of personnel willing and able to provide services to an ever-growing number of older adults.

ॐ

To the extent that this book advances teachers', students', and practitioners' capacity to understand and serve the elderly by providing imaginative and thought-provoking teaching and practice strategies for adult learners, we believe that we may contribute to the quality of life and care of older persons. Aging patients and clients can reap the benefit from professionals who have had teaching experiences that encourage personal change and offer opportunities to develop cognitive abilities and skills useful in problem solving situations relevant to older adult needs.

Nieli Langer
Terry Tirrito

1

PROGRAM AND SERVICES
FOR OLDER ADULTS:
A NATIONAL AND
INTERNATIONAL FOCUS

ಸಿಂ಄

Terry Tirrito

The longevity revolution promises to redefine aging and to create programs and services that will in some respects resemble the current continuum of services yet differ in order to reflect the next cohort of older persons, the Baby Boomers. While today's programs and services tend to focus on the "d-words" as described by Hagestad (1999)... "decline, dementia, dependency, disease, disability...disaster and deluge," the author hopes that future older generations will focus on the "h-words": ... "health, happiness, hope, help, harmony, humane, home, hardy, haughty, and heroic."

It has been suggested that the marker for old age is changing; chronological age will cease to be that marker. In a national survey of 3,048 adults of all ages, it was reported that 41% of the respondents saw physical decline as a marker for old age. Thirty-two percent saw mental decline as the marker and only 14% considered a specific age as the indicator of old age. Interestingly, 33% of those persons who were 70 years of age and older saw themselves as middle-aged and 45% of persons aged 65 to 69 years portrayed themselves as middle-aged (Takamura 2001). Changes are taking place in attitudes about aging, too. Contrary to the myth that younger persons do not respect older persons in the United States, researchers have found that over 80% of persons of all ages believe that older people are not accorded the respect they deserve (Takamura 2001). The social meanings of aging will be influenced by a number of variables. The largest elderly population in the history of the world will certainly change the structure and processes of the service delivery systems worldwide. Advances in communication technology will permit sharing of knowledge from countries worldwide in pursuit of the most effective service delivery systems possible.

The possibilities and opportunities for teaching about aging programs and services are far-reaching. Teaching students and preparing professionals to plan, develop, and manage programs and services for older persons requires that they have an understanding of the current state of services, can critically analyze them, and develop the skills to provide effective and competent programs to meet future needs while enhancing the quality of life for the current cohort of older persons.

This chapter will present the methods the author has developed in ten years of teaching about programs and services for older adults. In teaching any course, an effective instructor creates/modifies the materials and methods of instruction each time the course is taught in light of new advances and student/professional needs. The successful teacher learns from students, retools the objectives and course outline, and incorporates new teaching/learning strategies that will further promote the behavioral objectives of the course. The instructor must have current knowledge about the topics and issues that impact upon the target population studied, i.e., the elderly. The instructor learns about the existing programs from students, practitioners, colleagues, journals, newspapers, and books in the field. The wise instructor is one who learns while teaching and enjoys the challenge of trying new teaching methods to help students develop skills, values, and knowledge. In this chapter, information is presented on public support and health programs, housing initiatives, faith-based programs, educational programs, protective and legal services, and programs that encourage intergenerational problem solving. In addition to teaching activities, there is a description of recommended web sites and information on videos that have recorded reality-based service delivery specific topics. Teaching about programs and services for older persons provides an opportunity to view and explore the future of aging with students and professionals.

Programs and Services

Public support programs for older adults differ in each country but they are universally becoming increasingly expensive. S. Korea and Singapore are attempting to move from public support of older persons to mandatory family support of older persons (Global Ageing Report 1996). In the United States the costs of publicly supported programs such as Social Security, Medicare, Medicaid, and programs mandated by the Older Americans Act of 1965 are soaring. In Australia and New Zealand and in some European countries, public-supported programs are varied and more comprehensive than in the United States. Underdeveloped countries are at the beginning stages of public support programs since families continue to be the traditional means of support. Underdeveloped countries such as China and S. Korea are developing pension plans for retirement support.

Health care costs for the increasing number of older persons are a major expenditure in most countries. Long-term care at home or in nursing homes is a crucial component of healthcare services for older persons; the costs for these services are rising at alarming rates as is the cost of prescription drugs in the United States. The Insurance Association of America has a web site where consumers can find information about long-term care insurance. However, private insurance for long-term care is currently in its infancy (http:// www.hiaa.org/library/iguides/ltc.html). Australia, for instance, offers government funded home care packages (Gibson et al 1996).

Various types of housing in the U.S. are available for older persons, i.e. age-segregated retirement communities, assisted living centers, granny flats, home sharing, adult foster homes, residential care facilities, and a variety of private housing arrangements. The cost of nursing homes under Medicaid financing is a burden for state governments even though only five percent of older persons at any one time reside in nursing homes in the United States; nursing home placement is not a preferred choice of housing by older persons.

Hospice care is a program that provides services to the terminally ill. Day care programs offer short-term help with medical and social services and some respite from care giving responsibilities. Home health care services are extensive in some countries i.e., Australia, fledgling in North America, and almost non-existent in Asian countries. Social services both in the United States and other countries are provided by both senior centers and religious organizations. Programs that protect older persons from abuse and exploitation differ in each country and even in each of the fifty states in the United States.

Recreation and leisure activities enhance quality of life and older persons are involved in travel, sports, computer activities, and non-traditional hobbies such as skydiving, scuba diving, parasailing, mountain climbing, etc. Senior centers are common places for recreational activities in America. Family centers serve the same function in Europe, Asia, Australia, and New Zealand. Educational programs for older persons include returning to the classroom in pursuit of university programs or personal recreational advancement provided in learning in retirement centers (LRC) or elder hostels. Finally, intergenerational programs explore the mutually beneficial activities that enhance the lives of all generations.

Publicly-Supported Programs

In the United States, the Social Security Program remains in jeopardy of not meeting the future needs of the increasing number of older retired persons (CBS News | Hard Decisions On Social Security | January 15, 2003 13:57:53). Australia provides publicly-funded pensions to older persons. In addition to the public pension, Australia has a compulsory Superannuation System which facilitates the accumulation of private savings for retirement. The Superannuation Guarantee legislation requires employers to provide a minimum level of Superannuation support for employees earning $450 or more per month or become liable to pay a Superannuation Guarantee Charge. Employers are required to make contributions equivalent to 6% of an employee's earnings; contributions will reach 9% during 2003. As a result, Australians have a much higher retirement income than one could expect with an age pension. The Australian age pension was introduced in 1909 to provide a safety net for older people who are unable to support themselves. The Australian age pension is a flat rate. It is a non-contributory payment funded from general revenue and not linked to previous labor force participation. It is income and asset-tested and intended for the indigent. The age pension is payable to men at age 65 and to women at age 61. With the increasing number of older persons, Australians are encouraged to save for retirement (Australian Institute of Health and Welfare 1997). Public-supported pensions are unstable and are in flux in countries such as Chile, Argentina, the United States, and Germany.

Health Care Programs and Services

Long-term care provides services for those who are medically frail. They include nursing home, in-home, respite, day care, and caregiver supports. In the United States, Medicare, a national health insurance program for older persons, is linked to Social Security payments. Those persons who are eligible for Social Security payments are eligible for Medicare coverage. This health insurance program provides financial assistance to adults over 65 years of age who contributed to the Social Security System, those entitled to Social Security disability payments for 24 months or more, and those persons with end-stage kidney disease.

Medicare insurance is divided into two parts, A and B. Part A is funded by employee and employer contributions. Each pays 1.45% of payroll, and self-employed persons pay 2.9%. Part B is funded by monthly premiums paid by the beneficiaries and general fund revenues. Premiums cover about 36% of the costs and federal funds cover the remainder. All persons who are eligible for Social Security benefits or Railroad Retirement benefits are eligible. There is no cost for Part A, but those who participate in Part B pay a monthly premium ($58.70 in 2003) and an annual deductible for physician services. Part A covers costs associated with hospitalization and some post-hospitalization, skilled nursing facility care, home health care, hospice care, and blood transfusions. Part A pays for hospital services (90 days per benefit period), skilled nursing care (100 days following a 3-day hospital stay), home health care services, and hospice care. Part B pays for the costs of physician services, outpatient hospital services, medical equipment and supplies, some rehabilitation services, blood tests, urinalysis, blood transfusions, and some ambulatory surgical services (Wacker, Roberto, and Piper 1998). Older adults can supplement Medicare insurance by purchasing "medigap" insurance policies that are designed to pay deductible, co-payments, and the remaining 20% of the charges for physicians and hospitals that Medicare does not pay.

Medicaid provides medical assistance for low-income families and individuals, and state and federal governments jointly fund the program; it is a means-tested program. Each state develops its own range of services and eligibility requirements and, therefore, programs vary from state to state. Since each state determines eligibility guidelines, the state also determines coverage. Basic services are inpatient and outpatient hospital services, physician services, nursing home services, health clinics, home health care, laboratory and X-rays, dental services, drugs, optometrist services, and prosthetic devices. States can require beneficiaries to enroll in managed care plans. Delaware, Florida, Hawaii, Illinois, Kentucky, Maryland, Massachusetts, Ohio, Oklahoma, Oregon, Rhode Island, Tennessee, and Vermont have established inclusive managed care Medicaid programs (Wacker, Roberto, and Piper 1998).

Managed care programs i.e., health maintenance organizations (HMOs) in the United States have multiplied to control rising costs of health care. Managed care is defined as the effort to coordinate, rationalize, and channel the use of services to achieve desired access, service, and outcomes while controlling costs (Wacker, Roberto, and Piper 1998). HMOs provide managed care that includes comprehensive health services at a fixed cost. The advantages of managed care include a wide range of services in exchange for a small co-payment. The drawbacks to managed care are restrictions on services and physicians and cost denial of services by insurance companies. A Web site for additional information is http://www.ghc-hmo.com/abt_main.htm

While Australians over age 65 represent only 12% of the total population, they spent 35% of the 31 billion dollars in total expenditures for health services in 1993-1994. Health expenditures for persons over 65 years of age were 3.8 times higher than for those under 65 years. In Australia, one type of home care program is the brokerage-type or home-based care-community packages in which a person can purchase services as needed with government funding (Australian Institute of Health and Welfare (AIHW) 1997). Germany instituted a lump sum payment for caregivers with restrictions that services not be purchased in public programs, and that health care costs not include nursing home care. Long-term care, whether home-based or institutional, is an indispensable component on the continuum of healthcare services for older persons.

Nursing Homes

The quality and cost of nursing home care have been studied extensively over the last two decades. Nursing homes are heavily regulated to protect patients from emotional, physical, and financial abuses. However, nursing home abuses are still rampant. The failure of long-term care settings to aggressively address problems related to mental health remains a serious omission in their delivery of services (Cohen 1997). Older adults fear losing their independence because this major loss is a prime risk factor for nursing home placement. An ordinary nursing home does not feel like home. It is an amalgam. From the investor's perspective, it is a financial corporate entity. From the state regulator's perspective, it is a medical facility. From staff perspective, it is a labor- intensive workplace. Only for residents does it purport to be a home. The American value system has always placed a premium on self-reliance; those who could not make the grade were viewed with pity and disdain. However, dependency is a social reality. It is a by-product of industrialization. The tension between autonomy and dependency has special significance for the elderly and especially those who need nursing home placement. Nursing homes are total institutions that provide care for individuals who are incapable of self-care. Staff in nursing homes must conform to institutional demands for efficiency, cost-effectiveness, and uniformity. The needs of the individual for personal freedom and self-expression must be balanced with the needs of the institution to provide care. Nursing homes are an accepted mechanism to provide maintenance during old age. People are living longer and their physical conditions can be managed for many more years. An older population, with chronic physical problems remains in the community when social supports exist. Once these "old old" also become afflicted with a mental condition, and the social supports can no longer provide service, this population becomes nursing home patients. Therefore, an older and greater impaired senior population now makes up the resident population in nursing homes; greater custodial care is needed to accommodate their needs and the impact of total institutionalization is felt.

Some newer facilities are referred to as memory care residences. These facilities are small, intimate, and personal. They are structured to meet the individual needs of Alzheimer's patients. Circular walkways permit the residents to wander freely. Evaluation has shown that residents in these specialized facilities have slower rates of deterioration than those being cared for in conventional nursing homes. In addition, the operational costs are reported to be 20% lower than those incurred in traditional nursing homes (Global Aging Report 1997). However, these facilities often are private pay and access is limited to those who can afford them; rates average about $2000/month (2002 dollars).

Hospice Care

Hospice care began in the Middle Ages when monks cared for people dying in the streets. In England, St. Christopher's Hospice was founded in 1967 by Dame Cicely Saunders; it is the model for today's hospice. The

Saunders's book, *Hospice Care on the International Scene* (1997) is recommended for additional information about hospice programs in Africa, the Americas, Australia, Europe, Asia, and the Middle East. In 1973, there were no hospice programs in the United States; there are currently over 2000 programs. While there was public interest in improving terminal care, financial support was a major obstacle when hospice became a Medicare-funded option in 1982, with an emphasis on home care rather than institutional care. The goal of hospice is to provide terminally ill patients maximum care and comfort in their homes. However, requirements for eligibility can be barriers to service. For example, a patient must be certified by a physician to be terminally ill with only six months to live; a caregiver's presence in the home is another requirement that presents an obstacle for some patients. Hospice programs are underutilized and often market their services directly to the public.

Respite Services

Although respite services vary widely, the need for these services is recognized worldwide. Respite is defined as a period of temporary relief from pain, work, duty, etc. (Geralink 1974). The increased participation of women in the labor force, higher rates of divorce, family breakdown, increases in the number of single family households, the aging of major immigrant groups, and changes in lifestyle and patterns of disability are changing traditional methods of care and assistance. Women, who traditionally provided care for the frail, ill, or dependent parent or spouse, are no longer able to manage care and career responsibilities. The help of extended family members is often not an option when extended family members are also working and residing at a distance from the frail person.

In Australia, respite services are widespread with an active Carers' Association involved in policy making decisions. The Home and Community Care Program provides a variety of services which include respite care, a carer's pension payable to persons caring full-time for a person with a disability, and a Domiciliary Nursing Care Benefit paid to carers of people who require nursing home care. With this benefit, a carer can place a person in a nursing home for respite care for any number of days each year. The Australian government in 1991 increased nursing home bed days by 146% when respite care was offered to care providers. While there was an increase in respite service use in hostels (residential care facilities), less than 50% of approved respite bed days were actually used (Gibson et al 1997).

While Australia has an extensive national program for respite, the United States has fragmented services with modest federal or state support. Three types of respite programs are available in the United States: in-home respite care, adult day care, and institutional care. Volunteer respite programs include the Visiting Nurse Association and Senior Companion Programs. Adult day care programs offer short-term relief from daily care giving responsibilities. Institutional settings provide respite services in private nursing homes, hospital-based nursing homes, and the Veterans' Hospitals. Caregivers usually pay out of pocket for institutional respite care, and respite programs are not available in many areas.

Home Health Care Services

While it is widely accepted that older persons prefer to remain in their own homes and that home care service avoids premature institution-alization, home care services remain difficult to access in addition to being expensive; public funding for this service is minimal in the United States. Home care services include meal preparation, medical attention, house-keeping services, social services, nursing services, and mental health services. Although private and public home care agencies are available to provide these services, in addition to costs, both quality of care and avail-ability of trained and appropriate care providers remain major obstacles to the consumer.

Mental Health Programs

Community mental health programs provide inadequate geropsychiatric services to persons in need. The nursing home remains the primary site for psychiatric treatment for older adults with mental health problems. Estimates indicate that 50-80% of dementia patients are placed in nursing homes. In the over 65 age group, fewer than 2% visit private psychiatric offices, and only 4-6% visit community mental health clinics (Wacker, Roberto, and Piper 1998). Crisis intervention, case management, group therapy, case consultation, and day treatment are primary therapeutic interventions. The sheer number of elderly in the next decades will mandate the need for geropsychiatric specialists.

Adult Day Care Programs

Adult day care programs are considered an alternative to nursing home placement. These programs utilize either a medical or a socialization model. The medical model provides health care services, physical therapy, nursing care, and social services. In the socialization model, social and recreational activities are the focus. Adult day care programs can provide a temporary alternative to nursing home placement. These programs commonly are used as respite for family members as well as socialization and medical care for the older frail adult.

Housing Programs

Housing options for older persons are diverse and include age-segregated retirement communities, assisted living houses, granny flats, home sharing, adult foster homes, residential care facilities, and other private arrangements. Granny flats are self-contained housing units (i.e., mobile homes) located near the home of a family member. These units are sometimes called Elder Cottage Housing Opportunity (ECHO). This type of housing allows the older adult to live with or near families but insures privacy and independence. Congregate housing includes apartments or houses with shared facilities for meals and recreation. There are variations of congregate housing units from the house, to the apartment, to the single room. Continuing care retirement communities (CCRCs) provide a full range of housing options from independent living to nursing home care. One type of housing is the Assisted Living Center. In Assisted Living Centers, services can range from personal care to some nursing care. Some centers offer social services, nursing, and access to medical services; others offer supervision and care for cognitively impaired persons. Fees range from $1000 to $3000 per person/month (Wacker, Roberto, and Piper 1998). Public payments can be in the form of a Medicaid Waiver. Private payment is the most frequent source of payment. While less costly than nursing homes, the assistance provided in this type of facility is minimal. Potential problems are high costs and lack of oversight by government agencies. Board and care homes are another type of living arrangement for frail older persons. Boarding homes are privately owned or managed by large corporations. Adult foster care is an option for older persons who need the support and security of family living (Wacker, Roberto, and Piper 1998).

Residents in foster care homes are more likely to be residents with mental illness, mental retardation, and/or physical ailments.

While the multigenerational family has been the traditional provider for housing in many countries, change is expected in this pattern. For example, in Singapore projections indicate that in 2030 one million people aged 60 and older will comprise 26% of the population, while in 1990 only 9% were over 60 years of age. The older, vulnerable adult is the responsibility of the family. Singapore has a vigorous economy, the absence of slums or poor housing, and a lack of conspicuous poverty. Literacy rates at 99% are the highest in the world. The government encourages aging parents and young couples to live together or nearby. Priority for rental apartments is given to parents and children who live near one another. With falling birthrates and greater longevity, families may not always be able to support the needs of older family members. Special housing for seniors who live alone is the exception in Singapore (Harrison 1997).

Israel is a welfare state that assumes responsibility for the well-being of its older population. The government is involved in education, health, housing, employment, and personal care services. While the government maintains responsibility for housing, there is a shift toward privatization of housing. In 1948, persons over the age of 65 constituted 5% of the population; in 1997, well over 9.5% of the population was 65 or older. In a government study, over 75% of those surveyed were satisfied with their public-supported homes, and over 82% owned their own homes. The government is committed to a policy of aging in place and has instituted a number of services in each community in order to maintain this policy. These services include comprehensive medical services, mobile laundry service, meal distribution, an emergency call service, day care centers, provision of medical equipment such as wheelchairs, and personal counseling. The local authorities receive a budget from the Ministry of Labor and Social Affairs to finance repairs and improve the physical condition of homes of the elderly. The Ministry of Housing provides financial assistance to purchase homes for elderly persons who meet eligibility criteria. The government also provides subsidized rents for public housing. There is partial or full coverage for nursing home fees. Multigenerational housing complexes and housing for the elderly have been constructed in the kibbutzim. In the kibbutz, the lower floors are occupied by the elderly and the upper floors by families with children. Elderly persons who live in a kibbutz receive housing, meals, medical services, and nursing care. However, with the growing number of older persons, there is a shortage of housing for elderly persons in Israel (Katan and Werczberger 1997).

In South Korea, the aged population is growing dramatically while the tradition of supporting elderly parents is diminishing. In 2021, S. Korea expects its older population to be 13.1% of the total population. S. Korean families maintain traditional family values; 74% of adult children living with their parents consider this living arrangement to be their responsibility. However, only 13.9% of these adult children stated that they wanted to live with their children when they were older. Attitudes are changing and the tradition of children supporting their elderly parents is vanishing. There are free homes for the poor aged and free nursing homes for anyone who needs placement. Private homes and private nursing homes for the aged are on the rise. Housing prices in S.Korea have continuously increased at higher rates than consumer prices; land is scarce. The government is encouraging the building of *silver towns*, which are privately owned homes for the aged with medical care available for the residents. Over 74.5% of those over 65 years of age prefer to live in retirement communities rather than with their children (Kim 1997). S. Korea is at the beginning stages of senior housing development (Kim 1997).

In India, the elderly prefer to live with their children. Sons are responsible for the care of their parents. In 1991, India had a population of approximately 844 million. In 2000, the elderly population was 75.9 million. India has more elderly people than the total population of eleven countries including Iran, Egypt, Turkey, Thailand, Ethiopia, Germany, and France. In India, the majority of the population lives in rural areas where the family provides physical, social, and economic support for the aged members of their household. The care of elderly parents is based on mutual exchange over the lifetime. While the majority of older persons live with their children, 12,758,610 persons, or 30%, have no families to live with or cannot live with their families. For this group, old age homes are needed. Most old age homes are public charities. The existing number of homes available is not sufficient to meet the needs of older persons who need care (Kara 1997).

Denmark has changed its housing policies in the past fifteen years. Nursing homes are no longer being built. Staying home is the goal with support by home nursing care, given to everyone free of charge and according to need. Fifteen percent of the population is over 65 years of age, or 793,000 of a population of 5,213,000 persons. Families are smaller. Most elderly people live alone. There is little potential for informal care from daughters as most are in the labor market. Only 7% of the elderly live in institutions. Elderly Danes have economic resources and want to live an independent and secure life in retirement (Lindstrom 1997).

Japan's older population is increasing at phenomenal rates and the country is facing a housing problem. In 2020, over 30% of the population will be over 65 and the birth rate is declining; it was 1.43 in 1995. In 1969, paired apartments were constructed to enable elderly persons to live next door to their children. In 1975, large apartments were permitted to enable parents and children to live together. Children are moving to large cities, and elderly persons prefer to live independently in their neighborhoods. While policy over the last forty years has encouraged more housing for aged persons, a more recent plan has encouraged the construction of barrier-free independent living environments that can be used over the life course (Kose 1997). The issues confronting Japan today are pensions, long-term care, housing policies, and the legal system as it affects the elderly.

Social Support Programs and Services

Senior centers provide community social activities for older Americans. Family centers serve the same function in Europe, Asia, Australia, and New Zealand. According to the National Institute of Senior Centers, senior centers are based on the philosophy that: Aging is a normal developmental process; that human beings need peers with whom they can interact and who are available as a source of encouragement and support; and, that adults have the right to have a voice in determining matters in which they have a vital interest. As such, the center is a major community institution whose mission is to foster good mental health and to prevent the breakdown and deterioration of mental, emotional, and social functioning of the older person (Wacker, Roberto, and Piper 1998, 115).

In the United States, senior centers were created in 1965 with the passage of the Older Americans Act (OAA). In 1973, the OAA mandated that, with a new Title V program, senior centers are authorized to provide nutritional services for older persons. Seniors receive meals at congregate meal sites or can have meals delivered to their home sponsored by the Meals on Wheels program. Multipurpose senior centers deliver a range of services. Between 5 and 8 million older adults attend senior centers (Waker, Roberto, and Piper 1998). The participants are usually female and live alone or with a non-relative. About twenty years ago, senior center participants were in their sixties. The average age of current participants is

80+. A younger cohort of older adults does not participate in senior center activities and older adults of color are even less likely to attend senior centers. A national sample of recreation and senior center directors estimated the percentage of their participants by ethnic group and reported that 8% of older African Americans participate; older Hispanics, 5%; and, Asian and Native Americans, 2% (Wacker, Roberto, and Piper 1998). Some centers reach out to specific groups. A senior center for gay men and lesbians is the Gay and Lesbian Outreach to Elders Senior Center (GLOE). In some ethnic areas of San Francisco, New York, and New Mexico, senior center participants are primarily Chinese, Japanese, African American, or Native American.

Programs offered at senior centers vary from community services to group and individual programs. The centers sponsor recreational, health and mental health, educational, nutritional, travel, arts and music, employment , and intergenerational programs; information and referral services, support groups and counseling, social action, volunteer opportunities, fitness programs, blood pressure checks, vision and screen tests, adult day care, legal assistance, and even financial management skills. Senior centers attract the well elderly in their seventies and eighties. A web source providing links to senior centers throughout the United States can be located at: Administration on Aging: Links to Senior Centers http://www. aoa.dhhs.gov/AOA/webres/senior.htm.

Religious Organizations and Social Services

Religious organizations provide a variety of support programs for older adults such as transportation, organized recreational travel, educational programs, and social services. Brashears and Roberts (1996) report on an innovative social service program of the Second Baptist Church in Kansas City, Missouri. The Second Baptist Church is the oldest African American Baptist Church in Kansas City with a congregation of 700 members. In 1987 a social worker was recruited to the church staff. The social worker provides direct services to the members of the church and their families and serves as the program administrator in the church's organizational structure. She provides case management; support services to the homebound and institutionalized members; support services to members and families experiencing distress, health crises, and terminal illness; family counseling services; and referrals for emergency community services (Brashears and Roberts 1996).

Churches and synagogues offer a variety of programs for older persons, from medical assistance to financial assistance. The Brookland Baptist Church maintains a credit union for its members (Bilingsley1999). Religious organizations maintain nursing homes and housing for older persons and day care programs. However, the churches can do more to fill the gap that governments, worldwide, are not providing. The spirit of collaboration between church and government must be renewed to meet the needs of older persons in each community (Tirrito and Spencer-Amado 2000). For more information on religious organizations in community services see Tirrito and Cascio (2003) *Religious Organizations in Community Services.*

Adult Protective Services and Legal Services

Protection and advocacy programs for older adults are concerned with elder abuse, neglect, and legal issues. Legal problems for older adults are related to either civil or criminal concerns. Civil problems can include Social Security disputes, age discrimination, divorce, access to benefits, estate planning, income issues, pensions, medical insurance, advanced directives for health care, fraud, nursing home access or costs, and management of financial affairs. Criminal complaints are related to cases of assault, robbery, rape, larceny, and elder abuse. Social Security disputes involve negotiations with a very complex system for entitlements and benefits. Medicaid and Medicare eligibility may need legal intervention. Legal problems may result from financial disputes with Medicare and Medicaid regarding eligibility and/or payment of Medicare or Medicaid claims.

The U.S. Congress enacted the Age Discrimination in Employment Act in 1967 which prohibits discrimination against persons aged 40 or older. It is likely that the number of age discrimination cases will increase as the number of older persons increases in the workforce over the next few decades. Retirees may need assistance with pension benefits if benefits are unfairly denied or improperly managed.

Advanced directives are legal documents that direct health care providers to adhere to personal instructions for end of life treatment or treatment during an illness. The living will document describes the types of life support systems during a terminal illness that the individual, prior to the onset of the illness, has requested be honored by medical personnel. A durable power of attorney allows a health care agent to make health care decisions for an individual. A DNR (do not resuscitate order) mandates that health care professionals must not use extraordinary measures to revive a patient.

Divorce in late life today is more widespread than in previous eras and creates financial difficulty for some older women. Homemakers and women with sporadic careers or part-time employment are financially disadvantaged when divorced in late life. Estate planning protects assets for older persons.

Protection of rights for nursing home patients, assisted living residents, or independent housing residents may require legal intervention. In some states, an Ombudsman may be the resource provided by the state to protect the rights of residents in nursing homes. He/she may be asked to intervene when costs of care may be hidden in admission agreements and breaches may require legal interventions. The management of a resident's financial affairs may often require the legal appointment of a guardian, conservator, or state agency when family members are absent. Criminal problems involve fraud, personal theft, robbery, and assault. Studies suggest that although older persons are more afraid of being victims of crime than younger people, research has revealed that older persons are less likely to be victims of crimes (Wacker, Roberto, and Piper 1998).

Elder abuse and neglect is an underreported problem. Victims are likely to be women, 75 years or older, who are frail and dependent emotionally or financially upon a caregiver. Risk factors for abuse are a history of substance abuse or mental pathology by either the caregiver or older person, a previous history of elder abuse, the financial dependence of the caregiver, and a chronic illness which affects the older person and exceeds the capacity of the caregiver (Baumhover and Beall 1996). The estimates of the prevalence of elder abuse range from 3-10%. In the United States, all fifty states have legislation to protect vulnerable adults. However, responsibility for the investigation of these cases varies in different states from departments of social service to Area Agencies on Aging.

Elder abuse is a significant problem in countries such as Canada, Australia, and New Zealand (Global Aging Report 1997). Some programs include education, screening and early intervention, and removal of barriers for identifying, reporting, and managing cases of elder abuse. Education for professionals is vital in order to enhance reporting, screening, and management of elder abuse cases. Laws are required for mandatory reporting and prosecution of abusers. Self-neglect and rights to self-determination are not clearly defined. The older person's right to live in a self-determined environment may be in conflict with the state's laws. A worthwhile resource for information on the law and rights of older adults is the web site for the Institute on Law and Rights of Older Adults at the Brookdale Center on Aging at Hunter College (http://www.hunter.cuny. edu/health/htmls/iol_hp.html). This resource provides legal support for social workers, paralegals, attorneys, and other professionals who act as advocates for older persons.

Educational Programs and Services

Educational programs include degree programs, education for recreation, and education with travel (elder hostel). There has been a substantial increase in the educational level of all Americans, with a greater number of older adults than ever before having earned college degrees during their lifetimes. By the year 2030, more than half of older women and men will have at least a high school education, and 25% of older men and women will have earned college degrees (Wacker, Roberto, and Piper 1998).

The emphasis on lifelong education, or lifelong learning, is a new phenomenon that the Baby Boomers are expected to bring to the aging process. In 1987, almost 95,000 Americans aged 65 and older were enrolled in undergraduate programs in institutions of higher learning in the United States; women comprised 65% of the older undergraduate population. In addition, about 7,500 older adults were enrolled in graduate programs. Men made up 59% of the population of graduate students. Of the older students, 66% were part-time graduate students. Thirty-eight states have tuition waiver programs for older adults. Learning in retirement centers (LRC) has emerged on over two hundred American university and college campuses. Programs are structured to appeal to retirees and offer a broad range of educational opportunities.

Elderhostel combines the excitement of travel with the opportunity to learn. Elderhostel was founded in 1975 in New Hampshire, where older adults were offered an opportunity to participate in courses on a college campus. By 1980, all fifty states and several foreign countries offered an Elderhostel program. In 1999, there were programs in every American state, and in Canada and forty-five other countries, with over 300,000 participants. Elderhostel is a nonprofit educational organization with 135 full-time employees in the national office in Boston. Each state has an Elderhostel office, and a network of 1,900 participating institutions develop individualized programs. The Elderhostel program usually brings together fourteen to forty-five persons over the age of 55 to a college campus, conference center, or retreat for a five-six night stay. During this time, they take non-credit courses with field trips and extracurricular activities but no testing. The cost for domestic participation is low, around $300 to $400 dollars, which includes registration fees, accommodations, meals, classes and activities. Elderhostel also offers international programs with prices that range from $2,500 to $5,500, depending on the travel destination (Elderhostel web site: http://www.elderhostel.org).

Other educational opportunities for older adults are available in libraries, senior centers, civic organizations, and religious organizations. The Shepherd's Center is a nonprofit community organization that is sponsored by a coalition of religious organizations to provide learning programs for older adults in twenty-five states for a small fee. Classes are offered in current events, history, literature, religion, painting, health, and travel (Shepherd's Centers of America web site: http://www.qni.com/shepherd/index.html).

Learning has taken on new meaning in the age of technology and computer learning. Senior Net began in 1986 to offer computer training to older adults in learning centers where volunteers teach older adults computer technology. Many Baby Boomers will enter their old age already computer literate (SeniorNet website: http://www.seniornet.org).

Intergenerational Programs and Services

At the university in Canberra, Australian students attending classes bring their young children to a day care center where teenagers and older persons in the community provide day care without charge. In England, at St. Christopher's Hospice, a free community day care center for neighborhood children offers the terminally ill patients an opportunity to interact with young children; their parents can benefit from free day care for the children.

Most intergenerational programs focus on bringing the generations together to promote the development of relationships and to provide support and services. Many programs are structured so that all participants benefit from the interactions. However, in the majority of programs, one age group is the provider of services or support and the other age group is the recipient of services. In one high school program, students are linked to homebound elderly while in another program in New York City seniors who speak foreign languages are linked with students to help improve their foreign language skills. Linking students with hospitals and nursing homes helps students learn about various health professions. Younger children often participate in singing groups in nursing homes or senior housing developments. Church groups connect young and old together in church-related study programs. Senior centers link students and senior citizens as computer partners; working with computers removes language barriers. Day care programs for adults and day care for children provide valuable reciprocal arrangements for care.

In South Korea, the family center is a place where intergenerational programming occurs spontaneously. Children, adults, adolescents, and older persons come together in an exchange of services. The mission of these centers is to foster interdependence and all programs are structured to enhance reciprocity.

Programs and services for older adults are extremely diverse globally. From the Internet, it is possible to access additional information about hospice, adult day care, home care services, and advocacy programs in various countries. It is possible to learn about Elderhostel programs, intergenerational programs, nursing homes, and respite care in every state in America and around the world. There are a variety of methods for teaching about these programs and services which will be discussed in the following section.

Strategies for Teaching about
Services and Programs

Since the late 1970s, the University of South Carolina has offered a Graduate Certificate Program in Gerontology. The courses in the Program examine the psychological, biological, social, demographic, and economic conditions that affect older adults. One of the required courses in the Certificate Program is a course on programs and services for older adults. This course focuses on international, national, state, and local planning and delivery of services to the elderly. One of the course objectives is to teach students the skills that will prepare them for working with older adults in community settings. The students critically evaluate current programs and services for older adults. They learn to appreciate the influence of sociological theories of aging on program development and policymaking. They acquire knowledge of the major social policies and programs currently in place such as the Older Americans Act, Social Security, SSI, Medicare, and Medicaid. They learn to assess the strengths and weaknesses of programs in health, mental health, long term care, retirement, housing, and leisure. Students are evaluated at the end of the semester for their ability to achieve the following behavioral objectives:

1. Articulate knowledge of the values that shape the social welfare system with emphasis upon those values that inform and result in policies intended to promote social justice and meet the needs of older adults.

2. Describe the range of programs that serve diverse groups of elderly persons.

3. Recommend policy/program changes that will enhance the social functioning of the older population.

4. Demonstrate the ability to recognize the factors of ageism, sexism, and racism which impact on the services to older adults.

5. Evaluate both the need for programs and the process and impact of particular programs.

6. Demonstrate awareness, sensitivity, and competence in relating to a diverse cultural client pool.

Teaching Activities

The class is conducted with a lecture-discussion format with the use of multiple audio-visual materials and input from guest lecturers. Individual and group student presentations enhance the students' knowledge about social service programs to the elderly. Some modules of the course are offered on the Internet using Blackboard, a university web–based interactive program. Videos present case studies that portray the lives of the elderly and their bio psychosocial issues with discussion about the appropriate programs that are available to address these problems. Students bring in newspaper articles about local programs for older persons. Students are assigned to write a letter to the governor outlining a proposal for a specific program in their local community that addresses an unmet or "undermet" need. Students bring to class photographs of older adult family members, friends or neighbors. Students take a Life Expectancy Quiz on the Internet and discuss their results in class. These interactive learning activities help students familiarize themselves with issues that confront the elderly daily and encourage them to undertake identification of appropriate programs and services that address these needs and maximize quality of life.

One assignment requires students to choose a program in their local county or state and visit the program site. In this visit, the student must interview the administrator or executive director and determine if the program meets the needs of the participants it is intended to serve. The program is critically evaluated and the student reports findings to the class in a poster session. Students prepare a poster that describes the selected program. Presentations are mounted on poster boards following the guidelines of a professional conference presentation. Site visit materials are included in the presentation. Handouts are expected to be prepared for the entire class. Included in the handout is a reference list of web sources for this type of program. Students are expected to give evidence of a well-researched program. For example, if the student is presenting on a local assisted living program that is targeted to persons with dementia or Alzheimer's disease, the student is expected to have some basic knowledge about Alzheimer's disease, such as its prevalence and its treatment options. A critical analysis is expected which offers implications for gerontological study.

The letter to the Governor, family photos, newspaper articles of older persons or programs, self reflective materials such as Old Age Portrait of Me When I am 80 years of age, What is Your Aging I.Q.?, and Life Expectancy Calculators on the web prepare the student to think about psychosocial issues related to aging and the potential sources to seek out for remediation. Students search the Web for programs in Europe, Asia, and Latin America. Students explore international aging agencies and programs. Students investigate if their community is "aging friendly". What are some of the programs provided in their community for older persons? Students can investigate if their faith organizations are aging friendly and whether they provide programs and services for older members of their congregations.

Table 1: Suggested programs of study

Programs	*Programs*
Meals on Wheels	Elderhostel
Adult Day Care	Hospice
Ombudsman Programs	Shepherd Centers
Senior Centers	Nursing Homes
Assisted Living Centers	Senior Housing
Geriatric Private Practice	Respite Programs
Memory Clinics	Geriatric Mental Health Centers
Geriatric Care Managers	Senior Employment Programs
RSVP- Retired Seniors	Educational Programs
Older Women's League	Continuing Care Retirement Communities

Video Sources

These web sites provide a diverse selection of videos that are easily accessed on aging programs and issues: www.terranova.org; www.fan light.com; www.films.com.

The following are descriptions of some videos available at the above sites. These videos can be used for discussion on current programs and services for the elderly in order to challenge students to think about services that would help resolve conflicting situations and improve the lives of older persons.

The Personals is about improvisations on romance in the Golden Years by Keibo Ibi; the longing for love, sex, and relationships is never-ending. This film presents a surprisingly humorous and often candid portrait of a segment of society whose private lives are not often explored.

As Time Goes is produced by the Canadian Broadcasting Corporation. Baby Boomers should be especially relieved to learn that humans seek out sexual gratification until the very end. The seniors profiled in this documentary share their experiences of love and romance in their mature years.

Wandering: Is it a problem? Experienced caregivers demonstrate techniques for intervening with patients who wander. Through viewing actual provider-patient interactions, students and staff learn effective methods of redirecting the wanderer, providing a safe and secure space for residents, and avoiding client escalation to an agitated state.

Self Deliverance by Michael Lutzky. The hero, Australian John Grisham says that he has reached his "usefulness by date." Living with constant pain, John spends his days looking for a hospice program that will respect his wishes, or a doctor who will help him end his life when he decides it is time.

To Be Old, Black, and Poor is a gritty and painfully real exposition of what it means to be Black, poor, and elderly in the U.S.

The Aging Process examines the effects of aging on the human mind and body, explores the "damage" and "cell clock" theories about why cells wear out. It examines the lifestyle habits that affect both longevity and the quality of life.

Forever Young: An Elixir of Youth? analyzes the aging process, showing ways to enhance longevity. The benefits and perils of hormones as an elixir of youth are discussed by Dr. Ron Livesey, who runs an anti-aging clinic in New York, and Professor Stephen Shalet, an expert on human growth hormone who explains its link to cancer.

Accepting Life's Transitions is a discussion of how one's current behaviors and attitudes may impact on our future as we age.

Aging addresses the physical processes of aging, examining body systems to see how and why they change as we age. Not all changes over the life span are inevitable and some changes in the aging body can be slowed down or even reversed.

Grandparents Raising Grandchildren by Gloria Bailen for Context Media describes the burdens of a current cohort of grandparents who care for grandchildren in the absence of the children's parents. It was supposed to be their golden years, a time to relax and spoil the grandchildren. However, for nearly four million grandparents across America, a new reality has taken shape: grandparents are raising their grandchildren. The video tells the stories of three grandparents who have taken on sole responsibility for raising their children's children and the impact it has had on the lives of all the generations involved.

A Perspective of Hope by Ben Achtenberg, Christine Mitchell, RN and Susan Shaw, RN highlights a unique program which involves schools of nursing in improving the quality of care for nursing home residents. Through the lives of individual students, it presents a positive but realistic view of nursing on the frontiers of change.

Not My Home by Suzanne Babin, Tynette Deveaux and Bert Deveaux is a look at life inside a nursing home. In candid interviews, nurses and aides discuss the demands of caring for residents in the face of tight schedules and minimal staffing.

From Rules to Caring Practices from the Park Ridge Center for the Study of Health, Faith, and Ethics addresses the ethical issues faced by frontline home care workers providing services to the elderly. It poses four questions as the building blocks of everyday ethics:

- How can I build and maintain a trusting relationship with this person?
- How can I respect and affirm this client as a person of worth?
- What does it mean to care well for this person?
- What do I need in order to respect myself and affirm that I am a morally worthy person?

Something Should be Done about Grandma Ruthie by Cary Stauffacher is a moving and unsettling portrait of the filmmaker's family as they struggle to deal with her grandmother's deteriorating mental condition. Though a series of compassionate caregivers have been unable to deal with her growing disorientation, Grandma Ruthie refuses to leave her long-time home. The family must confront the necessity of medicating her against her will and, eventually, forcibly removing her to a long-term care facility.

Agitation—it's a Sign describes the agitation and aggressive behavior that is exhibited when an Alzheimer's disease patient tries to communicate with the world outside their dementia. Lashing out may often be their only recourse for expressing their fears and anxiety. Through real-life patient encounters, this video shows techniques which can prevent or diffuse patients' anxiety, agitation, and aggression.

Common Heroes: Choices in Hospice Care by Robert Ruvkun—Facing terminal illness can be terrifying, not only for patients, but also for family members who must choose how best to help and care for their loved one at the end of life. This new video follows the nurses, physicians, social workers, and clergy who make up the hospice team and demonstrates the way they collaborate to help families develop care plans that will maximize each patient's quality of life during the end stages of their illness.

Life Support Decisions by Peter Walsh, New World Media Alliance will help elders, their families, and the professionals who work with them to understand the rights and options regarding life-support technologies and end-of-life care. Its discussion of the many issues involved in preparing advanced directives encourages everyone to communicate their wishes to their loved ones and caregivers before becoming ill or hospitalized.

Gay and Gray in New York City by Nicholas Chesla, Cindi Creager and Julie Englander features interviews with several "gay and gray" men and women, as well as profiling two organizations who work to provide services and support to elders in the gay community. One estimate suggests that there are around 45,000 gay and lesbian seniors in New York City alone. They share all the usual problems of aging—retirement from work, the decline of physical health, grief over the loss of friends and loved ones—but they are more likely than "straight" seniors to be living alone without family or other social supports.

The Oldest Victims: Elder Abuse addresses a number of elder abuse-related topics including the embezzlement of elders' funds by family members; the criminal neglect and endangerment of housebound and bedridden elders by their children and friends; and alleged mercy killings of terminally ill elders by their spouses.

Chronic Anxiety in the Elderly describes the problem of anxiety in the elderly and the diseases associated with the problem. Interviews with sufferers of Geriatric Anxiety Disorder (GAD) provide insights into the agony of the condition.

A Desperate Act: Suicide and the Elderly come to grips with the chronic depression that leads many senior citizens to take their own lives. Promoting prevention, intervention, and follow-up, medical experts use three case studies as a basis for discussing the warning signs of depression and treatment through counseling, education, medication, electro convulsive therapy, and occupational therapy.

Ethics and Economics: *The Rising Cost of Health Care*—Dr. Willard Gaylin is a practicing psychiatrist and president of the Hastings Center, an institute devoted to studying the relationship between biology and ethics. In this video with Bill Moyers as moderator, Gaylin explores the growing conflict between the survival of communities and the survival of the individual.

Guest Speakers

Invited lectures from experts in various aspects of gerontological social work practice and related disciplines are included in the course syllabus. Experts provide the opportunity for students to learn about current policy trends and attitudes, the evolution of programs and services, and the effect of aging research on the target population. Guest speakers, often from local aging agencies, are also invited to address classes in order to present the reality of life in the community and what is currently available and still needs to be developed in order to improve the lives of older persons. There is a speaker's bureau of older persons. From the ranks of these community representatives, guest speakers are invited to speak about community programs and services as seen from the prospective of the users.

Future Projections

Population aging will change the focus and structure of future programs and services. Universal health care is inevitable in the United States. Older persons need prescription drug coverage, long term care insurance, and home health care as basic human rights. Retirement will take on new meaning and older persons will be active in various types of part time and full time work that is meaningful and interesting. Hobbies and leisure activities will begin at age 40, 50, 60, 70 or even 80 years of age. Older persons will travel (worldwide), become volunteers in greater numbers, be involved in life long learning, sports, and paid employment.

Takamura (2001) states that there will be no lack of issues to address as America prepares for the graying of its population. Debates will evolve regarding the role of government, family responsibility, enhancing respect and dignity of seniors, quality affordability, and access to a responsive service delivery system. The future will be significantly impacted by the global longevity revolution.

References

American Society on Aging Newsletter. Nov. 1999.

Australian Institute of Health and Welfare (AIHW) (1997). *Aged and respite care in Australia: Extracts from recent publications.* AIHW Cat. No. AGE. 5 Canberra.

Baumhover, L. A. and S.C. Beall. 1996. *Abuse, neglect, and exploitation of older persons: Strategies for assessment and intervention: 1-3.* Health Professions Press: Maryland.

Billingsley, A. 1999. *Mighty like a river: The Black church and social reform.* New York: Oxford University Press.

Brashears, F. and M. Roberts.1996. The Black Church as a resource for change. In Sadye L. Logan, ed. *The Black Family: Strengths, self-help and positive change*: 181- 193. Boulder, CO: Westview.

CBS Newshttp://www.cbsnews.com/stories/2003/01/15/national/main 5366 01.sh tml

Cohen, G. D. 1997. Gaps and failures in attending to mental health and aging in long- term care. In R.L. Rubenstein and M.P. Lawton, eds. *Depression in long term and residential care: Advances in research and treatment.* New York: Springer Elderhostel: Adventures in lifelong learning.1999. http://www.elderhostel.org

Geralink, D. 1974. *Webster's World Dictionary 2nd edition.* New York, NY: Williams Collins and World Publishing.

Gibson, D., E. Butkus, A. Jenkins, S. Mathur and Z. Liu.1996. The respite care needs of Australians: Prepared for the Respite review undertaken by the Aged and Community Care Division of the Commonwealth

Department of Health and Family Services. Canberra, Australia: Australian Institute of Health and Welfare. (Series: Respite review supporting paper; 1). (Series: Aged care series; no.3).

Global Aging Report 1997. Does the care suit the client? 2(6): 5. Washington, DC: AARP.

Global Aging Report 1997. Who are the likely victims? Reports on elder abuse, 2(5):4. Washington, DC: AARP.

Global Aging Report 1996. Charging children for care of aging parents: Two Asian nations turn to family for cash, 1(4): 4. Washington, DC: AARP.

Harrison, J. 1997 Winter/Spring. Housing for the ageing population of Singapore *International Ageing Journal.* 23(3 and 4):32-48.

Hagestad, G. 1999, October. Towards a society for all ages: New thinking, new language, new conversations. Paper presented at the United Nations, New York.

Katan, Y. and E.Werczberger.1997 Winter/Spring. Housing for the elderly people in Israel. *International Ageing Journal* 23 (3 and 4): 49-64.

Kara, S. 1997Winter/Spring. Housing facilities in India. *International Ageing Journal* 23 (3 and 4):107-114.

Kim, M. 1997 Winter/Spring. Housing policies for the elderly in Korea. *International Ageing Journal* 23 (3 and 4): 78-89.

Kose, S. 1997 Winter/Spring. Housing elderly people in Japan. *International Ageing Journal* 23 (3 and 4):148-164.

Lindstrom, B. 1997 Winter/Spring. Housing and service for the elderly in Denmark. *International Ageing Journal* 23 (3 and 4):115-132.

Saunders, D. C. 1997. Hospices worldwide: A mission statement. In Dame C. Saunders and Robert Kastenbaum, eds. *Hospice care on the international scene.* New York: Springer Publishers.

Stjernsward, J. 1997. The international hospice movement from the perspective of the World Health Organization. In Dame C. Saunders and Robert Kastenbaum, eds. *Hospice care on the international scene.* New York: Springer Publishers.

Takamura, J. 2001. The future is aging. In F.L. Ahearn Jr., ed. *Issues in Global Aging*: 3-16. New York: Haworth Press.

Tirrito,T, and T.Cascio.2003. Religious organizations in community services. New York: Springer.

Tirrito, T. and J. Spencer-Amado. 2000. A study of older adults willingness to use social services in places of worship. *Journal of Religious Gerontology.*11 (2):35-42.

Wacker, R., K.Roberto, and L. Piper. 1998. *Community resources for older adults: Programs and services in an era of change.* Thousand Oaks, CA: Pine Forge Press.

Additional Web Sources

Comparative Gerontology Quiz http://www.stpt.usf.edu/jsokolov/quiz.htm

Teaching Gerontology Newsletter http://www.pineforge.com/moody

Caregiving website http://www.thoushalthonor.org.

SAGE-SW http://www.cswe.org/sage-sw/curriculum/trk.htm

Source: National Vital Statistics System

Life Expectancy (2000) http://www.cdc.gov/nchs/fastats/lifexpec.htm

Single Age Life Table for the U.S. 1999: http://www.cdc.gov/nchs/fastats/pdf/nvsr50_06tb1.pdf

Trends in the Causes of Death of the Elderly http://www.cdc.gov/nchs/data/agingtrends/01death.pdf

Summary Measures of Population Health: Addressing the First Goal of Healthy People 2010, Improving Life Expectancy http://www.cdc.gov/nchs/data/statnt/statnt22.pdf

Summary Measures of Population Health: Methods for Calculating Health Life Expectancy http://www.cdc.gov/nchs/data/statnt/statnt21.pdf

Mortality Data from the National Vital Statistics System http://www.cdc.gov/nchs/ nvss.htm

Mortality by Statehttp://www.cdc.gov/nchs/datawh/statab/morttables.htm

Healthy Women: State Trends in Health and Mortality http://www.cdc.gov/nchs/ healthywomen.htm

Deaths: Preliminary Data for 2000 http://www.cdc.gov/nchs/data/nvsr/
nvsr49/nvsr49_12.pdf

Deaths: Leading Causes for 1999 http://www.cdc.gov/nchs/data/nvsr/
nvsr49/ nvsr49_11.pdf

United States Life Tables1999http://www.cdc.gov/nchs/data/nvsr/
nvsr50/nvsr50_ 06.pdf

Estimated life expectancy at birth in years, by race and sex: Death-
registration States, 1900–28, and United States, 1929–98
http://www.cdc.gov/nchs/fastats/ pdf/48_18t12.pdf

Method for Constructing Complete Annual U.S. Life Tables http://
www.cdc.gov/ nchs/data/sr2_129.pdf

Source: U.S. Census Bureau

The 65 and Over Population: 2000 http://www.census.gov/prod/2001
pubs/c2kbr01-10.pdf

Population by Age, Sex, Race, and Hispanic or Latino Origin for the
United States: 2000 http://www.census.gov/population/www/
cen2000/phc-t9.html

U.S. Census Population Projections by Age, Sex, Race and Hispanic
Origin, 1999-2001 http://www.census.gov/population/www/
projections/natdet-D1A.html

Age 65 and over in Cities, Counties, and States http://factfinder.census.
gov/servlet/BasicFactsServlet

Period Life Table, 1999 http://www.ssa.gov/OACT/STATS/table4c6.html

Life Expectancy for Social Security—Misinterpreting Life Expectancy
Statistics http://www.ssa.gov/history/lifeexpect.html

Population in the Social Security area: Estimated number and percent fully insured, by age and sex, 1998-2002 http://www.ssa.gov/OACT/STATS/table4c5.html

Report of the National Institute on Aging Advisory Panel on Exceptional Longevity (National Institute on Aging) http://www.nia.nih.gov/research/meetings/apelreport.pdf

Life Expectancy—Older Americans 2000: Key Indicators of Well Being (Federal Interagency 2000: Key Indicators of Well Being) http://www.aoa.dhhs.gov/agingstats/tables%202001/tables-healthstatus.html#Indicator%2012

Life Expectancy—Women of Color Health Data Book (The National Women's Health Information Center) http://www.4woman.gov/owh/pub/woc/figure 1.htm

Medicaid Life Expectancy Tables (Centers for Medicare and Medicaid Services) http://www.immediateannuities.com/content_pages/HCFA_life_expectancy_tables.htm

Source: Life Expectancy Calculators

The Living to 100 Life Expectancy Calculator (Alliance for Aging Research) http://www.livingto100.com/

What is Your Life Expectancy (Long to Life) http://www.longtolive.com/LongTo Live.asp

Longevity Game (Northwestern Mutual Life Insurance) http://www.northwestern mutual.com/nmcom/NM/longevitygameintro/toolbox--calculator--longevitygameintro--longevity_intro

The Human Mortality Data Base (University of California Berkeley and Max Planck Institute for Demographic Research) http://www.mortality.org/

Life Expectancy at Birth (World Policy Institute) http://worldpolicy.org/americas/econrights/maps-life.html

Estimates of Health Life Expectancy for 191 Countries in the Year 2000: Methods and Results (World Health Organization) http://www3.who.int/whosis/burden/ papers/GPE%20HALE%20discussion%20paper.doc

Infant Mortality Rates and Life Expectancy at Birth, by Sex, for Selected Countries, 1999 http://www.infoplease.com/ipa/A0004393.html

Life Expectancy at Birth for Selected Countries: 1950 and 1998 http://www.info please.com/ipa/A0774532.html

Canada

http://www.statcan.ca:80/english/Pgdb/People/Health/health26.htm

England

Healthy Life Expectancy in England at the Sub-National Level (Office for National Statistics) http://www.statistics.gov.uk/downloads/theme_health/HSQ14_v4. pdf

Ireland

Life expectancy and vital statisticshttp://www.doh.ie/statistics/health_statistics/ vital.html

Japan

Life Expectancy at Birth (1983-2000) http://jin.jcic.or.jp/stat/stats/02VIT24.html

International Comparison of Life Expectancy at Birth http://www.jinjapan.org/stat/stats/02VIT25.html

Islamic Countries

Average Life Expectancy at Birth http://www.sesrtcic.org/statistics/charts/chdq exp1.shtml

Russia

The Russian Epidemiological Crisis as Mirrored by Mortality Trends
http://www. rand.org/publications/CF/CF124/cf124.chap4.html

Male Life Expectancy http://www.cspp.strath.ac.uk/SC6-Male-life-expec
tancy-1.html

Ancient Rome

Life Table http://www.utexas.edu/depts/classics/documents/Life.html

Editorial Commentary

ഇരുൽ

Nieli Langer

A shortcoming of education in the social sciences has been its failure
to effectively integrate research and practice. To make sound decisions,
practitioners and students of gerontology need to be:

1. Able to read and critique research articles

2. Know the relevance of evidence-based research on their own professional activities in light of rapid changes, innovations in programs, and
   new technology

Evidence-based practice originated in health care as an alternative to
authority-based practice (i.e., basing decisions on uninformed opinions).
Evidence-based practice offers practitioners and administrators a philosophy that is compatible with professional codes of ethics (i.e., for informed
consent) and educational accreditation policies and standards. While most
people engaged in meaningful careers in gerontology will in all probability
never conduct empirical research, they will be reading research articles in
their professional journals that describe issues relevant to their practices.
Evidence-based practice is designed to enhance students'/practitioners'

ability to be good consumers of research. If professionals are not familiar with the evidentiary status of alternative practices and policies, they cannot pass this information on to their clients; they cannot honor informed consent obligations. In order to access, analyze, and apply research findings in aging studies, learners will need to understand why, by whom, and how research studies are conducted. Therefore, instructors will need to teach research design—the overall framework for collecting data once the problem has been formulated. In addition, instructors will need to teach how to read and interpret the data and what they mean. A key contribution of evidence-based practice is discouraging inflated claims of knowledge that mislead all involved parties including students and hinder the development of knowledge.

The main objective of this educational strategy is to integrate individual clinical expertise with critical evaluation of evidence discovered from a systematic literature search in order to solve a problem. Students are given examples of consumer research problem topics such as models to prevent elder abuse, factors that influence older adults' use of in-home services, staffing and stress reduction in social service/health care facilities, programs that enhance cultural competence, etc. The group votes on a single topic about which there are divergent opinions and students then search for peer-reviewed articles relevant to the topic. Based on both individual student and group analysis of the evidence, they will make a determination as to the veracity of the findings and its efficacy in practice. Students can use the following format to summarize and critique the soundness of an author's conclusions:

1. Was the research question properly framed? What methods were used? What is the major question or hypothesis? What are the independent and dependent variables? What are the operational definitions for the major variables?

2. Was the evidence appropriately collected and analyzed? What are the findings? What are the controlled and uncontrolled extraneous variables? How was the sample/population sampled? What are the author's conclusions?

Simulation is a powerful tool for isolating the learner's first frustrating and confusing encounter with problems raised by attempts to introduce new cognitive, skill, or attitudinal behaviors into the teaching environment.

Role-playing allows learners to experience and develop strategies for overcoming the conflicts inherent in change. Loss, grief, and transition are at the root of many problems that care providers need to address with older clients and their families. Simulating successive losses and the resultant move to a nursing home are provided in the game *Into Aging: A simulation game* (Hoffman & Dempsey-Lyle 1994). Societal avoidance of issues confronting frail elderly is immediately challenged in this game. It is an opportunity for students to experience "aging" through some of the myths and stereotypes perpetuated by the game operators and life event cards. Students examine prejudicial attitudes about aging and the implications that the perpetuation of these myths have for their own aging and their work environment (Langer 1999).

References

Hoffman, T. and S. Dempsey-Lyle. 1994. *Into aging: A simulation game.* New Jersey: Slack.

Langer, N. 1999. Gerontologizing health care: A train-the-trainer program for nurses. *Gerontology & Geriatrics Education* 19(4):47-56.

The "How a Law is Born" activity for small group development was proposed by Mr. Howard Shapiro, a graduate student in my Policy and Principles of Program Management course at the College of New Rochelle (2003).

1. The class forms 3-4 small groups in which they select a current State law that affects the elderly. Examples of these laws might include age discrimination or telemarketing statutes, school tax waiver for older property owners, free admission to State Parks for senior citizens, etc.

2. After selection of the law/statute, each group contacts a State Senator or Assembly person in order to obtain a complete copy of the law and its accompanying "Bill Jacket".

The Bill Jacket will provide information on:

a. why the bill was originally proposed, i.e., what new policies will be created
b. who is the target population for the proposed bill
c. what the bill seeks to accomplish or remedy, i.e., what new programs will be created
d. how the new law/statute is supposed to work

Students will learn that most bills that are enacted into law are a variation of the original proposal (often unrecognizable from the original) and a compromise deal negotiated by political parties and interest groups. Groups should present their findings to the class using creative strategies.

2

STRATEGIES FOR TEACHING AGING SOCIAL WELFARE PROBLEMS AND POLICIES

ഇരു

Julie Miller-Cribbs

Introduction

The social work profession has been increasing its involvement in all aspects of practice with the elderly. In 1998 the John A. Hartford Foundation encouraged this involvement with grants to fund programs that strengthen geriatric social work. Although social work has spurred increased activity relevant to the aging population, less emphasis has been focused on the development and assessment of aging policy. In addition, in the current climate of devolution, deregulation, a decreased interest in entitlement policies and panic over Medicare and Social Security, the safety net of policies for the aging population is at significant risk (Administration on Aging (AOA) 2002; Liebig 1994). Although these policies have consistently been considered 'untouchable' in the past– this is less the case than ever before. In this context, aging policy takes on new importance for social work and gerontology students and practitioners. Not only must they attain policy advocacy skills so that they can advocate for the benefits of the current cohort of elderly, but they must also develop the policy analysis skills that will enable them to 'think outside of the box' and engage in creative, proactive solutions for future Medicare and Social Security beneficiaries.

The 'demographic imperative' is well documented in both the research literature and popular media. American society is graying in unprecedented numbers and it is estimated that older adults will comprise 20% of the population in 2030 (Kisor, McSweeney and Jackson 2000; AOA 2002). The population of older individuals in the United States is increasingly multicultural, living longer, and will need access to diverse and more intensive social services (Torres-Gil and Moga 2001). Social workers and gerontologists must be involved in the planning, creation, and delivery of such services.

In the past, it may have been easier for geriatric social workers to practice with paucity of policy knowledge since access and delivery of services were more straightforward, funding streamlined, and fewer battles waged over program resources. However, in the current unstable climate of aging policy support, the increasing complexity of policies such as Medicare and Social Security require 'policy gerontologists' (Liebig 1995). A survey of aging network personnel taken ten years ago noted that knowledge of aging policies, i.e. specific legislation and regulations, was ranked as the top area needed for job acquisition and retention while knowledge of political trends ranked sixth (Peterson, Wendt, and Douglass 1991). Since that study, aging policy has become even more complex and embattled.

Ginsberg's (1999) six domains of policy education offer a useful framework for teaching policy to social work students. This framework is useful whether one is considering creating a stand-alone aging policy course or infusing aging policy content into different courses in the curriculum. Of these six domains, this chapter will emphasize four in particular: history, social problems, policy description, and policy practice. These domains are useful in terms of their consistency with the Council on Social Work Education's Educational Policy and Accreditation Standards (CSWE EPAS) statement on social welfare policy and services content.[1]

---

1. 4.4 Social Welfare Policy and Services: "Programs provide content about the history of social work, the history and current structures of social welfare services, and the role of policy in service delivery, social work practice, and attainment of individual and social well-being. Course content provides students with knowledge and skills to understand major policies that form the foundation of social welfare; analyze organizational, local,

Table 1 highlights the four domains addressed in this chapter and provides examples relevant to aging policy.

Table 1: Policy Teaching Domains Highlighted in this Chapter

Social Policy Teaching Domains	Description & Objectives	Emphasis on Aging Content
History	Teaching the history of the development of social welfare policy in the U.S.; important policy milestones; understanding the historical roots and development of social policy	Tracing the development of policies relevant to aging, with a focus on particular policy milestones such as the birth of Social Security, the Older Americans Act, and Medicare; emphasis placed on age cohorts and key individuals in history.
Social Problems	Teaching students to identify the link between ideology and policy responses; identification of current social problems at international, national, state and local level.	Identification of ideologies related to social problems and how such ideologies (i.e. ageism, social construction of aging, institutional vs. residual policy responses) shape policy development; identification of key social problem domains relevant to older adults such as financial well-being, health care, social services, caregiving.

---

state, national, and international issues in social welfare policy and social service delivery; analyze and apply the results of policy research relevant to social service delivery; understand and demonstrate policy practice skills in regard to economic, political, and organizational systems, and use them to influence, formulate, and advance for policy consistent with social work values; and identify financial, organizational, administrative, and planning processes required to deliver social services." (CSWE, 2001)

Description	Description of relevant policies	Description and under-standing of specific social policies relevant to older adults: Medicare, Medi-caid, Older Americans Act, etc.
Policy Advocacy	Development of policy advocacy skills and knowledge of relevant players in policy forma-tion, development, and implementation.	Awareness of key political players in aging policy field such as AARP and the Gray Panthers; devel-opment of advocacy skills related to aging policy issues.

Defining Aging Policy

Similar to other social welfare policy areas, such as child welfare, aging policy cuts across many other arenas. The typical domains in aging include policies related to financial security, health, social services, discrimination, housing, transportation, and caregiving. It is useful to think of teaching aging policy in a holistic fashion, considering all of the elements relevant to well-being of older adults. This conceptual framework ensures compre-hensive attention to issues that affect older adults. While such comprehen-sive coverage would be ideal, uniform agreement on a set of aging policy readings or issues has not been found in surveys of aging policy syllabi (Liebig 1995; Coberly and Wilber 1990). Liebig (1995) notes the three ways in which social policy content is typically included in courses: (1) a unit on policy is incorporated into an existing course, (2) stand alone policy course, and (3) specialized policy course. Policy 'hot topics' are frequently emphasized in aging policy courses and it has been argued that such cursory attention is not sufficient for the current complex and dynamic aging policy realities, particularly in the health care areas where policy changes have been extensive and dramatic (Coberly and Wilber 1990; Fahey 1996). As the "policy climate has become more turbulent and less predictable, affecting federal and state age based policy, people well trained in multidisciplinary research in aging and requisite policy research and policy analysis skills will be better prepared to help shape that policy" (Liebig 1995, 41). This chapter attempts to address four important areas relevant to teaching aging policy in a more holistic approach.

History

As previously noted, EPAS requires that content relevant to the history of social welfare services and policies be taught to students. Therefore, just as the history of the development of American social welfare is taught, the important milestones in aging policy, the lives of prominent older adults, and social movements relevant to the elderly should also be included. For example, passage of the Americans with Disabilities Act was spearheaded by important elderly advocacy groups and older women made significant contributions to the feminist and women's health movements. Maggie Kuhn and a group of her retired social work colleagues established the Gray Panthers, a notable advocacy organization. As will be discussed later in the section on advocacy, inclusion of such contributions to the development of social welfare policies in American society is important, particularly since this active participation refutes the notion that advocacy is only for the younger professional.

As social work students and practitioners understand that the foundation of social policy is embedded in history, they are more prepared to see the connections, repetitions, triumphs, failures, and gaps in the field of aging policy. Placing current policy debates in a historical framework allows for a more nuanced understanding of current trends in aging policy. For example, Torres-Gil and Moga (2001) provide an analysis of aging politics of five cohorts from the New Deal Generation (1900-1929) through Generation Y (1977-1994).

Table 2: Cohort Analysis: Politics of Aging

Cohorts	Historical Events	Attitudes/Moods
New Deal Generation,1900-1929	Depression, WWII, Welfare State Social Contract	Traditional Values Socially Conservative Politically Liberal
Silent Generation (Depression and WWII Babies) 1930-1945	Cold War Prosperity, Economic Opportunity, Stability, Golden Years	Conformity; Socially and Politically Conservative

Baby Boomers 1946-1964	Civil Rights, Kennedy, Vietnam, Watergate	Socially Tolerant; antipathy to Big Government, Big Labor, Big Business; Peter Pan Generation
Generation X 1965-1974	Ronald Reagan, Budget Deficit, Persian Gulf War	Materialism, 1950s Values, Cynical, Self-Reliant, Antipathy to Baby Boomers
Generation Y 1977-1994	Clinton; Challenger Explosion	Diverse; College and High School Students; Suburban Values

As can be observed from this Table, a cohort consists of "generations born at the same historical point and influenced by similar historical experiences" (Torres-Gil and Moga 2001, 18). The argument is that American society is continuously being impacted in different ways as these cohorts age, and "in a society becoming older and more diverse, these cohorts will influence and shape the demographic landscape" (Torres-Gil and Moga 2001, 18). Using an historical analysis such as this allows students to explore 'cohort' politics as they relate to age.

Since the 1990's, the idea that the American government will care for the elderly has received less public support (Torres-Gil and Moga 2001, 20) when groups such as the Concord Coalition and other anti-deficit groups have argued the growth of entitlement spending in the federal budget (Schulz 1996; Concord Coalition 2003). The erosion of public support for programs such as Medicare and Social Security cannot be viewed in a vacuum, however, but in the context of historical and current events and trends. The U.S. has experienced the growth of the aging population, exponential rise of health care technology and health care costs, the rise in age expectancy, deficit problems, depressions, recessions, reduced cohesiveness among aging advocacy groups, increased complexity of services needed for the elderly (especially long term care), and devolution and infighting over resources at the state level (Schulz, 1996; Torres-Gil and Moga 2001). If trends continue and larger structural, comprehensive, and developmental changes to programs are not made, most programs for the elderly will suffer from inaccessibility, unaffordability, and poor quality. More elderly will be at risk for poverty and poor health outcomes

(Torres-Gil and Moga 2001; Schulz 1996). Policies that address family well-being across all stages in the life course are needed (Moen and Forest 1995). Social workers with their practical understanding of person-in-environment are in an ideal position to advocate for comprehensive policy action if they are armed with the requisite policy knowledge.

In summary, connecting current policy debates to historical events is an important element of teaching aging policy. There are some interesting history timelines and web resources that detail the history of political movements and policy development that many aging policy educators would find useful. Some of the resources are highlighted in Table 3. For example, the AOA has a side-by-side comparison of the Older Americans Act as amended in 1992 and 2000 and the Centers for Medicaid and Medicare Services (CMS) provide many resources on the development of Medicare and Medicaid. The Social Security Administration's multi media history of Social Security in the United States is an outstanding resource for social work students.

Table 3: Timelines and History Resources

History of Medicaid and Medicare
http://cms.hhs.gov/about/history/ssachr.asp
Side-by-Side Comparison of OAA in 1992 and 2000
http://www.aoa.gov/oaa/2000/side-by-side-fin.html
Multi Media History of Social Security in America
http://www.ssa.gov/history/history.html
History of Gray Panthers (click on history & achievements)
http://www.graypanthers.org/
History of Long Term Care by ElderWeb
http://www.elderweb.com/history/default.php?PageID=2806
Historical Evolution of Programs for Older Americans (AOA)
http://www.aoa.gov/network/history.html

Social Problems

Researchers and advocates have worked diligently to put a 'new face' on aging. They have been resolute in trying to dispel myths and ageist attitudes and have focused on educating the public and practicing professionals about normal aging processes and the inherent strengths of the elderly. Despite these efforts, major social problems persist for this target population. Social workers need to become more aware of the salient social problems that impact upon the elderly.

Even more important, however, is acknowledgement that teaching social problems also includes an analysis of the relevant ideologies that frame policy responses. This enables social work students to understand the social problems that affect the elderly in addition to the different perspectives and ideologies that support or refute policies. This section of the chapter will address teaching about ideology as well as highlight some of the current social problems that face the elderly in American society.

Ideology

One important knowledge objective in an aging policy course could include the social construction of aging (Lee and Estes 1979) addressing the following components:
Old age is:

- A social problem
- 'Different,' 'deviant' and requires special needs
- 'Resolvable' with programs and services
- Inevitable physical problems and decline
- Dependency

The danger of such constructions is that these ideologies influence public opinion on aging policies. The policy result may be a reinforcement of social, racial, class and gender divides or the idea that old people are a burden, dependent, and unproductive people who failed to save for their retirement and over use health care (Lee and Estes 1979). The end result is a "wasteful patchwork of often contradictory solutions" (Lee and Estes 1979, 4) that occurs when the significant problems of older adults are socially constructed as a result of misinformed social conceptions (Estes, Linkins and Binney 1996). Challenging social work students' own implicit and explicit notions of what 'old age' means to them as well as to society is an important first step in making the ideology-policy response connection.

There are other useful ideologies related to aging policy worth exploring. *Cumulative disadvantage theory*, for example, explores the manner in which experiences based on social status, gender; ethnicity and race throughout the life course can influence, define, or possibly mirror experiences in old age (Meyer and Herd 2001). Posing questions to individual students or small groups in which they are asked to project into the future about their own age cohort might help students see this in perspective (Meyer and Herd 2001).

The *political economy perspective* emphasizes the idea that industries such as nursing homes or long term care facilities have "financial interest in controlling the definition and treatment of aging" and therefore are likely to pathologize aging in order to create a need for services (Estes, Linkins and Binney 1996). Such a notion is similar to the age old debate of the role of social workers as social control or social change agents. Similarly, Specht and Courtney (1997) believe that the current emphasis on individual private practice makes social workers 'unfaithful angels' who are more concerned with increasing their income than in fostering greater social change. It is important that social work students consider such debates. For example, small group assignments or short papers could require students to consider such questions as: Is social work complicit in the perpetuation of social problems rather than moving to change them? What would happen if nursing homes, home health care, etc. were no longer needed? Do social workers need social problems in order to justify their professional mission? Does reliance on individual solutions lead to the abandonment of the mission of social work, i.e., to advocate for poor and oppressed populations? Some of these discussions with students need to address the comparison and contrasts between universal entitlement based programs and selective means tested programs and their effects on aging policy. For example, although Medicare and Medicaid have similar goals, Medicaid is poorly regarded while Medicare remains popular with the public.

Overview of Social Problems

The following section highlights some of the important social problems that face older adults in our society. Web resources related to each topic are provided in tables throughout this section.

Ageism

Generally, ageism refers to the stereotypic bias against older adults (Butler 1969; Nuessel 1982). Such views (primarily negative) of older adults are present throughout society—for example, language used to describe older people and images viewed in the media (Nuessel 1982). These ageist attitudes and actions serve to subordinate people on the basis of age. The incidence of discrimination on the basis of age is on the rise, most likely due to the graying of America (U.S. Equal Employment Opportunity Commission (EEOC) 2002). In 2001, 21.5% of all filings to the EEOC were due to age discrimination (EEOC 2002). Job discrimination based on age affects certain groups of elderly workers more than others including displaced homemakers, workers in declining industries, and workers in high technology fields. It has been noted that the elderly employed in the technology fields are often stereotyped as 'out of date' (American Association of Retired Persons (AARP) 2002; Computing Research Association 2000; Steen 1998). After older adults lose their jobs, they face an even more challenging time getting rehired at another job (AARP 2002). Where they still exist, mandatory retirement policies are harmful as well.

Gay, Lesbian, and Bisexual Older Adults

It has been estimated that there are between one and four million Americans over 65 years of age who are gay, lesbian, or bisexual (GLB) in the United States (National Gay and Lesbian Task Force (NGLTF) 2003). The number of GLB older adults is expected to rise as the population ages and by 2030 it is expected that four million older adults will be GLB (National Gay and Lesbian Task Force (NGLTF) 2002). Despite this demographic fact, modest interest, expenditure, and planning have been focused on the social problems faced by gay and lesbian adults (Tirrito 2003; Quam 1993). Like all ages of most GLB individuals in the U.S., social policies often neglect older GLB adults while services are almost nonexistent. Although significant strides have been made in societal acceptance of GLB individuals, most GLB older adults were not raised in environments that accepted homosexuality. In fact, growing up and living as a GLB adult was often an unsafe and oppressive experience (Quam 1993). GLB older adults face many barriers to accessing ser-vices—particularly during periods of caregiving and post-caregiving when many GLB partners are ignored or excluded (NGLTF 2002). Such exclusion often leaves GLB older adults isolated in later life as most GLB older adults live alone (NGLTF 2002).

Minority Adults

Minority populations are also living longer and contributing to a racially diverse older American population (Torres-Gil and Moga 2001). Despite this, services to ethnically and racially diverse groups have not kept pace with demographic realities and the need for culturally sensitive services. Often, minority elderly face many of the same social problems and barriers to access and delivery of social services as minorities in the general population. Minority elderly are more likely to be indigent, in poor health, and have less access to health care and social services (AOA 2002; National Hispanic Council on Aging 2003; National Resource Center on Native American Aging 2002). Divorced African-American women (ages 65-74) have the highest rate of poverty (47%), more than any other subgroup of Americans (AOA 2002). Many barriers, such as language and poverty, impact the accessibility of services for minority elderly (AOA 2002; National Hispanic Council on Aging 2003). In fact, African-Americans and Hispanics are the most likely to report delays in obtaining health care due to costs (AOA 2002). Due to limited educational or employment histories, many minority elderly are reliant on Social Security as their primary income (AOA 2002). For example, immigrant groups who experience intermittent employment patterns and participate in non-traditional agricultural labor often tend to accrue limited retirement benefits (Hudson 2002; Kajakazi 2002). Hispanics are less likely to be covered by pension plans further eroding their economic foundation. Over the lifetime, poor people are less likely to be able to save or accumulate assets to be used later in life (Hudson 2002).

Women

Older women comprise the majority of the population over 65 and experience higher poverty rates than older men. Women also tend to have paucity of retirement funds, pension plans, or Social Security income primarily because of employment patterns over the life course (Kajakazi 2002). Women provide the bulk of informal caregiver support and often provide this care in the context of limited resources. Biases in health care research and services have also impacted upon older women's access to and quality of health care. Less than 3% of the federal budget for health and medical care goes to research devoted to health care for older women (Our Bodies Ourselves 2003).

Table 4: Diversity and Aging Resources

Michigan Center for Urban African American Aging Research
http://mcuaaar.iog.wayne.edu/
Center on Minority Aging
http://www.unc.edu/depts/cmaweb/
Center for Aging in Diverse Communities
http://medicine.ucsf.edu/cadc/
'National Resource Center on Native American Aging
http://www.und.nodak.edu/dept/nrcnaa/
National Hispanic Council on Aging
http://www.nhcoa.org/
'National Center on Women and Aging
http://www.heller.brandeis.edu/national/ind.html
'National Asian Pacific Center on Aging
http://www.napca.org/
'Gay and Lesbian Aging (resources compiled by Linda Woolf at Webster University) http://www.webster.edu/~woolflm/oldergay.html
'American Society on Aging: Lesbian and Gay Aging Issues Network
http://www.asaging.org/networks/lgain/index.html
'Gay Lesbian Association of Retired Persons
http://www.gaylesbianretiring.org/index.htm
Senior Action in a Gay Environment
http://www.sageusa.org/
Age Rights.Com
http://www.agerights.com/
Our Bodies Ourselves
http://www.ourbodiesourselves.org/)
National Women's Health Information Center
http://www.4woman.gov/
AOA: Ageism in Employment Resources
http://www.aoa.gov/NAIC/Notes/agesim.html#Ageism%20in%20Employment

Health Care

Health care issues regarding cost, access, and quality are of paramount concern to older adults. Recently, the cost of prescription drugs has become a top concern. On average, older adults spend 3.1% of their income on prescription drugs (RAND 1999). The high cost of health care is also a serious problem for many elderly Americans who pay a higher proportion of their incomes for health care than other groups (AOA 2002; Day 2002). Minority and low income elderly spend an even higher percentage of their incomes on health care and prescription costs and are more likely to have even less access to health care services (AOA 2000).

Table 5: Health Care Resources

Center of Medicaid and Medicare Services
http://cms.hhs.gov/
Aging for Health Care Research and Quality
http://www.ahcpr.gov/
Institute for Health, Health Care Policy, and Aging Research at Rutgers
http://www.ihhcpar.rutgers.edu/
Health Hippo
http://hippo.findlaw.com/hippohome.html
Medicare Reform from the 20th Century Fund
http://www.tcf.org/Publications/Basics/Medicare/
National Committee to Preserve Social Security and Medicare
http://www.ncpssm.org/
National Health Care Council
http://www.nationalhealthcouncil.org/

Financial Well Being

Poverty rates for older adults are alarming. Approximately 3.4 million older adults (1 of every 6) are poor or "near poor" (AOA 2002). Minority elderly are even more likely to be indigent (Torres-Gill and Moga 2001). For example, although African-American elderly comprise 8% of the total elderly population, this group constitutes 36% of low income elderly (Torres-Gil and Moga 2001). Women and individuals residing alone or with non relatives were most likely to be poor (AOA 2002).

The future of Social Security is certainly in question. Solvency is but one of the many problems and criticisms of the Social Security system. Issues related to equity and fairness have been raised. Social Security is unfair for low wage workers, minorities, working women, and young

Americans (Alliance for Worker Retirement Security 2000). Times have changed dramatically since 1935 when the Social Security Act was passed and its current form does not resemble its original design (Schulz 1996; Cutler 1997). Although the public by and large views Social Security as the mainstay of financial security for the elderly, it was not established as their primary source of retirement income (Cutler 1997). In fact, as elders have been living longer and retiring earlier, the wealth accumulation stage has decreased while the expenditure stage has increased (Cutler 1997). Gregg and Cutler (1991) refer to this as the human wealth span and report that this span has been changing dramatically since the 20th century. These changes have serious implications not only for the future of Social Security, but also for employment policy and social services. Originally constructed as a fairly simple retirement plan, the Social Security system now encompasses many programs. Due to the projected enormous demographic strain, the Social Security system is expected to run a deficit in about 15 years and most estimates report that without significant policy changes it will become bankrupt (Social Security Reform Center n.d.; Williamson 1997).

Despite the fact that Social Security was not designed to provide a full income for elderly retirees, it still comprises the majority of income for most of the elderly population and dependency increases significantly with age (Kisor, McSweeny, and Jackson 2000; Schulz 1996). The three most prevalent reform proposals: raising payroll taxes, modifications of retirement age, and privatization have been criticized (Quinn 1996; Social Security Reform Center n.d.). One of the biggest concerns with current reform proposals is that they represent a disproportionate threat for women, low wage workers, and minorities who experience higher rates of poverty and are more likely to depend on Social Security benefits for the majority of their income. Since for the poorest 20% of the elderly Social Security benefits provide 81% of their income (Tanner 1996), privatization reform policies may pose a serious threat to their economic security (Alliance for Worker Retirement Security 2000; Kisor, McSweeny, and Jackson 2000; Tanner 1996). This disproportionate threat of privatization has led Tanner (2001) to remark that current proposals for privatization of Social Security are a civil rights issue. African-Americans gain less from Social Security benefits mostly as a result of shorter life expectancies and paying a higher percentage of their incomes in payroll taxes (Tanner 2001). As a result, many poor elderly have little discretionary cash to save and invest (Hudson 2002). Obviously, the more income a person has, the more money he or she can place in pensions, private accounts and investments, and other retirement funds (Tanner 1996; Hudson 2002).

Table 6: Financial Security Resources

Social Security Online
http://www.ssa.gov/
'The Cato Institute Project on Social Security Choice
http://www.socialsecurity.org/index.html
'For Our Grandchildren: A Social Security Education Project
http://www.forourgrandchildren.org/
'Social Security Reform Center
http://www.socialsecurityreform.org/index.cfm
'Alliance for Worker Retirement Security
http://www.retiresecure.org/
'National Center for Policy Analysis and Social Security
http://www.mysocialsecurity.org/filters/index.html
'National Senior Citizens Law Center
http://www.nsclc.org/index.html

Social Services: Elder Abuse, Nutrition, Transportation, Housing

Elder Abuse

Elder abuse is a significant problem in today's society. In 1996 there was more than half a million individuals over 60 who experienced abuse. Risks for abuse increase with age (AOA 2001a). Most domestic abuse typically involves relatives in caregiving roles (AOA 2001a; National Center on Elder Abuse 2002b). Categories of elder abuse can include domestic or institutional (such as nursing home) and self neglect or self abuse (National Center on Elder Abuse 2000b). The elderly are also susceptible to predatory lending practices, fraud, and financial abuse.

Malnutrition

Malnutrition is a problem for older Americans in a variety of living situations—in their own homes, in nursing homes or other care facilities

(35-50%) or even hospitals (65% estimated) (National Policy and Resource Center on Nutrition and Aging 2002). Malnutrition is especially problematic for the elderly who have special nutritional needs or diseases where diet is important, such as hypertension and diabetes. The number of older adults living in their own communities who are malnourished is in the hundreds of thousands, with one estimate that over one million homebound elders may be malnourished (National Policy and Resource Center on Nutrition and Aging 2002).

Transportation

Despite its apparent importance, transportation policy has been a neglected domain of aging policy (Bush 2001; Kisor, McSweeny, and Jackson 2000; Coughlin 2001). Older adults comprise a large percentage of the 'transportation disadvantaged' (Surface Transportation Policy Project 1996-2003) and face a variety of transportation problems including a lack of reliable, affordable and flexible transportation options. There is limited transportation available on weekends or evenings. Further, mass transit is often not equipped to assist individuals with mobility issues (e.g., working lifts to accommodate wheelchairs). For older adults, locating and securing transportation to medical appointments or health care services is a serious problem as "transportation provides the necessary links between activities that support healthy living and hence healthy aging" (Bush 2001, 1). Transportation provides vital links between the elderly and their families and driving has been linked to quality of life and active aging (Coughlin 2001). Very few older adults plan for the inevitable time when they must stop driving; driving cessation in older adults has been linked to depression (Coughlin 2001). Without adequate transportation, many older adults become socially isolated. There are risks to the general population as well as it has been projected that without adequate transportation policy, fatalities due to motor vehicle accidents will increase (Bush 2001).

Housing

Housing is a significant problem for many older adults. Many of the poorest elderly pay more than half of their incomes on housing, often of poor quality (American Association of Housing and Services for the Aging 2003). Although a high demand for elderly housing exists, few units are built (under 6000 units yearly as part of HUD Section 202 program) (American Association of Housing and Services for the Aging 2003). Currently, some of the subsidized housing used by the elderly has been converted to housing that is unaffordable. Programs that encourage preservation and renovation of housing for older adults are not widespread and when they do exist, they are managed with few resources.

Table 7: Social Service Resources

National Committee for the Prevention of Elder Abuse
http://www.preventelderabuse.org/
Sustainable Transportation—US Department of Energy
http://www.sustainable.doe.gov/transprt/trintro.shtml
Surface Transportation Policy Project
http://www.transact.org/
Ford-MIT Alliance Library (see Active Safety Articles)
http://ford-mit.mit.edu/Library.htm
Senior Citizens and HUD
http://www.hud.gov/groups/seniors.cfm
American Association of Homes and Services for the Aging
http://www.aahsa.org/

Caregiving

There is great need for caregiving in our society but it comes at great cost both financially and emotionally. Certainly, as people age, caregiving needs intensify. Caregiving is a tremendous responsibility and as the population continues to age, it will soon be the normative experience for most Americans. It is estimated that about one of every three persons over 65 needs some form of care or assistance and over 30% of the adult population provides informal caregiver services (National Family Caregivers Association (NFCA) 2000; Older Women's League (OWL) 2003). This translates into roughly 50 million caregivers in the United States (NFCA 2000). Despite these overwhelming statistics, very little formal support is given to caregivers.

State expenditures for institutional care far exceed resources allocated for informal caregivers. Informal caregivers (family, friends, neighbors, church members) providing unpaid care provide the majority of care. Their contribution goes largely unnoticed, unpaid, and under-appreciated.

Informal caregivers are generally reluctant to access or use supportive services and provide services without much assistance or support (Alzheimers Association 1991; Cantor 1992; Montgomery and Borgatta 1989). It has been estimated that the 'free' services that family caregivers provide amounts to approximately $257 billion dollars per year (Arno, Levine and Memmott 1999). If people currently living in their own homes would go into institutional care, the state and federal expenses would increase dramatically. The typical caregiver is female, middle aged, and related to the recipient of care (Beckett, et al. 2000; Brody 1985; OWL 2003; Williams 1995), although some research has noted that this gender discrepancy is changing as men now comprise 44% of the caregiving population (NFCA 2000). Brody (1985) calls the widespread myth that families are unwilling to provide care for older adults as the 'Myth of Abandonment'. Clearly, the societal expectation that families should bear the significant financial and emotional costs of caregiving is present in current policy. Many caregivers care for both their children and older adults making them a part of what has been termed the 'Sandwich Generation'.

The 'woodwork effect' is used as a rationale for limiting resources for community and home based care. This argument stems from the notion that there is a hierarchy of assistance where individuals and family have responsibility before government (Ginsberg 1999). In other words, if benefits were extended to home and community based services, people would 'come out of the woodwork' and overtax the formal service system. This flies in the face of evidence that suggests that very few people seek institutional care and prefer to keep family members at home even *without* payment (Bass et al. 1994; Biegel et al. 1993; Collins et al. 1991). Even if families enhance their caregiving responsibilities with paid home care, they do not abandon their involvement (Brody 1985; Doty 1986; Hamilton et al. 1996; Tennstedt, Crawford, and McKinlay 1993). Further, often intensely involved caregivers do not receive consistent help from others, including other family members, and provide much of the care in isolation (NFCA 1998).

Costs to caregivers are many. Caregiving is stressful, demanding, and expensive. The typical caregiver works full time and provides care an average of 18 hours a week for 4.5 years, although this time frame is expected to increase as life expectancy increases (OWL 2003; Williams 1995). Yet, depending on the situation, caregiving can entail 24-hour around the clock care. Full time caregivers suffer from depression and other mental health problems at higher rates than non-caregivers (NFCA 1998).

It is estimated that businesses lose between $11-29 billion yearly due to time off for caregiving and that individual caregivers lose over $600,000 in income because of caregiving responsibilities (Family Caregiver Alliance 2002; Metropolitan Life Insurance Company 1997). Caregivers often have little leisure time and must balance other caregiving responsibilities (Family Caregiver Alliance 2002). Finally, there are fewer family caregivers available. In 1990, the ratio of caregivers to recipient was 11:1, and in 2050 the ratio is projected to be 4:1 (Institute for Health and Aging 1996).

Table 8: Caregiving Resources

The Sandwich Generation http://www.thesandwichgeneration.com/ The Sandwich Generation: A Cluttered Nest http://www.ianr.unl.edu/pubs/family/g1117.htm National Alliance for Caregiving http://www.caregiving.org/ Family Caregiver Alliance—National Center on Caregiving Policy http://www.caregiver.org/policy.html National Family Caregivers Association http://www.nfcacares.org/

Description of Aging Policies

As noted in the social problems section, there are many social policy areas related to aging. These include: health care, financial security, social services (abuse, nutrition, transportation, and housing) and caregiving. It would be difficult to cover each of these policy areas in great detail. Table 14 at the end of the chapter highlights, in chronological order beginning with the 1920's, social welfare policies relevant to aging and is basically an extended version of the AOA list of historical evolution of programs for older Americans as listed in the history section of this chapter. Many of the most important aging policies (OAA, SSA and Medicare) have been amended many times since their original conception and these amendments are noted in Table 14 as well. It is suggested that social work educators use this chart when considering what aging policy content to consider, whether one is considering developing an aging policy in its entirety or infusing aging policy content in an existing course.

Aging Policy Hot Topics

In terms of current policy topics, it is essential that policy educators remain in touch with current 'hot topics' relevant to aging policy. This can be accomplished quite easily by subscribing to various alert lists. Table 9 provides a list of policy alert email lists, news alerts, or action alerts. Participation in such lists often provides the subscriber to up-to-date policy events such as legislative action, progress or status. These updates can provide current information on policy-relevant issues often minutes before class as the instructor checks email! These lists can be a valuable tool in policy instruction.

Table 9: Example of Policy Alert E-mail Lists or New Events

AARP Citizen Advocate Registration
http://www.capitolconnect.com/aarp/recruitment/Registration.asp
OMB Watch
http://www.ombwatch.org/article/articlestatic/11/1/7/
National Health Council Advocacy Page
http://www.nationalhealthcouncil.org/advocacy/adv_index.htm
American Association of Geriatric Psychiatrists—Action Alerts, Legislative Action Center
http://www.aagponline.org/advocacy/default.asp
American Association of Housing and Services for the Aging, Advocacy and News alerts
http://www.aahsa.org/
Friday Alerts from the Alliance for Retired Americans
http://www.retiredamericans.org/fridayalerts.htm

Hot Topics

It is essential that social work students have a solid grasp of health policies in the United States, particularly if they plan to work with older adults. Understanding the basics of Medicaid and Medicare would be an important start. There are important professional and ethical issues that would provide a lively course discussion on the topic of health care. Medicare is the largest public health insurance program in the United States and provides the major source of health coverage for the elderly and enjoys a fair amount of public support. Before the program was initiated, very few older Americans enjoyed adequate health insurance. Currently, Medicare is faced with several challenges. Moon (1999) notes that solutions aimed at revitalizing Medicare must entail meeting three main challenges (1) the rising costs of spending on health care; (2) exponential growth of Medicare beneficiaries; and, (3) inadequate revenue contributions into the Medicare fund. Finally, as noted previously, prescription drug coverage for older adults remains a significant problem which needs to be addressed.

For many elderly, disparities in health care, housing, transportation, and social services exist. It is important to teach social work students to see the connections between poverty and other aspects of aging and well being. A large part of this discussion relates to retirement security and the Social Security system. The solvency of the Social Security system is obviously of paramount concern to many Americans. The current administration is interested in privatization of Social Security and several researchers have questioned the impact such a policy would have on women, low wage workers, and minorities. Life course planning on the part of all Americans is poor, as a whole; Americans do not save money well (Takamura 1999). Until the problem is resolved, one should expect Social Security to remain a priority aging policy topic.

The Older Americans Act was hailed as a significant piece of legislation. The establishment of the Administration of Aging ('aging network') and the goal to coordinate public services and resources for the elderly was and remains a significant contribution of the OAA. In fact, it has been noted that the SSA and OAA are core components of services to the elderly population (Carlton-LaNey 1997). However, current funding of OAA is a significant issue and is "insufficient to support its broad and comprehensive network of programs" which has resulted in a "symbolic gesture of commitment to elders" (Carlton-LaNey 1997, 287). Further, OAA programs are not immune from charitable choice provisions which may have impacts on funding and accessibility of social services. As noted in Table 14, the OAA has been amended numerous times and some have noted that this has resulted in its 'scatter shot' implementation approach (Kisor, McSweeney, and Jackson 2000).

The OAA has also had to keep pace with a growing and changing population of older adults. As the needs of the older population have shifted from 'meals on wheels' to more comprehensive needs such as long term care, the OAA has been criticized for falling behind (Hudson 1995). Another criticism of the OAA is that it creams the non poor or non needy elderly and fails to reach those older adults who need services the most.

The flip side to this, however, is that as OAA expands into home and community based care by targeting services and establishing eligibility, controversy follows it (Hudson 1996). The shift from age-based entitlement policies to policies targeted by means tests, membership in a minority group, income, and functionality has caused rifts in the aging lobby as well as problems with implementation (Liebig 1995).

Perhaps not as much in the forefront as Social Security or Medicare reform, issues related to transportation and housing are still important and will need serious debate in the near future. A solid and comprehensive plan for housing and transportation for the elderly has never had a solid foundation despite the growing demand for both.

Finally, caregiving has emerged as a vitally important policy topic for all Americans. Caregiving will be the normative experience for most Americans, yet policy initiatives to address the variables related to caregiving have lagged far behind. Caregiving affects the elderly, their families, employers of caregivers, and society.

Debates, discussions, small group assignments or short papers can be a useful way to enable students to explore current policy topics. Engaging in debates also gets students to consider the various ideological perspectives related to policy issues, policy responses, and the acquisition of critical thinking skills. The following table enumerates policy topics with suggestions for teaching.

Table 10: Policy Area, Hot Topics and Possible Questions and Debates

Policy Area	Current Hot Topic	Possible Questions/Debate Topics
Financial Security	▪ Privatization of social security ▪ Cash balance plans ▪ Solvency of Social Security ▪ Fairness of Social Security	▪ Should Social Security be an entitlement? ▪ Why don't Americans save? How do we encourage saving? ▪ How do we save Social Security? ▪ How and why are public perceptions of TANF and Social Security different? The same?

Policy Area	Current Hot Topic	Possible Questions/Debate Topics
Health Care	<ul><li>Prescription Drug Coverage</li><li>Medicare managed care</li><li>Current proposed cuts to Medicaid and Medicare</li><li>Health disparities</li></ul>	<ul><li>Is health care a right?</li><li>How much coverage is enough?</li><li>How can we justify end of life care and costs?</li><li>How do we address health care disparities? Why do health care disparities exist?</li><li>Should health care services to the elderly be rationed?</li></ul>
Social Services, Older Americans Act	<ul><li>Charitable Choice</li><li>Cuts in funding for social services</li><li>Devolution</li><li>Shift from age entitlement policies to targeted residual policies for social services</li></ul>	<ul><li>What are the advantages and disadvantages of delivering social services through faith-based initiatives to older adults?</li><li>What does the shift from entitlement to residual polices represent?</li><li>Is it a good idea to 'target' groups of the elderly or to require eligibility tests for OAA programs?</li></ul>
Transportation	<ul><li>Lack of affordable, accessible and reliable public transportation</li><li>Public safety</li></ul>	<ul><li>How do we balance needs of the elderly and public safety?</li><li>How do we provide safe access to services?</li></ul>
Housing	<ul><li>Lack of affordable, safe, quality housing</li></ul>	<ul><li>How will we address housing needs? Who will be able to afford it?</li></ul>

Policy Area	Current Hot Topic	Possible Questions/Debate Topics
Caregiving	<ul><li>Woodwork effect</li><li>Nursing home bias</li><li>Myth of abandonment</li><li>Increased need for long term care in the U.S.</li><li>Sandwich generation</li></ul>	<ul><li>Are families responsible for the care of older relatives? Does this view vary by cultural factors?</li><li>How is caregiving a gender issue?</li><li>What is another type of 'unpaid' labor by women in our society and how does it compare to caregiving?</li><li>Does the 'woodwork effect' argument make sense in relation to caregiving?</li><li>What is the ideal way to care for older adults?</li><li>Is the 'nursing home bias' warranted?</li><li>Is the 'myth of abandonment' true for you? For your family? For others you know?</li></ul>

Implementation: The Forgotten Discussion

Finally, when discussing current policies in aging, it is often useful to discuss issues related to implementation and the relationships between federal, state and local agencies. Sometimes in the rush to describe policy, the many ways in which policies are shaped by implementation are ignored. Examination of the organizational structure of the National Aging Network can provide an excellent opportunity for student exploration of policy implementation. Such an exercise will provide for a more direct and useful understanding of the responsibilities and activities at the various levels of government. The organizational chart of the National Aging Service Network is available online (http:www.aoa.gov/aoa/PAGES/orgchart-med2.gif).

Advocacy and Public Policy

Despite the fact that the Social Security Act of 1935 remains the mainstay of public programs designed to assist older people, the United States has seen a dramatic disinterest in entitlement based policies and even such popular programs as Social Security and Medicare are not immune (Torres-Gil and Moga 2001). In response to increased devolution, states often find themselves in intense debates about the allocation of scarce resources. Frequently 'children' and 'the elderly' are pitted against one another as potential recipients of scarce resources. Although some have thought of the elderly as an 'untouchable' group, recent evidence suggests that the once wholesale support for policies that impact the elderly has been in serious decline in the last decades (Kisor, McSweeny, and Jackson 2000; Torres-Gil and Moga 2001). Such a decline in support has serious implications for support of policies related to aging. This is happening during a time that requires a more nuanced approach to policy and social service delivery due to the changing demographics of aging population and diversity or the 'Nexus of Aging and Diversity' (Torres-Gil and Moga 2001). Torres-Gil and Moga (2001) note that "between 2010 and 2020, we will see an entitlement crisis in which our inability to make structural changes to programs for the elderly will make the programs untenable and unaffordable; ... lack of preparation for aging will put a large portion of older persons at risk for poverty and poor health" (Torres-Gil and Moga 2001, 21). Aging advocates must be skilled at policy analysis while also "seeking common reference points that lessen separation, segregation and disunity" (Torres-Gil and Moga 2001, 19).

The "politics of aging refers to older persons and their organized interest groups shaping public policy and influencing the political agenda" (Torres-Gil and Moga 2001, 20). Since the OAA was enacted in 1965, the number of aging interest groups has dramatically increased. These groups are actively involved in politics and have made themselves quite visible to the public (Binstock and Day 1996). The rise of aging interest groups and the elderly as a political force to be contended with has developed in the United States over time. It is important that social work students become familiar with these organizations and their missions, history, and current activities.

There are many active and important advocacy organizations in the field of aging. The Association of Retired Persons (AARP), with its 35 million members, is the most prominent but is by no means the only organization that lobbies on behalf of older adults (Binstock and Day 1996). One of the challenges for social workers is to find ways to lessen the divide between the various aging interest groups as there are few collaborative relationships or coalitions among these groups (Torres-Gil and Moga 2001). Thus, social work students must be taught that "advocacy around gerontology and social work must accommodate the reality of shifting alliances" and work to build more sophisticated alliances among groups (Torres-Gil and Moga 2001, 28). The voice of advocacy of aging groups has been defensive as opposed to proactive including such activities as opposing tax hikes or protecting entitlement programs with acknowledged problems.

The fragmentation of aging policies makes it even more difficult to advocate for unified change (Binstock and Day 1996). The fact that aging interest groups are not unified makes them more vulnerable to failure. Further, "the current attraction of conservative thinking around aging politics is well beyond that associated with the long-standing political popularity of the old and the real or alleged strength of the organized aged… current assaults on aging-related programs are nothing less than attempts to reresidualize the old and deinstituionalize the policies" (Hudson 1999, 359). The evidence is clear: there is an aging advocacy imperative. Social work students must be given information not only about the history and current trends of social problems or knowledge of current policies but they must also possess a thorough understanding of the relevant aging advocacy organizations, political players, and the barriers to advocacy in the field of aging.

Interestingly, at the last annual program meeting of CSWE (2003), the National Gerontological Social Work Conference sponsored several presentations addressing advocacy and aging (Hermanoso, Overly, Tompkins, Simons (2003); Karjala (2003); DeHope and Joyner 2003). These presentations included a partnership between the National Committee to Preserve Social Security and Medicare (NCPSSM) that developed an intergenerational policy and advocacy course (Hermanoso, Overly, Tompkins, Simons (2003) and the development of a Town meeting for the dissemination of information on resources and services for the aging (DeHope and Joyner 2003). Another interesting project presented older adults in the roles of social activists (Deines and Richart 2003). Model assignments specific to activism were prominent. Table 11 highlights some of the notable advocacy resources available online.

Table 11: Advocacy Resources

American Association of Retired People (AARP)
http://www.aarp.org/
Capital Hill Basics from AARP
http://capwiz.com/aarp/issues/basics/?style=comm
AARP Legislative Action Center
http://capwiz.com/aarp/home/
Aging Research and Advocacy Groups—compiled by Monika Deppen at
Rutgers University
http://crab.rutgers.edu/~deppen/advocacy.htm
Association of Retired Americans
http://www.ara-usa.org/
National Association of Retired Federal Employees
http://www.narfe.org/
National Committee to Preserve Social Security and Medicare
http://www.ncpssm.org/
National Senior Citizens Law Center
http://www.nsclc.org/index.html
Raging Grannies of Boston
http://www.wilpfboston.org/raging.html
Gray Panthers
http://www.graypanthers.org/
Seniors Active in a Gay Environment (SAGE)
http://www.sageusa.org/
Advocacy—Family Caregiving Alliance
Fact Sheet: Advocacy Tips for Family Caregivers
http://www.caregiver.org/factsheets/advocacy_tips.html

Other Aging Policy Teaching Strategies and Ideas

For those educators interested in finding more specific classroom exercises, strategies and resources related to aging policy, Table 12 highlights the teaching resources and syllabi related to aging policy available on the internet. Table 13 highlights clearinghouses of aging related information available online. Aging policy case studies are also available (Adams 2003; Kisor, McSweeney, and Jackson 2000). Adams (2003), in particular, describes using the SSA website and video to teach social work students about Social Security. Cooperative learning environments provide students with opportunities to talk, share learning, and self manage based on strengths (Cianciolo, Henderson, Kretzer and Mendes 2001). These authors highlight several collaborative learning strategies and modules related to aging and public policy (1) Social Security reform; and, (2) international aging policy and women. Brown (1999) suggests using two conflicting schools of thought to frame a debate on a policy topic, i.e., using devolutionists versus safety netters to argue Medicare or Social Security in light of the current climate whereby entitlement—institutional age based policies—are being questioned.

Table 12: Teaching Resources and Syllabi on Aging Policy

Association for Gerontology in Higher Education

http://www.aghe.org/aghe/
Introducing Public Policy Issues in Aging into the Curriculum, Syracuse University
http://www-cpr.maxwell.syr.edu/gero_ed/wrkshp00.htm
Aging Policy Issues Carolyn M. Shrewsbury, Mankato State University (exercises)
http://krypton.mankato.msus.edu/~cbury/web/Courses97-8/aging.html
Links to several Syllabi related to aging policy
http://crab.rutgers.edu/~deppen/syllabi.htm
Internet Resources for teaching Sociology of Aging
http://www.crab.rutgers.edu/~deppen/aging.htm
Policy oriented Gerontology Curriculum
http://www-cpr.maxwell.syr.edu/gero_ed/index.htm
Women's Health Syllabus - resources for Women aging and health
http://www.twu.edu/hs/hs/ws3133/whsched.htm
Women and Old Age Syllabus
http://www-cpr.maxwell.syr.edu/gero_ed/family.htm
Topics on Aging Policy
http://uwadmnweb.uwyo.edu/Pols/courses/471001011as.html'

Table 13: Internet Resources or Clearinghouses on Aging Information

AARP Guide to Internet resources on aging
http://www.aarp.org/cyber/guide1.htm
GeroWeb
http://geroserver.iog.wayne.edu/GeroWebd/GeroWeb.html
Aging Policy Sources Online
http://www.lib.umich.edu/socwork/agingpolicy.html
AOA
http://www.aoa.gov/aoa/PAGES/aoa.html
AOA: Resources for Practitioners and Other Professionals in Aging
http://www.aoa.gov/practice/default.htm
AOA: The Many Faces of Aging: Resources to Effectively Serve Minority
Older Persons Promising Practices and Programs
http://www.aoa.gov/minorityaccess/promising-practices.html
ElderWeb
http://www.elderweb.com/default.php?PageID=1

Table 14: Aging Policies over Time

Time Period	Policy/ Event/Type	
1920-1960		
1920	Civil Service Retirement Act	Provided a retirement system for some governmental employees.
1935	Social Security Act	Established basic federal old-age benefits programs and federal-state system of unemployment insurance.
1937	Railroad Retirement Act	Provided pensions for retired railroad employees/spouses.
1946	Hill-Burton Act	Provided direct grants for construction of 350,000 beds in health care facilities; amended in 1954 to provide grants for construction of nursing homes.

1950	First National Conference on Aging	Initiated by President Truman, sponsored by the Federal Security Agency.
1952	First Federal funds appropriated for social services programs	First federal funds appropriated for social service programs for older persons under the Social Security Act.
1956	Special Staff on Aging	Established within the Office of the Secretary of Health, Education and Welfare, to coordinate responsibilities for aging.
	Federal Council on Aging	
	Social Security Amendments	Added new insurance program for disabled workers50 and older; changed OASI to OASDI.
1959	Housing Act	Authorized a direct loan program for non-profit rental projects for the elderly at low interest rates. Lowered eligibility ages for public-low-rent housing.
1960-1980		
1960	Extension of Social Security Benefits	Eliminated age 50 as minimum for qualifying for disability benefits, and relaxed the retirement test and requirement for fully insured status.
1961	First White House Conference on Aging	
	Social Security Amendments	Lowered the retirement age for men, relaxed the retirement test, and increased minimum benefits and benefits to aged widows.
1965	Medicare	Title XVIII: a health insurance program for the elderly

	Medicaid	Title XIX: health insurance for low income people.
	The Older Americans Act	Established the Administration on Aging and initiated state units on aging.
1967	Older Americans Act extended for 2 years	Provisions made for the Administration on Aging to study the personnel needs in the aging field.
	Age Discrimination in Employment (ADEA)	Under ADEA, it is unlawful to discriminate against a person because of his/her age with respect to any term, condition, or privilege of employment or benefits.
1969	Older Americans Act amendments	Grants for model demonstration projects given: Foster Grandparents, and Retired Senior Volunteer Programs.
1971	Second White House Conference on Aging	
1972	Older Americans Act amendments	Title VII added: authorizes funds for a national nutrition program for the elderly.
	Social Security amendments	Indexed SS benefits to Consumer Price Index (CPI)so benefits increased with prices.
1973	Older Americans Act Comprehensive Services amendments.	Established Area Agencies on Aging. Title V: authorizes grants to local community agencies for multi-purpose senior centers; created the Community Service Employment grant program.
	Comprehensive Employment and Training Act	Included provisions for older persons.
1974	Supplementary Security income (SSI)	Replaced federal-state programs for the blind, disabled and older Americans with a direct federal aid program.

	Employee Retirement Income Security Act	Established 10 year vesting standard & regulated portability.
	Title XX of Social Security amendments	Title XX of the Social Security Amendments authorized grants to states for social services to the elderly.
	Older Americans Act amendments	Title III: added transportation under model projects.
	Housing and Community Development Act	Provided for low-income housing for the elderly and handicapped.
	Title V of the Farm and Rural Housing Program	Expanded to include the rural elderly.
	National Institute on Aging	Created to conduct research and training related to the aging.
	Employment Retirement IncomeSecurity Act (ERISA)	Regulated private pensions.
1975	Older Americans Act amendments	Title III: grants provided to Indian tribal organizations. Mandated transportation, home care, legal services, and home renovation/repair as priority services.
1977	Older Americans Act amendments	Changed the Title VII nutrition program
	Social Security amendments	Raised SS tax rates to bring in additional revenue.
1978	Older Americans Act amendments	Title III: Area Agency on Aging administration and social services; Title VII: nutrition services; Title V: multipurpose senior centers were combined into a new Title III.
		Added Title VI: for grants to Indian Tribal Organizations.

		The former Title V became the Community Service Employment grant program for low-income persons, aged 55 and older.
	Congregate Housing Services Act	Authorized contracts with local public housing agencies and non-profit corporations, to provide group independent living service programs.
	OAA amendments	States required to establish a long-term care ombudsman program to cover nursing homes
1980-2000		
1981	Third White House Conference on Aging	
	Social Services Block Grant Program	Amended Title XX. It funds states for the provision of social services to be directed towards economic self-support or self-sufficiency; preventing or remedying neglect, abuse, or exploitation of children and adults; preventing or reducing inappropriate institutionalization; and, securing referral for institutional care where appropriate.
	Older Americans Act reauthorized	Emphasis placed on supportive services to help older persons remain independent in the community. Expanded ombudsman coverage.
1983	Social Security amendments	Introduced a gradual increase in the normal beneficiary age.
1984	Reauthorization of the Older Americans Act	Strengthened and clarified the roles of State and Area Agencies on Aging; coordinated community-based services; established accountability for the funding of national priority services.

1986	Age DiscriminationAct	Elimination of the upper age cap of 70 from ADEA; exempted state and local governments when hiring or retiring firefighters or law enforcement officials from age limitations; provided that colleges and universities involuntarily retire professors at age 70.
1987	Omnibus Budget Reconciliation Act (Nursing Home Reform Act)	Nursing home residents were guaranteed certain rights; mandated that nursing facility residents have access to ombudspersons; provides for nursing home reform (nurse aid training, certification procedures, pre-admission screening, and annual reviews for patients with mental illness).
	Reauthorization of the Older Americans Act	Added 6 specific authorizations of appropriations for services: 1. in-home services for frail elderly; 2. long-term care ombudsman; 3. assistance for special needs; 4. health education and promotion for aids; 5. prevention of elder abuse, neglect, and exploitation; 6. outreach activities for persons who may be eligible for benefits under SSI, Medicaid, and food stamps; emphasis given to serving those in greatest economic and social need, i.e., low-income minority groups.
1988	Age Discrimination Claims Assistance Act (ADCAA)	Reinstated the rights of ADEA charging parties to file a private lawsuit beyond the two or three year statute of limitations for an additional 18 months.
1990	Americans with Disabilities Act	Extended protection from discrimination in employment and public accommodations to persons with disabilities.

	National Affordable Housing Act	Elderly Housing program reauthorized and provided demonstration programs or supportive services.
	The Older Workers Benefit Protection Act (OWBPA)	Amended the ADEA to specifically prohibit employers from denying benefits to older employees.
	Age Discrimination Claims Assistance amendments (ADCAA II)	Provided (ADEA) charging parties an additional 450 days in which to file their own private ADEA lawsuits.
1991	Civil Rights Act	Amended Title VII of ADEA; it provided that the charging parties can request jury trials and that successful plaintiffs can recover compensatory and punitive damages in intentional employment discrimination cases; expanded protection to include Congressional and high level political appointees. It eliminated the two and three year statute of limitations period. for filing private lawsuits under the ADEA.
1992	Reauthorization of the Older Americans Act	Added Title VII: Vulnerable Elder Rights Protection Program. Designed to protect and enhance rights and benefits of older adults.
1995	Fourth White House Conference on Aging	
1996	Age Discrimination in Employment amendments	Reinstated an exemption that permits state and local governments to use age as a basis for hiring and retiring law enforcement officers and firefighters.
1997	Balanced Budget Act of 1997 (BBA)	Made the most significant changes to Medicare since its origination.

1998	Higher Education amendments	Amended ADEA to permit colleges and universities to offer special age-based retirement incentives for tenured faculty members at institutions of higher education.
1999	Medicare, Medicaid, and SCHIP Balanced Budget Refinement Act of 1999 (BBRA).	It made numerous changes to the Medicare program aimed at reducing the impact of the payment reductions to providers in the BBA of 1997.
2000	Benefits Improvement and Protection Act of 2000 (BIPA).	It made numerous changes to the Medicare, Medicaid and SCHIP programs.
	OAA Amendments	Creation of the National Family Caregiver Support Program
2001	Long-Term Care and Retirement Security Act of 2001	Tax credits for caregiving expenses and tax deductions for long term care insurance premiums provided. Employers to include long term care insurance in cafeteria plans. Federal employees, retirees, and military personnel allowed to purchase long-term care coverage.

Conclusion

This chapter has highlighted many topics related to teaching aging policy to social work students. Resources and ideas have been provided throughout the chapter. The importance of the development of advocacy skills for 'policy gerontologists' has been emphasized.

References

Adams, P. 2003 March. *Teaching Social Security: Classroom activities and assessment techniques.* Paper presented at the meeting of the Council on Social Work Education, Atlanta, GA.

Administration on Aging. 2000. *Older Americans 2000: Key indicators of well-being.* Retrieved March 23, 2003, from http://www.aoa.gov/agingstats/chart book2000/healthcare.html

Administration on Aging (AOA). 2001a. *Elder abuse prevention.* Retrieved March 23, 2003, from http://www.aoa.gov/factsheets/abuse.html

Administration on Aging. 2001b. *Profile of older Americans: 1999.* Retrieved March 23, 2003, from http://www.aoa.gov/aoa/stats/profile/profile99.html# Poverty2

Administration on Aging. 2002a. *Facts and figures: Statistics on minority aging in the U.S.* Retrieved March 23, 2003, from http://www.aoa.gov/minorityaccess/stats.html#Poverty

Administration on Aging. 2002b. *Selected highlights: Side by side comparison of 1992 and 2000 amendments to the Older Americans' Act (OAA).* Retrieved March 20, 2003, from http://www.aoa.gov/oaa/2000/side-by-side-fin.html

Alliance for Worker Retirement Security. 2000. *Social Security reform: Confronting the challenges to women's retirement security.* Retrieved March 20, 2003, from http://www.retiresecure.org/articles.php?id=6

Alzheimer's Association. 1991. *Time out! The case for a national family caregiver support policy.* Washington, DC.

American Association of Homes and Services for the Aging. 2003 March. *Talking Points Issue: HUD's FY04 Appropriations.* Retrieved March 22, 2003 from http://www.aahsa.org/member/Advocacy/FASC2003/TalkingPoints/HousingFY04appropsTPMarch.pdf

American Association of Retired Persons (AARP). 2002. *The policy book: AARP public policies 2003.* Retrieved March 23, 2003, from http://www.aarp.org/ legipoly.html#ppa1

Arno, P., C. Levine, and M. Memmott. 1999. Economic value of informal caregiving. *Health Affairs, 18(2),* 182-188.

Bass, D., C. McCarthy, S. Eckert, and J. Bichler. 1994. Differences in service attitudes and experiences among families using three types of support services. *American Journal of Alzheimer's Care and Research, 9*(3), 28-38.

Beckett, J. O., R.L. Schneider, E. Vandsburger, and E.J. Stevens. 2000. Aging women. In R. L. Schneider, N. P. Kropf, and A. J. Kisor, eds., *Gerontological social work: Knowledge, service settings, and special populations:* 2nd ed: 65-95. Belmont, CA: Wadsworth Brooks/Cole.

Biegel, D.E., D.M. Bass, R. Schulz, and R. Morycz. 1993. Predictors of in-home and out-of-home service use by family caregivers of Alzheimer's disease patients. *Journal of Aging and Health, 5*, 419-438.

Binstock, R. and C.L. Day. 1996. Aging and Politics. In R.H. Binstock and L.K. George, eds., *Handbook of aging and social sciences:* 4th ed: 410-429. San Diego, CA: Academic Press.

Brody, E. 1985. Parent care as a normative family stress. *Gerontologist, 25*, 19-29.

Bush, S. 2001. Does future elderly transportation demand pose a "pending crisis"? Challenges for research and policymaking. MIT AgeLab. Retrieved April, 18, 2003   http://ford-mit.mit.edu/Library.htm

Butler, R. N. 1969. Age-ism: Another form of bigotry. *The Gerontologist, 9*, 243-246.

Cantor, M. A. 1992. Families and caregiving in an aging society. *Generations, 16*(3), 67-70.

Carlton-LaNey, I. 1997. Social workers as advocates for elders. In M. Reisch and E. Gambrill, eds., *Social Work in the 21st Century:* 285-295. Thousand Oaks: Pine Forge Press.

Coberly, S., and K.H. Wilber. 1990. Comparability in gerontology core courses: An analysis of policy and aging course syllabi. *Educational Gerontology, 16*, 481-469.

Cianciolo, P. K., T.L. Henderson, S. Kretzer, and A.Mendes. 2001. Promoting collaborative learning strategies in aging and public policy courses. *Gerontology and Geriatric Education, 22*(2), 47-67.

Collins, C., M. Stommel, C.W. Given, and S. King. 1991. Knowledge and use of community services among family caregivers of Alzheimer's disease patients. *Archives of Psychiatric Nursing, 5*(2), 84-90.

Computing Research Association. 2000. Women, minorities, and older workers. In *The supply of information technology workers in the United States* (chap. 7). Retrieved March 19, 2003, from http://www.cra.org/reports/wits/chapter_7.html

The Concord Coalition 1995. *The zero deficit plan: A plan for eliminating the federal budget deficit by the year 2002,* New York: 9-10.

Coughlin, J. 2001 October. Beyond health and retirement: placing transportation on the aging policy agenda. MIT AgeLab. Retrieved March 2, 2002, from

Council on Social Work Education. 2001. *Educational policy and accreditation standards.* Retrieved February 3, 2003, from http://www.cswe.org/accreditation/EPAS/EPAS_start.htm#iv

Cutler, N.E. 1997. The financial gerontology birthdays of 1995-1996: Social Security at 60 and the "Baby" Boom at 50. In M. Reisch and E. Gambrill, eds., *Social Work in the 21st century:* 143-151. Thousand Oaks: Pine Forge Press.

Day, T. 2002. *About caregiving.* Retrieved March 23, 2003, from http://www.ltclink.net/about_caregiving.html),

Deines, H. and R. Richart. 2003, March. *Older adult social activists: Challenging stereotypes about aging across the curriculum.* Paper presented at the meeting of the Council on Social Work Education, Atlanta, GA.

DeHope, E. and M. Joyner. 2003 March. *Transforming curriculum through the intergenerational lens.* Paper presented at the meeting of the Council on Social Work Education, Atlanta, GA.

Doty, P. 1986. Family care of the elderly: The role of public policy. *Milbank Quarterly, 64,* 3475.

Estes, C.L., K.W. Linkins, and E.A. Binney. 1996. The political economy of aging. In R.H. Binstock and L.K. George, eds., *Handbook of aging and social sciences:* 4th ed.: 410-429. San Diego, CA: Academic Press.

Fahey, C. J. 1996. Social work education and the field of aging. *The Gerontologist, 36,* 36-41.

Family Caregiver Alliance. 2002. *Fact sheet: Caregiving and depression.* Retrieved April 12, 2003, from http://www.caregiver.org/factsheets/ caregiving_depression.html

Ginsberg, L. 1999. *Understanding social problems, policies, and programs* (3rd ed.). Columbia, SC: University of South Carolina Press.

Gregg, D.W. and N.E. Cutler. Winter 1991. The human wealth span and financial well-being in older age. *Generations, 15: 45-52..*

Hermoso, J., L. Overly, C. Tompkins, K. Simons, A. Rosen. 2003 March. Intergenerational advocacy: A pilot project. Paper presented at the meeting of the Council on Social Work Education, Atlanta, GA.

Hudson, R. 1994. Social Protection and Services. In R.H. Binstock and L.K. George, eds., *Handbook of aging and social sciences:* (4th ed.: 410-429. San Diego, CA: Academic Press.

Hudson, R. 1995. The Older Americans Act and the defederalization of community-based care. In P. Kim, ed., *Services to the aging and aged: Public policies and* programs: 45-75 New York: Garland.

Hudson, R. B. 1999. Conflict in today's aging politics: New population encounters old ideology. *Social Service Review, 73,* 358-379.

Hudson, R. 2002. Getting ready and getting credit: populations of color and retirement security. *Public Policy and Aging Report*, National Academy on an Aging Society. 12 (3), 1-2.

Institute for Health and Aging and the University of California, San Francisco. (1996). *Chronic care in America: a 21ˢᵗ century challenge.* Princeton, NJ: Robert Wood Johnson Foundation.

Kajakazi, K. 2002. Impact of unreported social security earnings on people of color and women. *Public Policy and Aging Report*, 12(3), 9-12.

Karjala, Y. 2003 March. Transcultural intergenerational outreach and advocacy: Searching an innovative macro practice teaching model. Paper presented at the meeting of the Council on Social Work Education, Atlanta, GA.

Kisor, A., E. McSweeney, and D. Jackson. 2000. Social problems and policies and the elderly. In R. L. Schneider, N. P. Kropf, and A. J. Kisor, eds., *Gerontological social work: Knowledge, service settings, and special populations:* 2ⁿᵈ ed.: 65-95. Belmont, CA: Wadsworth Brooks/Cole.

Lee, P. R., and C.L. Estes. 1979. Public policies, the aged, and long-term care. *Journal of Long-Term Care Administration, 7*(3), 1-15.

Liebig, P. S. 1994. Decentralization, aging policy, and the age of Clinton. *Journal of Aging and Social Policy, 6*(1/2), 9-26.

Liebig, P. S. 1995. Social policy and professional identity. *Generations, 19*, 39-42.

Metropolitan Life Insurance Company. 1997 June. *The MetLife study of employer costs for working caregivers.* Retrieved April 12, 2003, from http://www.metlife.com/WPSAssets/88881768001015600333V1F5.1.066.pdf

Meyer, M. H., P. Herd. 2001. Aging and aging policy in the USA. In J. R. Blau, ed., *The Blackwell companion to sociology:* 375-388. Malden, MA: Blackwell.

Moen, P. and K.B. Forest. 1995. Family policies for an aging society: Moving to the 21ˢᵗ century. *Gerontologist, 35*, 825-830.

Montgomery, R. J., and E. Borgatta. 1989. The effects of alternative support strategies on family caregiving. *Gerontologist 29*, 457-464.

Moon, M. 1999. *Growth in Medicare spending: What will beneficiaries pay?* Retrieved March 3, 2003, from 'http://www.urban.org/url.cfm?ID=407788

National Center on Elder Abuse. 2002b. *What are the major types of elder abuse?* Retrieved March 3, 2003, from http://www.elderabusecenter. org/basic/index. html

National Family Caregivers Association. 1998. *Caregiving across the life cycle* [Electronic version]. Kensington, MD: Author. Retrieved March 3, 2003, from http://www.nfcacares.org/

National Family Caregivers Association (NFCA). 2000 October. *Caregiver Survey-2000* [Electronic Version]. Kensington, MD: Author. Retrieved March 3, 2003, from http://www.nfcacares.org/

National Gay and Lesbian Task Force (NGLTF). 2003. *What do we know about GLBT elders?* Retrieved March 12, 2003, from http://www. ngltf.org/issues/ agingweknow.htm

National Hispanic Council on Aging. 2003. *Welcome to the NHCOA.* Retrieved January 20, 2003, from http://www.nhcoa.org/

National Resource Center on Native American Aging. 2002. *National Resource Center on Native American Aging.* Retrieved January 20, 2003, from University of North Dakota Center for Rural Health website: http://www.und. edu/dept/nrcnaa/

Nuessel, F. H. 1982. The language of ageism. *The Gerontologist, 22,* 273-276.

Older Women's League (OWL). 2003. *OWL: The voice of midlife and older women.* Retrieved February 3, 2003, from http://www.owl-national.org/

Our Bodies Ourselves. 2003. *Our bodies ourselves: Inspiring a movement of women's health around the world.* Retrieved February 3, 2003, from http://www.ourbodiesourselves.org/

Peterson, D., R. Wendt, and E. Douglass. 1991. Determining the impact of gerontology preparation on personnel in the aging network. Washington, D.C., Association for Gerontology in Higher Education.

Quam, J. (Ed.). 1993. Gay and Lesbian aging. SEICUS Report, 10-12.

Quinn, J. 1996. *Entitlements and the federal budge*t. Washington, DC: National Institute on Aging.

RAND. 1999. *Prescription drugs and the elderly: Policy implications of Medicare coverage.* Retrieved February 3, 2003, from http://www.rand.org/publications/ RB/RB5028/rb5028.html

Senior Action in a Gay Environment (SAGE). 2003. *Home.* Retrieved January 24, 2003, from http://www.sageusa.org/

Schulz, J. 1996. Economic security policies. In R.H. Binstock and L.K. George, eds.,   *Handbook of aging and social sciences:* 4th ed.; 410-429. San Diego, CA: Academic

Social Security Reform Center. (n.d.). *Fast facts.* Retrieved March 12, 2003, from http://www.socialsecurityreform.org/fastfacts/index.cfm

Specht, H. and M.Courtney. 1997. *Unfaithful angels: how social work has abandoned its mission.* New York: The Free Press.

Steen, M. 1998 July. *Many older IT workers are fishing for jobs despite labor shortage.* Retrieved March 12, 2003, from 'http://www.cnn.com/TECH/computing/9807/23/age.idg/

Surface Transportation Policy Project. 1996-2003. *Transportation and social equity.* Retrieved   March 30, 2003, from http://www.transact.org/library/factsheets/equity.asp

Takamura, J. C. 1999. Getting ready for the 21st century: The aging of America and the Older Americans Act. *Health and Social Work, 24*(3), 232-238.

Tanner, M. 1996 July. *Privatizing Social Security: A big boost for the poor* (Social Security Choice Paper No. 4).   Washington, DC: Cato Institute.

Tennstedt, S. L., S. Crawford, and J.B. McKinlay. 1993. Is family care on the decline? A longitudinal investigation of the substitution of formal long-term care services for informal care. *Milbank Quarterly, 71*, 601-6-24.

Tirrito, T. 2003. *Aging in the new millennium: A global view.* Columbia, SC: University of South Carolina Press.

Torres-Gil, F., and K.B. Moga. 2001. Multiculturalism, social policy, and the new aging. *Journal of Gerontological Social Work, 36*(3/4), 13-32.

U.S. Equal Employment Opportunity Commission. 2002. *EEOC issues fiscal 2001 enforcement data.* Retrieved March 12, 2003, from http://www.eeoc.gov/press/2-22-02.html

Williams, M. 1995. *The American Geriatrics Society's complete guide to aging and health.* New York: Harmony Books.

Editorial Commentary

ℰℭ

Nieli Langer & Terry Tirrito

Structured Debates

Curriculum standards where aging studies are taught generally include policy, planning, and the political process. With this expectation of policy education, the use of structured debates has a great potential for promoting competence in policy practice and knowledge of topics relevant to social policy as it affects the elderly. Debates offer an effective transformative teaching strategy. The benefits of debates include the necessity to prepare thoroughly by researching the topic and logically thinking about the presentation of information. The process involved in debates encourages students to develop and exercise skills that may translate to political activities, such as testifying before legislative committees. This educational strategy helps adult learners to confront their biases and appreciate the complexities involved in policy decision-making. Effective policy practice involves analytic as well as persuasive activities. According to Jansson (1984, 57-58), five fundamental skills underlie policy practice:

- Value clarification: identifying values inherent in policy positions
- Conceptual skills: identifying and evaluating different policy options
- Interactional skills: interpreting the values of others as well as expressing your own
- Political skills: development of strategies, i.e., coalition building
- Position-taking skills: advocacy of a position

Significant parallels exist between policy practice skills and the characteristics of critical thinking (Brookfield 1987; Freeley 1996; Gambrill 1997). Critical thinkers are aware of multiple and legitimate points of view and each, when thoroughly analyzed, may yield valuable insight. If we seek to encourage students to be creative thinkers, to explore their own attitudes and values, to encourage investigation and analysis of competing alternatives, and motivate them to articulate a point of view in a persuasive manner, then structured debates are a valuable strategy to engage students in active learning.

The Use of the Novel and Film to Transform Social Issues

Across the professional curricula, syllabi are anchored by required readings of textbooks, journal articles, book chapters, and reference books. Though essential to the education and training of the practitioner, students often report experiencing difficulty integrating their content into actual practice. The humanities in social welfare education can provide a means for translating abstract material into more concrete terms. The humanities transmit multiple reflections on human life that have shaped our heritage, for good or ill. They increase understanding of social, cultural, and psychological phenomena, and afford a context for applying classroom learning to the life stories of "real" people. Long before the social sciences emerged as academic disciplines, literature encapsulated what people felt and did and how societies were constructed. Literature and the arts not only reflect society's conventions, but also help to create them. In striving to differentiate stereotype from reality, students benefit not only from studying positive examples presented in both literature and the arts, but also from questioning traditional concepts. Through this process, they may realize that many of the stereotypes portrayed in the humanities as natural and universal, such as attitudes about aging, are actually socially con-structed values. Through studying literature, the arts, and popular culture, they can question the negative stereotypes that they encounter while also using these media to construct more positive images. In this regard, literature approached interpretively, can make a unique contribution to gerontology's evolving interests in teaching practice, social policy analysis, as well as history. Students of social policy who learn how to analyze relationships between social realities and an author's intentions are able to understand historical trends and ideologies. Feature films, too are a useful and entertaining art form to illustrate abstract theories in practical, concrete terms.

Fiction is not a substitute for systematically accumulated knowledge. Nevertheless, literature and the cinema provide the student and practitioner with a wealth of sociologically relevant material and with manifold clues and departure points for theory and research. The instructor asks students to select a novel or a movie from a suggested list. After reading the book or viewing the film, students are required to write an essay of approximately five pages using the following outline:

1. Describe the setting of the story (when and where the story takes place). This information is important for placing the story's societal and cultural environment in a historical framework. Also of significance is where the film or novel's characters interact with other people. For example, *Fried Green Tomatoes* (1991) initially confines Mrs. Threadgood to a nursing home but the setting changes to the community as the relationship with Ms. Couch evolves.

2. Briefly outline the plot (the sequence of events or the process used to tell the story). *Driving Miss Daisy (1989)* illustrates how plot is used to mark the development of friendship and the simultaneous deterioration of a person's mental and physical health.

3. Select one character to describe. In the twists and turns of a character's life, the reader or viewer, develops skills at diagnosing and problem-solving that helps them to understand the complexities of character development from a person-in-environment perspective. Integral to any feature film or novel is character analysis that examines the conscious and subconscious components of personalities. This aspect is critical in regard to older adults because film and novel characters can either support or defy stereotypes associated with the aging process. Many of the films and novels on the lists have been selected primarily because the lead characters display behaviors or attitudes that challenge ideas about older adults and the aging process.

4. In one or two sentences, define the central theme of the novel or film. The theme involves person-in-environment. For example, *That's Life* (1986) is a film that examines the impact of retirement on a life-long businessperson.

5. Discuss the major social policy issue of either the film or novel.

6. Describe a brief history of organized attempts to cope with each social issue in the book or film.

7. Be prepared to critique your selection in a ten minute oral presentation. Select an excerpt to read or describe to the class that is representative of the book or film's theme or main character.

Recommended Novels, Tales, and Short Stories

...Some of these books have been made into movies.

Anderson, R. *I never sang for my father*.
Barker, P. *Union Street: The Century's Daughter*.
Beauvoir, S. de. *A Very Easy Death*.
Beresford-Howe, C. *The Book of Eve*.
Cooper, S. and Cronyn, H. *Foxfire*.
Cook, L. *Love as Strong as Ginger*.
Edgerton, C. *Walking Across Egypt*.
Gale, P. *Rough Music*.
Gould, J. *Tales from Rhapsody Home*.
Hemingway, E. *The Old Man and the Sea*.
Irwin, H. *The Lilith Summer*.
Jenkins, M. *A House in Flanders*.
Lessing, D. *The Summer Before the Dark*.
Lessing, D. *The Diary of a Good Neighbor*.
Lively, P. *Mood Tiger*.
Mann, T. *Death in Venice*.
McNally, T. *Love! Valour! Compassion! And a Perfect Ganesh*.
Meyerhoff, B. *Number Our Days*.
Miller, A. *Death of a Salesman*.
Perriam, W. *Tread Softly*.
Rhodes, E. *The Prince of Central Park*.
Rooke, C. *Night Light: Stories of Aging*.
Sarton, M. *As We Are Now*.
Sarton, M. *The House by the Sea*.
Sennett, D. *Full Measure: Modern Short Stories on Aging*..
Shakespeare, W. *King Lear*.
Stegner, W. *Angle of Repose*.
Swann, E. *Night Gardening*.
Swift, G. *Last Orders*.
Tan, A. *The Bonesetter's Daughter*.
Tyler, A. *A Patchwork Planet*.
Van Velde, J. *The Big Ward*.

Two reference volumes by Yahnke and Eastman on the literature of aging and older adults are dedicated to the issue of aging in creative literature and contain detailed annotations for each citation. They offer a set of literary examples of the life experiences of older African-Americans and Native Americans.

Yahnke, R.E. and R.M. Eastman. 1995. *Literature and gerontology: A research guide.* Westport, CT: Greenwood Press.
Yahnke, R.E. and R.M. Eastman . 1990. *Aging in literature: A reader's guide.* Chicago: The American Library Association.

Feature Films.

The Color Purple—triumph over adversity of a sharecropper's daughter in Georgia .
Hard Knox—retirement.
The Old Man and the Sea—a once strong, proud man comes to terms with his failing abilities and age.
Izzy and Moe—out-of-work vaudeville actors turn prohibition agents.
No Surrender—Pensioners on a bus trip traveling to celebrate New Year's Eve.
That's Life—an architect struggles with the celebration of his 60th birthday.
Tough Guys—two legendary bank robbers are released after 30 years imprisonment and decide to plan their boldest train heist.
Roommates—a retired grandfather raises his orphaned grandson.
Pals—two retired fishing buddies find over $3million.
Dirty Rotten Scoundrels—two con artists specialize in bilking rich women on the Riviera.
Side by Side—three lifelong buddies decide to pool their resources and create a clothing line designed for older people by older people.
Dad—a son is shocked to discover his father has deteriorated under the over protectful eye of his mother.
Driving Miss Daisy—depicts a 25-year friendship between an older woman and her aging African American chauffeur.
Mr. and Mrs. Bridge—after years of a comfortable life and marriage, a woman reevaluates her life and values.
Fried Green Tomatoes—an older woman from a small town in Ala.bama describes her life and inspires her middle-aged friend to change her life.

Over the Hill—a 60 year old woman asserts her independence by taking a road trip across the Australian continent.

Used People—a woman from Queens, New York unexpectedly discovers love and happiness on the day of her husband's funeral.

Grumpy Old Men—examines the love-hate relationship between two neighbors.

The Autobiography of Miss Jane Pittman.

The Crew—how resilience and group support affect retirement of four "wise guys" in Miami.

Cocoon—the rejuvenating waters of a pool promise eternal life to some seniors.

A Woman's Tale is about an old woman who exemplifies integrity and hope in the face of death.

The Gin Game—how the meaning of the game becomes apparent and deadly serious when losing (and never winning) takes on great significance for the male character at this time of his life and in this setting.

The Straight Story depicts the fiercely independent spirit of an older resident of Iowa who drives his lawnmower 240 miles to Wisconsin to visit his estranged and ailing brother.

Wild Strawberries (Sweden) focuses on the reminiscences and dreams of an older man as he travels to Lund to receive a lifetime achievement award.

Brookfield, S. 1987. *Developing critical thinkers: Challenging adults to explore alternative ways of thinking and acting.* San Francisco: Jossey-Bass.

Freeley, A.J. 1996. *Argumentation and debate: Critical thinking for reasoned decisionmaking* (9th ed.). Belmot, CA: Wadsworth

Gambrill, E. 1997. *Social work practice: A critical thinker's guide.* New York: Oxford University Press.

Jansson, B.S. 1994. *Social welfare policy: From theory to policy practice* (2nd ed.). Belmont, CA: Wadsworth.

3

TEACHING THE ADULT LEARNER ABOUT MENTAL HEALTH ISSUES IN AGING

෨෨

Vicki Murdock

Vital, successful, optimal aging: these are current phrases used to positively describe a process every person faces each day (Baltes and Baltes 1990; Erickson, Erickson, and Kivnick 1986; Qualls 2002). These expressions represent the gerontology professional's perspective on growing old, i.e. a perspective that recognizes the normalcy of aging and the strengths and adaptations inherent in having lived a long life (Hooyman and Kiyak 1999). One goal of gerontological education is to encourage each new learner (whether beginning student or seasoned professional) to adopt this positive, holistic, and realistic viewpoint which may require that some be helped to dispense with ageist stereotypes and myths (Butler 1963; Schaie and Willis 2002).

The field of mental health is also changing since professionals and advocacy groups are focusing awareness on adaptation, independence, and recovery (Lin 1995). Again, a goal of education is to dispel myths and decrease stigma while increasing knowledge and skills for helping. Combining aging and mental health issues yields an educational arena burdened with personal, societal, and cultural biases that instructors will need to address with students and professionals (Tan, Hawkins, and Ryan 2001). This chapter seeks to use the recognized learning potential of experiential activity to explore attitudes, increase knowledge, and offer skills practice (Knowles 1972; Meyers and Jones 1993).

The foundation of the chapter is the three domains of educational objectives: values clarification, knowledge building, and skill building. The conceptual basis for experiential teaching and learning about mental health issues of older adults is introduced, and an overview is given of the knowledge base needed to provide appropriate services. The chapter then presents a series of attitude, knowledge, and skill-based activities that cover aspects of gerontological mental health theory, practice, research, and policy. The chapter concludes with a list of resources pertaining to mental health in older adulthood: selected professional books and articles, quizzes/workbooks/measurement tools, case studies, websites, films, and drama/literature/self help/creative arts sources.

What Should Students/Practitioners Learn?

The educational content for the creation of a syllabus in mental health issues in the elderly is derived, like all curricula, from two foundations: the *cognitive* domain, encompassing the knowledge and skill-building components, and the *affective* domain, which gives students and profession-als the opportunities to examine their attitudes and values about the discipline/topics. Once instructors have determined the syllabus for the course, they then need to clearly state, in behavioral terms, the knowledge, skills, and attitude outcomes their students should have at the conclusion of the course. In this way, instructors clearly define the goals of the course and the students/practitioners are fully aware of the instructors' expecta-tions for student realization of course objectives. In addition, it is then possible for the instructor to evaluate student performance according to the objectives originally selected.

Knowledge is basic to all the other ends or purposes of education. Problem solving cannot be carried on in a vacuum, but must be based upon knowledge of some of the "realities" in a discipline. For the topic of mental health in the elderly, which is undergoing rapid transition, knowledge is taught as a basis for learning the methodology of the field and as a basis for attacking the problems therein. If the instructor believes in the importance of mental health as a topic to be addressed in the aging curriculum and communicates the importance of it to students, students will, in all likelihood, have little difficulty in realizing knowledge objectives. Instructors, as the architects of the syllabus in mental health, need to consider these variables when making the determination on the knowledge content to select.

The student and helping professional needs knowledge of thorough, holistic assessment, appropriately tailored interventions, and follow-up care for the older adult client, particularly when mental health problems are evident. Students and practitioners must also think critically about the tendency to diagnose, rather than looking at environmental barriers to good health. A social, rather than medical model may help to reduce the daunting statistics on mental illness in older adulthood cited here (Thomas 1999). Students and practitioners also need to be trained to the primacy of a medical examination for thorough assessment of the older adult (Hooyman and Kiyak 1999). The ability to differentiate between organic and non-organic causes of dysfunctional behaviors is a starting point for proper treatment of late life mental health problems.

"More than 80% of older adults served by nursing homes and other long term care facilities have significant psychiatric or behavioral problems" (Bartels and Smyers 2002, 15). More than one fourth of all older adults (living in the community and institutions) have a mental disorder (Bartels and Smyers 2002). However, many practitioners do not receive sufficient training in the assessment and treatment of mental health disorders in the elderly. The knowledge base should necessarily include a comprehensive introduction to the epidemiology, causes, and assessment of mental health disorders as they are experienced by the mature older adult. Specific attention should be directed towards issues of race, ethnicity, culture, class, gender, sexual orientation, religion, physical and mental disabilities, and national origin as they influence the manifestations and assessment of mental health problems.

Depression is quite common in the older population; NIH figures suggest 15% of all older adults experience chronic depression (Bartels and Smyers 2002). Dementia is also a syndrome most commonly seen in late life, although in smaller numbers. Drug and alcohol problems affect the older person in numbers similar to younger adults, and drug interactions and misuse (polypharmacy) affect the older population due to the combination of physical problems of late life and any newly formed or longstanding psychological problems (Schaie and Willis 2002). Prevalence estimates for problem drinking (the "drug of choice" for the current older adult population) are approximately 15%; most of this population goes unidenti fied by the healthcare system (Blow, Oslin, and Barry 2002). Suicide in the older population is far higher than for other groups. Alerting students to the warning conditions such as loss of spouse or serious medical illness can help them anticipate suicidal tendencies with clients, and prepare them for their own response and skills in addressing this difficult area of helping (Schaie and Willis 2002). Grief and loss are inescapable for older adults: loss of youth, health, social support, financial growth potential, work and career identity, and for some, spouse/partner/friends. Loss can be an opportunity for adaptation and growth, but for many, the losses become a cause for at least situational or temporary depression. Research is growing on issues of cultural diversity among older adults, and mental health and mental illness assessment and treatment must be considered in light of new knowledge and awareness of cultural differences (Abramson, Trejo, and Lai 2002).

Although information is recognized as an important outcome of education, few instructors will be satisfied to regard this as the sole outcome of instruction. Students need to exhibit evidence that they can do something with their knowledge. It is also expected that students will acquire the technical strategies needed to address new problems. Therefore, identification of the social service skills and the specific behavioral outcomes that will measure the acquisition of these skills as they impact the elderly compromised with mental health problems should also be included in the course outline. Skills for helping are where the background knowledge of theories, research, policy, and working models are tried and tested. The competent professional must begin as a student and continue to be a student, willing to learn new skills by practicing them. Because the educational research supports the use of doing and reflecting as the most lasting competence-building methodology, the activities are designed to appeal both to the student and to the in-service participant and provide them with skills-enhancing material to take with them, to be applied in the world, with confidence and competence.

Affective behaviors develop when appropriate learning experiences are provided for students much the same as cognitive behaviors develop from appropriate learning experiences. The goals in the affective domain are to acquaint students with attitudes and values that they may learn to incorporate as part of themselves from awareness to internalization.

The educational objectives are the explicit ways in which students and professionals will be changed by the educative process; that is, the ways in which they will change in their thinking, their actions, and their values/attitudes. The selection of objectives as well as the determination of the relative emphasis to be given to various objectives will be determined by the instructor and the mission of the institution providing the educational modality.

Creating and Administering the Means of Teaching Mental Health in the Elderly

The human services student must graduate with knowledge, values, and skills on the vast array of material that addresses human living: from pre-birth to post-death, from the genetic to the global level. Both social service practitioners and educators acknowledge that the student's education is just the beginning, and that lifelong learning is part of the commitment. Research has confirmed that we remember much more of what we do than what we only hear or see (Meyers and Jones 1993). In fact, believing oneself competent may be the key to confident and competent practice (Bandura 1997). So how do we help students/practitioners learn even some of what they will ultimately need to know? Instructors need to clearly specify the outcomes or objectives they intend their instruction to accomplish. The facilitative instructor then selects and arranges learning experiences for students in accordance with the principles of learning. He/she offers opportunities for the student to learn the knowledge, values, and skills of the profession in theory and in practice by doing and reflecting on the doing. Experiential learning, that is, the learning that relies on doing and reflecting provides opportunities for actual skill practice, for critical thinking, for self-awareness, for the application of the theoretical or abstract into practical or do-able activities. The more active the classroom or the workshop, the better the chances are that material will be retained, reflected upon, transferred to other settings, and applied in the workplace (Meyers and Jones 1993).

Both mental health and aging have been stigmatized topics in the past. Chronic mental illness still causes alarm in its unpredictability and its power to create problems in living. Declines in mental health and function that were once assumed to be the normal course of aging for all people are now beginning to be viewed as correlated to physical and mental illness that affects some older adults, but by no means all (Hooyman and Kiyak 1999). Aging itself is still disparaged by popular culture, and ageism in policy and practice is still far too prevalent in American society (Kosberg and Kaufman 2002). Therefore, the first educational imperative for students is the expectation that they will explore these negative attitudes, identify them in themselves and others, work to change their own thinking and societal thinking about aging, and be given tools to work from a positive aging model.

Material on aging is complex, multidisciplinary, and multidimensional, and has been underrepresented in the curricula of many helping professions (Kosberg and Kaufman 2002). Discussing normal aging processes, Qualls (2002, p. 13) writes that while we have the *Diagnostic and Statistical Manual* (APA 1994) we have "no codification for describing mental strengths or well-being." The older adult needs a very individualized assessment and plan of intervention; older adults are the most unique of clients, bringing a variety of physical/medical concerns, a long social history, perhaps longstanding psychological problems, and a history of loss and adaptation to loss unique to those who have lived long (Hooyman and Kiyak 1999). Mental health and mental illness in late life are crucial topics for every student, not only those who specialize in gerontology. Every helping professional must be able to assist the support network of a client because even the professional working with children or teens will likely interact with older adults when considering family issues impacting upon the client. It is imperative that students have access to gerontological mental health knowledge with which to create a foundation for appropriate professional practice. According to Bartels and Smyers (2002, 16), generalists (in all disciplines) are providing "...the vast majority of geriatric healthcare," and the "...research findings are not being fully translated into clinical practice" quickly enough for the surge in elder population that is approaching.

Many of the activities suggested here are intended to promote a positive perspective on both aging and mental health, reinforcing normal aging processes, and helping students to think in terms of holistic assessment and intervention; to rule out disorders, rather than imposing general, and generally negative broad categories of illness, such as senility or dementia. Many activities reflect the need for a working knowledge of signs and symptoms, because, even though a medical examination must take place for thorough assessment, professional helpers in gerontological settings are often those who first see the symptoms, signs, and side effects (Bartels and Smyers 2002). This chapter also suggests methods for learning about the most common mental illnesses, syndromes, and problems associated with mental health in aging: depression, dementia, alcohol/drug use and polypharmacy, grief and loss issues, suicide, and the cultural variations seen in late life mental health.

Experiential Learning Activities

Activities for Exploring Attitudes

1. Take a memory recall test to remind you of how easy it is to forget at any age.

2. Ask each student to bring to class an object that represents a significant loss for them; allow time for presentation and discussion.

3. Do sentence completion exercises designed to identify biases, misconceptions, etc. Old people's stories are _____. As people age, they think_____. Memory loss is _____. Old people don't _____. Old brains_____. Alzheimer's disease is _____. Old age is _____. Old people don't _____, etc.

4. List rituals that older adults might engage in as part of cultural or religious traditions, with an effort to think outside your own cultural/religious box; discuss your list with others; how could rituals assist in promoting positive mental and emotional aging? Could they cause harm?

5. Find popular examples of ageism and/or age-celebration (myths, television, movies, advertising, greeting cards), particularly looking for mental health issues.

6. Conduct a self-appraisal using the Strengths Assessment Interview Guide (Kivnick and Murray 2001).

7. Use the case vignette on countertransference in Altschuler and Katz (1999), or ask students to create a vignette from their experience to discuss in small groups the potential for positive attitudes toward aging.

8. Complete "A Look Back from the Future" (Frank, in Kropf and Tompkins 2002).

9. Have students line up from oldest to youngest without speaking. While visualizing their place in the continuum, have students share (or write) the things they like and don't like about their age. Allow students to change places in line or to suggest another place to another student. Follow this activity with small group discussion of age-related stereotypes (Kline 1998).

10. Invite a massage therapist to discuss, and perhaps demonstrate, how massage and touch can help (or frighten) an older adult who is anxious, depressed, or suffers from dementia. Close with small group discussions on the use of touch with older adults; include ethics as part of the discussion.

11. Have students talk with or assess a mentally healthy older adult, using the definition of a mentally healthy person offered by Qualls (2002, 12). Alternatively, use the definition to brainstorm a list of how elements of this description would look in real life.

12. Use a process recording of an interview with an older person to examine student values, hidden agendas, and countertransference issues. An alternate method would be a student videotape or audiotape of an interview.

13. Using Grinnell's (1997, 626-627) "Six Basic Steps to Consider when Conducting a Cross-Cultural Research Study," ask students to explore all the steps while considering age (their ages vs. the older adults' ages) as a cultural difference (examples: asking about preference or resentment to labels such as elderly, old, or aged; explore the concept "reasonable opposites to biased assumptions").

14. Write about your first childhood death experience: how old were you; how do you remember it; how were you related to the deceased; what explanations were given to you? (Klick 1999).

15. Write an assessment or summary based on issues in a case study on mental health and aging; examine this writing for your own attitudes or exchange papers and examine for others' attitudes; observe what was/was not addressed in the assessment.

16. Write and bring in your own obituary; discuss the writing process as well as the content in small groups. Alternatively, plan your funeral and discuss the thoughts and feelings around this activity (Cohen, in Kropf and Tompkins 2002, 62).

17. Design an "intelligence test" that would be biased in favor of older adults. Use a minimum of 10 items from the test to use with the 1-3 persons younger than 30, and 1-3 persons older than 65. Critique the validity of your test, i.e., does it accurately reflect or measure intelligence? (Evans 1981).

18. Allow students to play the role of the older adult (with depression, dementia, anxiety, grief and loss issues, etc.) while another student uses infantilizing speech, gives too many verbal prompts at one time, speaks impatiently, or asks a probing life review question. Ask participants and observers to respond orally or in written form.

19. Brainstorm about some of the new ways to think about mental health and aging: "successful aging," "well-being," "productive aging," "vital aging," "vibrant aging." What do these terms mean? Each small group could develop the meaning of one phrase.

20. Debate issues in mental health and aging in small groups: the right to die, the right to refuse medical treatment; who decides competence: autonomy vs. safety; disengagement theory/activity theory; genetic screening and/or cure for Alzheimer's disease; late life wisdom, late life creativity and the meaning of life in a youth-oriented culture; mandatory or "encouraged" retirement; older adult suicide, lifesaving medical care for the person with Alzheimer's disease; purpose/benefits of mental health therapy with the old.

21. Fill out a Living Will for yourself (not to be signed or witnessed within the context of class assignment); write a reflection paper on your thoughts and feelings after completing the exercise (Haulotte and Kretszchmar 2001).

22. List the things that define good quality of life for you—what makes life worth living for you. Rank the items on your list, placing the most important first. Now try to imagine yourself as Uncle Bert in the case

study "Uncle Bert's Bad Judgment." List the things that would
constitute a good quality of life for you at that age. Is your second list
the same as your first? What conclusions can you draw from the
comparison? (Moody 1998).

23. Have all students watch a television show segment that depicts older
    people in normal life situations (perhaps a taped segment to show in
    class). Ask students to do a simple form of structured observation as
    they tally the number of references to aging and mental health.

24. Imagine you have just received a letter from an old friend who is
    contemplating suicide. Write a detailed letter to the friend giving your
    reasons for agreeing or disagreeing with the conclusions he or she has
    reached (Moody 1998).

25. Gather mission statements from various mental health and aging
    services agencies; critique for inclusion of life-span issues and
    approaches to growth/change/strengths.

26. Read a description of an ethical research issue (for example,
    Buckingham's "Living with the Dying" study of 1976, 1211-1215).
    Discuss not only the ethical considerations, but also student thoughts
    and feelings during the recitation of the case.

27. Assign separate small groups of students to write (and possibly
    illustrate) a short story about aging and mental health issues for
    toddlers, K-5th grade, middle, and high school students (e.g., "Grandpa
    Doesn't Know My Name," "Aunt Helen's Wisdom," "Why Did Mr.
    Edmonds Kill Himself?").

28. Complete a spiritual history (survey or interview) on yourself or
    another student; discuss in class, particularly acknowledging the effects
    of a positive or negative past role of spirituality on emotional well-
    being (for example, Genia 1991, or Hodge 2001).

29. Create an intergenerational classroom for one or two sessions of the
    course; invite several older adults to speak, participate, be interviewed,
    and comment on classroom activity. Ask students to write a reflection
    on the older adults' presence in the classroom, using a positive aging

model (such as Qualls' 2002 definition of a mentally healthy person or Kivnick's 2001 assessment tool) as a guide to their reflections.

30. Have students write down five things they highly value. Have them share their sense of loss and despair that accompanies the loss of each of the five things they have listed. Alternatively, have students list roles they have actually or imaginatively held and mourn their loss (Morano, in Kropf and Tompkins 2002, 162).

31. Require that a personal reflection log be kept of reactions to guests, to site visits, to videos shown, to new knowledge gained, to attitudes changed, to skills learned.

32. Take a longevity test (available online, see quiz list). Discuss or write about your feelings about the questions asked and the results. Would you discuss this test and the results with your parents or grandparents? Explain.

Activities for Knowledge-Building

1. Explore aging and disabilities websites or local stores, nursing homes, or hospitals for current technology designed to assist older persons with memory deficits, wandering problems, etc.

2. Visit an Alzheimer's unit, a nursing home, a senior day center, an alcohol and drug treatment facility, an open AA meeting, a hospital geriatric unit, a hospice, a geriatrician's office, or go along on a Meals-on-Wheels delivery.

3. Use the "Signs and Symptoms of Potential Substance Misuse and Abuse in Older Adults" chart (Blow, Oslin, and Barry 2002, 51), but remove its heading, or offer symptoms one at a time. Have students consider what mental health problems these symptoms describe. The complexity of differential diagnosis will be evident as various issues are considered.

4. In small groups, have students consider the activities taking place in dementia care unit, a hospice, or an alcohol or drug treatment facility. Participants should then list the different activities/behaviors they think

can be measured for assessing outcomes of patient care. How would they measure these activities/behaviors?

5. Critique a visited site, or a site observed in a film on the use of music, art, dance, exercise, games, crafts, sensory input, and the holistic perspective on care. In a similar exercise critique staff attitudes, milieu, food, cleanliness, etc.

6. Use DSM-IV criteria to differentially diagnose a person described in a case study. Have students work from the whole manual, or guide their use by giving only certain mental illness criteria to consider.

7. Critique DSM criteria for alcohol or substance misuse regarding the reference to "failure to fulfill major role obligations at work, home, or school" (DSM/APA 1994; Blow, Oslin, and Barry 2002). Encourage a discussion of "role obligations" as it applies to a nursing home resident.

8. Invite a Medicare or insurance policy specialist (from a local nursing home or state agency) to describe the much higher co-payment for mental health treatment than for medical treatment (Bartels and Smyers 2002; Shea 2002). Have students evaluate this discriminatory policy, and develop/send letters to the legislature on this issue.

9. Gather local assessment tools and treatment plan forms from aging and mental health agencies where students are in field placement, work, or go to visit; compare and contrast.

10. Use a free copy (from www.samhsa.gov) of *Anger Management for Substance Abuse and Mental Health Clients: A Cognitive Behavioral Therapy Manual and Participant Workbook* (DHHS Publication No. 02-3661) to stimulate discussion of interventions, to critique for use by older adults, or to simulate a treatment group.

11. Have students report on JCAHO standards or the Minimum Data Set standards (for nursing homes) as they pertain to mental health issues (see Elderweb website).

12. Invite a pharmacist, geriatrician, or nurse to speak on commonly prescribed medications for older adults and their side effects. Create a fact sheet of common medications used to treat older adults' mental health issues.

13. Use DSM criteria to make a chart that offers possible cultural alternatives to symptoms often seen in older adults (feelings of hopelessness vs. fatalism, illusions associated with delirium vs. religious dreams/visions).

14. Critique various assessment and treatment planning forms for holistic, strengths-based approach and inclusion of termination of services and follow-up care.

15. List local, regional, national, and international agencies that provide mental health services to older adults; discuss who would benefit from a resource list such as this (i.e., caregivers, agencies, area students and professionals).

16. Brainstorm underlying causes for misuse of alcohol, drugs, or medications, and then devise alternative coping measures for these causes of distress. Do the same with triggering events and locations.

17. Have students estimate alcohol usage by several older acquaintances (or have them actually inquire) and then review the alcohol guidelines for older adults (Blow, Oslin, and Barry 2002, 52).

18. Explore websites that address mental health and aging issues; have each student report on one to the class, or report on any that were particularly helpful.

19. Create a chart that distinguishes between organic mental illness from functional mental illness; list causes, medications, recommended therapies, typical prognoses.

20. Research an aging and mental health policy issue (e.g., autonomy, competence, psychiatric patient rights, prescription drug coverage) and then discuss in a small group; think outside the box to list as many alternatives as possible to address this policy/program need; spend part

of the assigned time brainstorming "if money were no object" or "if a reasonable amount of funding were available."

21. Have each student prepare a brief fact sheet and "teach" on one aspect of aging and mental health (e.g., depression symptoms, reminiscence therapy, elder suicide statistics, causes of dementia, medication side effects). Use these sheets to create simple quizzes that test for knowledge development (not necessarily for grading).

22. Assess a video as it represents theoretical perspectives (e.g., did you see examples of disengagement? Did you see evidence of coping and adaptation?).

23. Have students develop a mnemonic device to remember the warning signs of dementia, the common symptoms of depression, or common medication effects.

24. Student 1 calls out a symptom or warning sign of depression, anxiety, suicidality, or dementia and student 2 gives an example of this symptom. Student 2 then calls out a symptom for an example given by student 3 (e.g., symptom-change in sleeping habits: older person starts waking at 4 a.m.; warning sign of poor judgment: wearing a coat on a hot day). Throwing a soft toy or calling out student names will provide randomness, so that all students must remain prepared to respond.

25. Divide up a case study into sections and read or give out only a section at a time so that students only know a little about the person in the case (simulating how we often learn details progressively over time). Address differential diagnoses by brainstorming and listing what could be happening to the person, and rule these out as more of the client's story unfolds.

26. Brainstorm how different cultural or cohort groups might respond to recommended group techniques for working with older adults: empowerment, expression of negative feelings, assertiveness training, or a focus on individual strengths.

27. Compare and critique several similar assessment tools (e.g., 2-3 anxiety scales). Considering the special needs of older adults, how do each of

the tools address validity (is it measuring what it is intended to measure), ease of use, comprehension level, and timing of administration.

28. Invite guest speakers to address issues in mental health and aging: personal caregivers, professionals, older adults.

29. Use an article that addresses cultural competence with older adults (such as Abramson, Trejo and Lai's 2002 "Culture and Mental Health: Providing Appropriate Services for a Diverse Older Population") to help students create role-plays of worker-client interactions on varying diversity and mental health issues.

30. Expose students to "The Eden Alternative" through their reading of *Learning from Hannah* or viewing an Eden video. Then, visit a nursing home or dementia unit to observe groups or environments: therapy, education, reality orientation, milieu, pet, art, and music. Use the lens of the philosophy of the Eden Alternative to view all activities and behaviors (Thomas 1999).

31. Locate and critique a peer-reviewed article that uses quantitative or qualitative research to explore an aging and mental health question; present the research results to the class in pictorial form (examples: correlating depression and medical illness, evaluation of an Alzheimer's unit on reduction of aggressive behaviors, or results that support spiritual involvement as an anxiety reducer).

32. Have students use the CSWE/SAGE-SW Social Work Gerontological Competencies to identify topics for research papers and presentations.

33. Identify mental health symptoms and disorders common to older adults in the DSM-IV and match appropriate interventions to symptoms.

34. Give quizzes for learning (not for grading purposes), on mental health and aging in theory, practice, policy, and research; alternatively, have students/practitioners create the quizzes.

Activities for Skill Development

1. Create a daily schedule for one week on an Alzheimer's unit for either a single patient or for a group of patients.

2. Assign students roles in gathering a family together to discuss planning for a cognitively impaired family member: the patient, the physician, the social worker, the spouse, the children, the family's religious representative, the family attorney, etc.

3. Students design a graph/chart/diagram that shows the variations in depression: chronic, situational, early, mid or late life, cyclical, organically/pharmacologically induced.

4. Have students create learning modules for nursing assistants (for example, on communication with dementia patients, matching skills with capacities, handling aggressive behavior or speech). Ideally, arrange for these modules to be presented.

5. Fill out an Adult Protective Services form from your local social services department using a case study to provide the client information.

6. Have students record their own moods for one week; working in pairs, have them list natural mood enhancers used or ones to be considered for the next week.

7. Create a timeline of losses with a partner; discuss feelings engendered and potential for this graphic intervention to normalize the grieving process.

8. Fill in a "Book About Me" with an Alzheimer's caregiver about the patient; this could be done with an imaginary client, with certain factors given by the instructor and the book completed by the student by imagining the client's preferences and peculiarities (see Carlton and Sessions 2002).

9. Have students complete a life review or spiritual history of themselves with another student or with an older adult (for example, Hodge 2001).

10. Using individual treatment plans from *The Older Adult Psychotherapy Treatment Planner* (Frazer and Jongsma 1999), have students practice with various interventions according to assigned roles.

11. Have students prepare a short, interactive module on mental health and aging to offer as a presentation to elementary or middle school students.

12. Ask students to list symptoms of anxiety, loneliness, interpersonal conflicts, substance misuse, or depression that they have experienced. They then rank the symptoms by how much each one interferes with daily living. Record these symptoms (of a single problem area) across one week by frequency and intensity (1-10 scale of how anxious or how depressed). List symptom reducers. Develop a symptom-reducing behavioral contract to follow for one week (Frazer and Jongsma 1999).

13. Have students facilitate and participate in a relaxation group activity such as deep breathing, muscle relaxation, or guided imagery. The facilitator practices using slow, clear, strong speech and words and imagery appropriate to older adults.

14. Develop a chart of symbols that might facilitate communication across languages, or with communication deficits.

15. Have students plan and lead various arts-related therapies. Each art center will be comprised of a facilitator and 2-3 students participating in the therapy (i.e., music therapy, painting or drawing, sculpting, sewing, gardening, etc.)

16. Practice engaging a cognitively impaired person in an initial meeting: how would you speak, what would you include in this meeting, how would you adjust as you learn more about their deficits? Students and instructor alternate portraying the older clients.

17. Using any of the assessment tools in the resource list of this chapter, or an assessment instrument used at a local social service agency, assess yourself, another student, or an older adult, friend, or family member.

18. Use diagrams (ecomap, genogram, timeline, pie analysis chart, life history grid, family exchange analysis or family diagram) to accompany the assessment process.

19. Create a resource guide for a family with an older adult with dementia, depression, or emotional problems, such as grief or loneliness.

20. Give a memory test to an older client, friend, or family member.

21. Assign each student a role to play as part of a therapeutic group for older adults: an 85 year old woman with dementia, a 70 year old man with chronic depression, a 60 year old woman recently widowed, a 55 year old man with schizophrenia, a 95 year old woman who has lost all her relatives and friends, a 70 year old man who talks about suicide, a 60 year old woman with alcoholism. (Instructor or student can role-play the facilitator). Process the experience and debrief after spending some time in the roles.

22. Using the same roles as above, add a diversity component to the description (e.g., an 85 year old Chinese American woman, a 70 year old gay man with chronic depression, etc.).

23. Create a suicide contract working with a class partner; check it for thoroughness and for its effect on both "worker" and "client;" process your feelings about preparation of this document and contemplate its use with a client. Critique the contract regarding risk management and liability. Alternatively, use the "Suicidal Ideation" treatment planner in *The Older Adult Psychotherapy Treatment Planner* (Frazer and Jongsma 1999, 233-242).

24. Develop research questions that seek to explore, describe, and/or explain issues of aging and mental health; identify resources to support the research; describe the research method that would best answer the questions raised.

25. Separate students into small groups. Each group simulates a different kind of group therapy used with older adults (e.g., social, recreational, validation, reality orientation, reminiscence, educational, support, advocacy, grief/loss/change, substance abuse). Use readings or fact

sheets to prepare students on topics, props and directions as appropriate (ball or music for recreational group, policy brief for advocacy group, fact sheet for educational group); assign leader and member roles. Process experience post-activity.

26. Simulate a group of older adults from different cultural backgrounds. Use language, behaviors, and value differences to add an additional layer to whatever the group is already gathering to address (socialization, reality orientation, grief/loss, etc.).

27. Using Grinnell's (1997, 626-627) "Six Basic Steps to Consider when Conducting a Cross-Cultural Research Study," develop as a class or in small groups a research method to be used with a group that includes older persons from various cultures. Students should be able to develop a chart that lists how to conduct culturally sensitive research.

28. Have students lead small groups in "Mental Aerobics:" verbal games for high or low functioning mental ability (i.e., list words that contain the word "and"; create a list of animals or items in a grocery store in alphabetical order; list as many animals as you can in one minute; repeat a list of 10 words after hearing them and again several minutes later; list the names of well-known couples who have been romantically involved); math games (O-T-T-F-F-S-S-?; 4-61, 5-52, 6-63, 7-94, 8-46, 9-?; counting backwards), spatial games (puzzles, rebuses, using geometric shapes to create a picture) (Paggi and Hayslip 1999).

29. Allow students to practice using appropriate professional behavior to work with simulated aggressive behaviors, as seen in organic brain syndrome or dementia (instructor portrays older person acting aggressively).

30. Make labels in the classroom building that would help a person with memory loss, wandering behaviors, or communication deficits to find their way, perform tasks, stay safe, etc. or assign students to do this at home and report on their learning.

31. Have students use the Face-Hand Test (for organic brain syndrome) on one another. Facing one another, client sits with hands on knees and eyes closed. Tester uses one finger to touch one cheek and one hand at

a time and asks client to tell where they were touched. Order is right cheek and left hand, left cheek and right hand, right cheek and right hand, left cheek and left hand, both cheeks, both hands (Kane and Kane 2000). Discuss the experience of and ethics of touching and being touched from both the practitioner and client perspectives.

32. Practice giving a depression scale, mental status exam, or anxiety checklist aloud to another person. Discuss how different an experience it is to speak about psychological issues than to give a paper assessment instrument to someone.

33. Use the DSM Global Assessment of Functioning Scale (APA 1994) criteria to practice assessing for strengths. If possible, students could assess an older family member or friend, or an older adult in their field agency or workplace.

Resources for Learning about
Mental Health in Older Adults

This final section contains teaching resources for instructors. Films, books, and articles, case studies, websites, plays and poems, and question-naires, workbooks, and quizzes are listed as resources for engaging students in active and affective learning. While the lists are by no means complete, the hope is that these resources may contribute to the change in thinking about mental health/mental illness and the mature adult for students and teachers alike. By teaching with methods that involve the learner, we touch heart and mind. Mental health and aging issues have been too long ignored or stigmatized. With joy and activism let us change the focus toward vital, successful, optimal long life.

Books and Articles

Complete references are provided at the end of the chapter.

General Mental Health Issues

Baltin, M.P. and L.1997. Should older persons have the right to commit suicide? In Scharlach, A.E. and L.W. Kaye, eds. *Controversial issues in aging.* Boston: Allyn and Bacon.

Blazer, D. 1998. *Emotional problems in later life: Intervention strategies for professional caregivers.*

Buckingham et al. 1976. Living with the dying.

Butler et al. 1998. *Aging and Mental Health: Positive psychosocial and biomedical approaches.*

Emlet et al. 1996. *In-home assessment of older adults: A multidisciplinary approach.*

Frazer, D.W. and A.E. Jongsma. 1999. *The older adult psychotherapy treatment planner.*

Hooyman, N. and H.A. Kiyak. 1999. *Social gerontology* (5th ed.).

Kane, R.L. and R.A. Kane, eds. 2000. *Assessing older persons: Measures, meaning, and practical applications.*

Kivnick, H.Q. 1993. Everyday mental health: A guide to assessing life strengths.

Kivnick, H.Q., and S.V.Murray. 2001. Life strengths interview guide: Assessing elder clients' strengths.

Kline, P.M. 1998. Aging sensitivity.

Knight, B.G. 1996. *Psychotherapy with older adults* (2nd ed.).

Kropf, N. P. and C.J.Tompkins, eds. 2002. *Teaching aging: Syllabi, resources, & infusion materials for the social work curriculum.*

Lichtenberg, P.A. ed.1999. *Handbook of assessment in clinical gerontology.*

McDonald, P. and M. Haney.1997. *Counseling the older adult: A training manual in clinical gerontology* (2nd ed.).

Paggi, K. and B. Hayslip. 1999. Mental aerobics: Exercises for the mind in later life.

Smyer, M. and S. Qualls. 1999. *Aging and mental health.*

Tice, C. and K. Perkins. 1996. *Mental health and aging: Building on the strengths of older adults.*

Turner, F. 1992. *Mental health and the elderly.*

Whitbourne-Krauss, S. (Ed.). 2000. *Psychopathology in later adulthood.*

Zarit, S.H. and J.M. Zarit. 1998. Mental disorders in older adults: Fundamentals of assessment and treatment.

Grief/Loss/Death/Dying

Klick, A. 1999. Death and bereavement. (In Richardson, 1999).
Morgan, J.P.1994. Bereavement in older adults.
Worden, J.W. 1991. Grief counseling and grief therapy: A handbook for the mental health practitioner (2nd ed.).

Depression, Dementia, Delusions

Cheston, R. 1998. Psychotherapeutic work with people with dementia: A review of the literature.
Dilworth-Anderson, P. and B. Givson. 1999. Ethnic minority perspectives on dementia, family caregiving, and interventions.
Duffy, M. (Ed.) 1999. *Handbook for counseling and psychotherapy with older adults.*
Toseland et al.1997. The impact of validation group therapy on nursing home residents with dementia.

Addictions and Suicide

Barry-Lawton, C., D.W. Oslin and F.C. Blow. 2001. *Prevention and management of alcohol problems in older adults.*
Gurnack, A.M. 1997. *Older adults' misuse of alcohol, medicines, and other drugs.*
Pearson, J.L and Y. Conwell.1996. *Suicide and Aging.*
Tice, C. and K. Perkins. Alcohol use and misuse in late life. (In Tice and Perkins, 1996).
Tice, C. and K. Perkins. Suicide and older adults. (In Tice and Perkins, 1996).
Vandeputte, C. 1991. Alcohol, medications, and older adults: A guide for families and other caregivers.

Cultural Issues in Mental Health

Biegel, D.E., K.J. Farkas, and L. Song. 1997. Barriers to the use of mental health services by African-American and Hispanic elderly persons.
Burlingame, V.S. 1998. *Ethnogerocounseling: Counseling ethnic elders and their families.*

Damron-Rodriguez, J.A. 1998. Respecting ethnic elders: A perspective for care providers.

McDougall, G.J. 1993. Therapeutic issues with gay and lesbian elders. Special issue: The forgotten aged: Ethnic, psychiatric, and societal minorities.

Padgett, D. 1995. *Handbook on ethnicity, aging, and mental health.*

Quam, J.K. ed.1997. *Social services for senior gay men and lesbians.*

Yeo, G. and N. Hikoyeda.1993. Differential assessment and treatment of mental health problems: African American, Latino, Filipino, and Chinese American elders.

Ethical Issues in Mental Health and Aging

Kane, R.A. and A.L. Caplan. eds. 1990. Everyday ethics: Resolving dilemmas in nursing home life.

Moody, H.R. 2000. Should people have a choice to end their lives? In H.R. Moody, *Aging: Concepts and controversies* (3rd ed., 123-150).

National Association of Social Workers. 1996. Code of Ethics.

National Center for Cost Containment. 1997. *Assessment of competency and capacity of the older adult: A practice guide for psychologists.*

Smith, G. 1996. *Legal and healthcare ethics for the elderly.*

Strauss, P.J. and N.M. Lederman. 1996. The elder law handbook: A legal and financial survival guide for caregivers and seniors.

Scales/Measurement Tools/Workbooks/ Knowledge-Attitude Quizzes

A Look Back From the Future (Frank, 2002, in Kropf and Tompkins, 2002, 25).

Alcohol Beliefs Scale. (Connors and Maisto 1988, 24-26).

Beck Anxiety Inventory. (Beck and Steer 1990).

Beck Depression Inventory. (Beck et al 1961).

Brief Depression Rating Scale. (Kellner 1986).

Center of Epidemiologic Studies Depression Scale (CES-D). (Radloff 1977).

Center of Epidemiologic Studies Depression Scale (CES-D), abbreviated version. (Health and Retirement Study, online).

Clinical Anxiety Scale. (Hudson 1992).

Cognitive Capacity Screening Exam. (Jacobs et al 1977).

Cognitive Slippage Scale. (Miers and Raulin 1985).

Cognitive-Somatic Anxiety Questionnaire. (Schwartz, Davidson, and Goleman 1978).

Concern about Death-Dying Checklist and Coping with Death-Dying Checklist. (Fry 1990).

Emotional Assessment Scale. (Carlson et al 1989).

Emotional/Social Loneliness Inventory. (Vincenzi and Grabosky 1987).

The Facts on Aging Quiz. (Palmore 1998).

Generalized Contentment Scale. (Hudson 1992).

Geriatric Depression Scale. (Yesavage and Brink 1983).

Geriatric Hopelessness Scale. (Fry 1986).

Hypochondriasis Scale for Institutional Geriatric Patients. (Brink et al 1978).

Index of Alcohol Involvement. (MacNeil 1991).

Irritability/Apathy Scale. (Burns et al 1990).

Longevity Calculator. http://diskworld.wharton.upenn.edu/~chuac/References/DemoCalc.html

The Longevity Game. www.nmfn.com/tnetwork/longevity_game_popup.html#

McMullin Addiction Thought Scale. (McMullin and Gehlaar 1990).

Michigan Alcoholism Screening Test-Geriatric Version (MAST-G). (Blow et al 1992).

Mini-Mental State Exam. (Folstein, Folstein, and McHugh 1975).

NIA Aging Quiz. www.nia/nih.gov

Patient Health Questionnaire Nine-Item Depression Module (PHQ-9). (Spitzer et al. 1994).

Penn State Worry Questionnaire. (Meyer et al. 1990).

The Pleasant Events Schedule-AD. (Teri and Logsdon 1991).

Reasons for Living Inventory. (Linehan et al 1983).

Scale for the Assessment of Positive and Negative Symptoms. (Schuldberg et al 1990).

Scale for Suicidal Ideation. (Beck, Kovacs and Weisman 1979).

Self-Rating Anxiety Scale. (Zung 1971).

Self-Rating Depression Scale. (Zung 1965).

Strengths Assessment Interview Guide. (Kivnick and Murray 2001).

Symptom Questionnaire. (Kellner 1987).

Templer Death Anxiety Scale. (Lonetto and Templer 1983).

Wechsler Adult Intelligence Scale-Revised. (Wechsler 1981).

What You Need to Know About Me: A Notebook for Families and Caregivers. (Carlton and Sessions 2002).

Case Studies that Address Mental Health Issues in Older Adults

Ageist attitudes: "Case Histories" (Weisberg and Wilder 1985).

Alcohol abuse/drug misuse: "Mr. Phillipson" and "Mrs. Carteret" (Blazer 1990).

Alzheimer's disease and other dementias: "Mr. Adams" (Hooyman and Kiyak 1999); "The Gray Family" (Kropf, in Richardson 1999, 122); "Mrs. Preston" (Kropf, in Richardson 1999, 127).

Anxiety: "Angela Martini" (McDonald and Haney 1985, 127-128); "Frances" (Knight 1992, 35-42); "Mrs. Jensen" and "Mr. Barnes" (Blazer 1990, 108-109); "Mrs. Spinoli" (Edinburg 1985, 172-173).

Anxiety and developmental disability: "Mrs. Vishnick and Meta" (Kropf, in Kropf and Tompkins 2002, 178-179).

Anxiety/Spiritual Dilemma: "Spiritual Dilemma Exercise" (Emlet, in Kropf and Tompkins 2002, 161).

Caregiving: "A Group for Relatives and Friends of Institutionalized Aged" (LeCroy 1992, 186-197); "Elaine and Warren" (Knight 1992, 43-57); "Friends Don't Really Understand: The Therapeutic Benefit of Social Group Work for Caregivers of Older Persons" (LeCroy 1992, 147-153).

Communication problems: "Mrs. Freeman" (Blazer 1990, 18-19); "Kate and Albert" (Sundel and Sundel 1993, 231-232).

Cultural competence: "She Doesn't Need To Know" (Fletcher et al 1997, 149-150).

Delirium: "Mrs. Bishop" (Blazer 1990, 41).

Depression: "Harold," "Helen," and "John" (Knight 1992, 1-34); "Homebound" (Haulotte and Kretzschmar 2001, 64); "Isobelle Banet" (McDonald and Haney 1985, 123); "Marie" (Rife 1998, 77-78); "Mrs. Sawyer," "Mrs. Johnson," and "Mr. Paxton" (Blazer 1990, 63-65); "Nancy Sue" (McDonald and Haney 1985, 127); "Sam" (McDonald and Haney 1985, 126).

Ethical decision making, competency: "Hard to Forget" (Haulotte and Kretzschmar 2001, 80); "Suffering and the Sanctity of Life" (Fletcher et al 1997); "Uncle Bert's Bad Judgment" (Moody 1998, 161-162).

Grief/Loss: "Agnes," "Jerry and Bea," "JoAnn," "Rena," and "Rose" (Knight 1992, 58-120); "Dear One" (McDonald and Haney 1985, 83-85); "Mr. Taylor" (Blazer 1990, 203-204); "Mrs. Johnson" (Hooyman and Kiyak 1999, 131); "My Mother" (McDonald and Haney 1985, 85-86); "Saying Goodbye" (Haulotte and Kretzschmar 2001, 86); "The Widow" (Edinburg 1985, 198-199).

Grief/loss and countertransference: "Mr. T." (Altschuler and Katz 1999, 83).

Memory loss: "May Smith" (McDonald and Haney 1985, 87-88); "Mr. Jones" (Blazer 1990, 34-35); "Phillip S" (Morano, in Kropf and Tompkins 2002, 180-181).

Organic brain syndrome: "Mr. R and Mrs. A" (Edinburg 1985, 102).

Physical illness' emotional effects: "Mr. Gibson" (Blazer 1990, 182-183).

Schizophrenia and other psychotic disorders: "Lila and Sophia," and "Mildred" (Knight 1992, 147-169); "Schizophrenia Complicates Care Needs" (Wacker, Roberto, Piper 1998, 227-228).

Somatization: "Nora," and "Lana" (Knight 1992, 121-146); "Mrs. Samuels" (Blazer 1990, 125-126).

Successful aging: "The Old Professor" (Blazer 1990, 240-242).

Suicide/Right to Die: "A Request for a 'Humanized' Death" (Fletcher et al 1997, 148).

Suspiciousness: "Mrs. Evans" and "Mrs. Arnold" (Blazer 1990, 90-92).

Websites/Phone Contacts on Mental Health and Aging

Alzheimer's Association, Inc. www.alzheimers.org or www.alz.org

American Association for Geriatric Psychiatry www.aagpgpa.org

American Association for Retired Persons www.aarp.org

Canadian Mental Health Association www.cmha.ca/english

Eden Alternative www.edenalt.com

Eldercare Web (includes Minimum Data Set information) www.elderweb.com

Emotional Support Guide http://asa.ugl.lib.umich.edu/chdocs/support/emotion.html

Federal Interagency Forum on Aging-Related Statistics www.agingstats.gov

Health Care Financing Administration www.hcfa.gov

Hospice Association of America www.nahc.org
Live Well, Live Long: Steps to Better Health Website. www.asaging.org/
   cdc
Medicare 1-800-772-1213
Mental HealthNet 'www.cmhc.com
MIND (British mental health association) www.mind.org.uk
National Alliance for the Mentally Ill www.nami.org
National Asian Pacific center on Aging www.NAPCA.org
National Association for Hispanic Elderly 1-626-564-1988
National Caucus and Center on Black Aged www.ncba-blackaged.org
National Hispanic Council on Aging www.nhcoa.org
National Indian Council on Aging www.nicoa.org
National Institute of Mental Health 1-301-443-4513.
National Hospice and Palliative Care Organization www.nhpco.org
National Institute on Aging www.nia.nih.gov
National Institute on Drug Abuse www.nida.nih.gov
National Mental Health Association www.nmha.org or 1-703-684-5968
National Mental Health Information Center 800-969-6642
National Self-Help Clearinghouse 212-642-2944
Native Elder Health Care Resource Center www.uchsc.edu/sm/nehcrc
Older Women's League www.owl-national.org
Psych Central www.coil.com/grohol/web.htm
Substance Abuse and Mental Health Services Administration (DHHS)
   www.samhsa.gov
   or www.mentalhealth.org

Films on Mental Health and Aging

Aging with Grace. Northwest Media.
Alzheimer's Care Series. Assisted Living Federation of America, Fanlight
   Productions.
Amanda's Choice (early onset Alzheimer's). Canadian Broadcasting Co.,
   Filmakers Library.
An Alzheimer's Story. Rosenberg and Neuwald, Filmakers Library.
And Thou Shalt Honor (caregiving and mental illness). www.thoushalt
   honor.org
Caring at the End of Life. Achtenberg, Fanlight Productions.
Choices and Challenges: Caring for Aggressive Older Adults. Bosch,
   Fanlight Productions.

Common Heroes: Choices in Hospice Care. Ruvkun, Fanlight Productions.
Communicating with severely confused older adults. Mental Health Outreach Network.
Complaints of a Dutiful Daughter. Terra Nova Films.
Dax's Case: Who Should Decide? (the right to die). Unicorn Media, Inc., Filmakers Library.
Defining Life: Should One Help a Loved One Die? Peterson, Filmakers Library.
Depression in Older Adults. Clark, Fanlight Productions.
Depression in Older Adults: The Right to Feel Better. Terra Nova Films.
Driving Miss Daisy. Commercial release.
Dying with Dignity: Experiences in the Netherlands. NOS, Filmakers Library.
Grief in America (cross cultural perspective). Atkinson, Fanlight Productions.
I Know a Song: A Journey with Alzheimer's Disease. King, Filmakers Library.
In and Out of Time. Finlayson, Fanlight Productions.
Iris *based on the true story of author Iris Murdoch's dementia, R-rated. Commercial release.*
It Can Happen to Anyone: Problems with Alcohol and Medications Among Older Adults.
AARP Films.
It's Better to Live in a Garden. Eden Alternative.
The Journey Home: Stories from Hospice. Green, Fanlight Productions.
Learning from Hannah. Eden Alternative.
Long Day's Journey into Night. Commercial release.
Mental Health Problems of Older Adults. Mental Health Outreach Network.
More Than a Failing Heart (end-of-life decisions). Barey and Burson, Fanlight Productions.
Mr. Nobody (self-neglect and competence). National Film Board of Canada, Filmakers Library.
My Mother, My Father. Terra Nova Films.
On Golden Pond. Commercial release.
On Our Own Terms: Moyers on Dying: Living with Dying. Films for the Humanities and Sciences. www.pbs.org
On Wings of Song: Music Therapy at the End of Life. Beitel/Lazar Productions, Filmakers Library.

The Road to Galveston. 1996. Commercial release.
Shadowlands. 1994. Commercial release.
Something Should be Done about Grandma Ruthie (Alzheimer's disease). Stauffacher, Fanlight Productions.
Stolen Memories: Alzheimer's Disease. *Greenstone Pictures, Filmakers Library.*
The SUPPORT Project: To Improve Care at the End of Life. Achtenberg, Fanlight Productions.
To Dance with the White Dog. 1993. Hallmark Films. Commercial release.
Tuesdays with Morrie. Jackson, M. 1999. American Broadcasting Company. Commercial release.
Two Videos on the Validation Method (Alzheimer's Disease/ Disorientation). Edward Feil Productions, Filmakers Library.
The Way We Die: Listening to the Terminally Ill. Mednick, Fanlight Productions.
Who Owns My Life? The Sue Rodriguez Story (the right to die). Canadian Broadcasting Co., Filmakers Library.
Who's Afraid of Virginia Wolff? Commercial release.
You Must Remember This: Inside Alzheimer's Disease. Bowden and MacKinnon, Filmakers Library.

Drama, Literature, Creative Arts, and Self-Help Books for Reading, Reading Aloud, Writing, Acting Out, Performing

Albom, M. 1997. *Tuesdays with Morrie: An old man, a young man, and the last great lesson.*
Alzheimer's disease poetry. www.zarcrom.com/users/yeartorem/ADpoetry/contributed.html
Audio Stories. Audio taped stories of the Eden Alternative.
Bayley, J. 2001. *Elegy for Iris.*
Browning, R. Rabbi Ben Ezra (poem, "Grow old along with me...").
Burns, D. 1989. *The feeling good handbook.*
Covey, H. 2000. Shakepeare on old age and disability.
Davis, M., E. Eshelman, and M. McKay.1988. *The relaxation and stress reduction workbook.*
Diamond, T. and C.R. Stimpson.1992. *Making gray gold: Narratives of nursing home care.*

Dowling, J.R. and N.L. Mace. 1995. *Keeping busy: A handbook of activities for persons with dementia.*

Feil, N. 1993. *The validation breakthrough: Simple techniques for communicating with people with Alzheimer's-Type Dementia.*

Frazer, D.W. and A.E. Jongsma. 1999. Appendix A: Bibliotherapy suggestions (e.g., on aggression, anxiety, communication deficits, decision-making, depression, grief, loneliness, memory impairment, substance abuse, suicide). In *The older adult psychotherapy treatment planner*, 253-259.

Kushner, H. 1991. *When bad things happen to good people.*

Lapp, D.C. 1995. *Don't forget! Easy exercises for a better memory.*

"Life Worth Living: A Celebration of Elders and Those Who Care for Them." Song CD by Allen Powers, Eden Alternative.

Mace, N.L. and P.V. Rabins. 1991. *The thirty-six hour day: A family guide for caring for persons with Alzheimer's Disease, related dementing illnesses, and memory loss in later life.* .

O'Neill, E. 1956. *Long day's journey into night.*

Schmidtke, C.R. 2000. Using a dramatic persona for a classroom life review.

Scott-Maxwell, F. 1979. *The measure of my days.*

Senior Theatre Research and Performance. www.seniortheatre.com and www.accad.ohio-state.edu/~jreilly/html/senior_connections.html and www.accad.ohio-state.edu/~jreilly/index.html and www.dramatic pub lishing.com/theatreresources.html

"She Misses Him" a ballad about Alzheimer's, lyrics by Tim Johnson, sung by Tim Rushlow, produced by David Malloy

Thomas, W. H. 1999. *Learning from Hannah: Secrets for a life worth living.*

Tolstoy, L. 1960. *The death of Ivan Ilyich.*

Wood, M.D. 2002. Books and short stories. In *Literature and Aging*, http://crab.rutgers.edu/~deppen/literature.htm

Weisberg, N. and R. Wilder, R. eds. 1985. *Creative arts with older adults: A sourcebook.*

Yahnke, R.E. and R.M. Eastman.1995. Literature and gerontology: A research guide.

Online as *The poets of aging-a selected bibliography.*

References

Abramson, T.A., L. Trejo, D.W.L. Lai. 2002. Culture and mental health: Providing appropriate services for a diverse older population. *Generations, 26* (1), 21-27.

Albom, M. 1997. *Tuesdays with Morrie: An old man, a young man, and the last great lesson.* Bantam Doubleday Publishing Group.

Altschuler, J. and A.D. Katz. 1999. Methodology for discovering and teaching countertransference toward elderly clients (p. 83). *Journal of Gerontological Social Work, 32* (2), 81-93. American Psychiatric Association. 1994. *Diagnostic and Statistical Manual of Mental Disorders* (4th ed.). Washington, DC: Author.

Baltes, P.B. and M.M. Baltes, eds.1990. *Successful Aging.* Cambridge, UK: University of Cambridge Press.

Bandura, A. 1997. *Self-efficacy: The exercise of control.* USA: W.H. Freeman and Company.

Barry-Lawton, C., D.W. Oslin, and F.C. Blow. 2001. *Prevention and management of alcohol problems in older adults.* New York: Springer.

Bartels, S.J. and M.A. Smyer. 2002. Mental disorders of aging: An emerging public health crisis? *Generations, 26* (1), 14-20.

Bayley, J. 2001. *Elegy for Iris.* New York: St. Martin's Press

Beck, A.T., M. Kovacs and A. Weisman. 1979. Assessment of suicidal ideation: The Scale for Suicidal Ideation. *Journal of Consulting and Clinical Psychology, 47,* 343-352.

Beck, A.T. and R.A. Steer. 1990. *Beck Anxiety Inventory: Manual.* The Psychological Corporation.

Beck, A.T., C.H. Ward, M. Mendelson, J. Mock, and J. Erbaugh. 1961. An inventory for measuring depression. *Archives of General Psychiatry, 4,* 561-571.

Biegel, D.E., K.J. Farkas, and L. Song. 1997. Barriers to the use of mental health services by African-American and Hispanic elderly persons. *Journal of Gerontological Social Work, 29,* 23-44.

Blazer, D. 1998. *Emotional problems in later life: Intervention strategies for professional caregivers.* New York: Springer.

Blow, F.C., K.J. Brower, J.E. Schulenberg, L.M. Demo-Dananberg, J.P.Young, and T.P. Beresford. 1992. The Michigan Alcoholism Screening Test-Geriatric version (MAST-G): A new elderly-specific screening instrument. *Alcoholism, 16,* 372.

Blow, F.C., D.W. Oslin, and K.L. Barry. 2002. Misuse and abuse of alcohol, illicit drugs, and psychoactive medication among older people. *Generations, 26* (1), 50-54.

Brink, T.L., J. Bryant, J. Belanger, D. Capri, S. Jasculca, C. Janakes, and C. Oliveira. 1978. Hypochondriasis in an institutional geriatric population: Construction of a scale. (HSIG). *Journal of the American Geriatrics Society, 26*, 552-559.

Buckingham, R., S. Lack, B. Mount, L. MacLean, and J. Collins. 1976. Living with the dying. *Canadian Medical Association Journal, 115*, 1211-1215. [Summary and discussion of Buckingham study in A. Rubin and E. Babbie. 1997. *Research methods for social work* : 28-29 and 64-65. Pacific Grove, CA: Brooks/Cole.]

Burlingame, V.S. 1998. *Ethnogerocounseling: Counseling ethnic elders and their families.* New York: Springer.

Burns, A., S. Folstein, J. Brandt, and M. Folstein. 1990. Clinical assessment of irritability, aggression, and apathy in Huntington and Alzheimer Disease. *Journal of Nervous and Mental Disease, 178*, 20-26.

Burns, D. 1989. *The feeling good handbook.* New York: Plume Penguin.

Butler, R.N. 1963. *Why survive? Being old in America.* New York: Harper and Row, Publishers.

Butler, R., M. Lewis, and T. Sunderland. 1998. *Aging and Mental Health: Positive psychosocial and biomedical approaches.* Boston: Allyn and Bacon.

Carlson, C.R., F.L. Collins, J.F. Stewart, J. Porzelius, J.A. Nitz, and C.O. Lind. 1989. The assessment of emotional reactivity: A scale development and validation study. *Journal of Psychopathology and Behavioral Assessment, 11*, 313-325.

Carlton, S.R. and N.S. Sessions. 2002. Columbia, SC: The SC Respite Coalition and The Center for Child and Family Studies, USC College of Social Work. Contact 1-803-799-9819.

Cheston, R. 1998. Psychotherapeutic work with people with dementia: A review of the literature. *British Journal of Medical Psychology, 71*, 211-231.

Connors, G.J. and S.A. Maisto. 1988. In Hersen, M. and A.S. Bellack, eds. *Dictionary of Behavioral Assessment Techniques*, 24-26. New York: Pergamon Press.

Council on Social Work Education. 2001. CSWE/SAGE-SW Gerontological Competencies. Alexandria, VA: Author.

Covey, H. 2000. Shakespeare on old age and disability. *International Journal of Aging and Human Development, 50* (3), 169-183.

Damron-Rodriguez, J.A. 1998. Respecting ethnic elders: A perspective for care providers. *Journal of Gerontological Social Work, 29* (2/3), 53-72.

Damron-Rodriguez, J., V. Villa, H.F. Tseng and J.E. Lubben. 1997. Demographic and organizational influences on the development of gerontological social work curriculum. *Gerontology and Geriatrics Education, 17*, 3, 3-18.

Davis, M., E. Eshelman, and M. McKay. 1988. The relaxation and stress reduction workbook. Oakland, CA: New Harbinger.

Diamond, T. and C.R. Stimpson. 1992. *Making gray gold: Narratives of nursing home care (women in culture and society).* Chicago: University of Chicago Press.

Dilworth,-Andrson, P. and B. Givson. 1999. Ethnic minority perspectives on dementia, family caregiving, and interventions. *Generations, 23*(3), 40-45.

Dowling, J.R. and N.L. Mace. 1995. *Keeping Busy: A handbook of activities for persons with dementia.* Baltimore: Johns Hopkins.

Duffy, M. ed. 1999. *Handbook for counseling and psychotherapy with older adults.* New York: Wiley.

Edinburg, M.A. 1985. *Mental health practice with the elderly.* Englewood Cliffs, NJ: Prentice-Hall, Inc.

Emlet, C.A., J.L. Crabtree, V.A. Condon, and L.A. Treml. 1996. *In-home assessment of older adults: A multidisciplinary approach.* Gaithersburg, MD: Aspen.

Erickson, E.H., J.M. Erickson, and H.Q. Kivnick. 1986. *Vital involvement in old age.* New York: W.W. Norton.

Evans, J.D. 1981. Personal involvement projects in the psychology of aging: Some examples and an empirical assessment. *Teaching of Psychology, 8*, 4, 230-233.

Fanlight Productions, 4196 Washington St., Boston, MA, 02131; www.fanlight.com or 1-800-937-4113

Feil, N. 1993. *The validation breakthrough: Simple techniques for communicating with people with Alzheimer's-Type Dementia.* Baltimore: Health Professions Press.

Filmmakers Library, 124 E. 40th St., NY, NY 10016, 212-808-4980, www.filmakers.com

Films for the Humanities and Sciences, www.films.com

Fletcher, J.C., P.A. Lombardo, M.F. Marshall, and F.G. Miller, eds. 1997. *Introduction to clinical ethics* (2nd ed.) (p.149). Frederick, MD: University Publishing Group, Inc.

Folstein, M.F., S.E. Folstein, and P.R. McHugh. 1975. Mini-mental state: A practical method for grading the cognitive state of patients for the clinician. *Journal of Psychiatric Research, 12*, 189-198.

Frazer, D.W. and A.E. Jongsma. 1999. *The older adult psychotherapy treatment planner.* New York: John Wiley & Sons, Inc.

Fry, P.S. 1986. Assessment of pessimism and despair in the elderly: A Geriatric Scale of Hopelessness. *Clinical Gerontologist, 5*, 193-201.

Fry, P.S. 1990. A factor analytic investigation of home-bound elderly individuals' concerns about death and dying and their coping responses. *Journal of Clinical Psychology, 46*, 737-748.

Genia, V. 1991. The spiritual experience index: A measure of spiritual maturity. *Journal of Religion and Health, 30*, 4, 337-347.

Grinnell, R. 1997. *Social work research and evaluation: Quantitative and qualitative approaches* (5th ed.). Itasca, IL: F.E. Peacock Publishers, Inc.

Gurnack, A.M. 1997. *Older adults' misuse of alcohol, medicines, and other drugs.* New York: Springer.

Haulotte, S.M. and J.A. Kretzschmar. 2001. *Case scenarios for teaching and learning social work practice,* 64. Alexandria, VA: CSWE.

Health and Retirement Study. Center of Epidemiologic Studies Depression Scale (CES-D), abbreviated version: www.agingstats.gov

Hillier, S. and G.M. Barrow. 1999. *Aging, the individual, and society* (7th ed.). Belmont, CA: Wadsworth Publishing Company.

Hodge, D. 2001. Spiritual assessment: A review of major qualitative methods and a new framework for assessing spirituality. *Social Work, 46*, 3, 203-214.

Hooyman, N.R. and H.A. Kiyak. 1999. *Social gerontology: A multidisciplinary approach* (5th ed.). Boston: Allyn and Bacon.

Hudson, W.W. 1992. *The WALMYR assessment scales scoring manual.* Tempe, AZ: WALMYR Publishing Co.

Johnson, T. 2002. Alzheimer's ballad: She Misses Him.

Kane, R.A. and A.L. Caplan, eds. 1990. *Everyday ethics: Resolving dilemmas in nursing home life.* New York: Springer.

Kane, R.L. and R.A. Kane, eds. 2000. *Assessing older persons: Measures, meaning, and practical applications.* New York: Oxford University Press.

Kellner, R. 1986. Brief Depression Rating Scale. In N. Sartorius and T.A. Ban, eds. *Assessment of Depression*, 179-183. New York: Springer-Verlag.

Kellner, R. 1987. A symptom questionnaire. *The Journal of Clinical Psychiatry, 48*, 268-274.

Kivnick, H.Q. 1993. Everyday mental health: A guide to assessing life strengths. *Generations, 17*, 13-20.

Kivnick, H.Q. and S.V. Murray. 2001. Life strengths interview guide: Assessing elder clients' strengths. *Journal of Gerontological Social Work, 34*, 7-32.

Klick, A. 1999. Death and bereavement. In V. Richardson (Ed.) *Teaching gerontological social work: A compendium of model syllabi,* 73. Alexandria, VA: Council on Social Work Education.

Kline, P.M. 1998. Aging sensitivity. *Activities, Adaptation, and Aging, 23,* 2, 101-108.

Knight, B.G. 1996. *Psychotherapy with older adults* (2nd ed.). Thousand Oaks, CA: Sage.

Knowles, M. 1972. Innovations in teaching styles and approaches based upon adult learning. *Education for Social Work,* 32-39.

Kosberg, J.I. and A.V. Kaufman. 2002, February 15. Gerontological social work: Issues and imperatives for education and practice. *Electronic Journal of Social Work, 1,* 1, Article 9. Retrieved 3-1-02, from http://www.ejsw.net/Issue/Vol1/Num1/Article9.pdf

Kropf, N. P. and C.J. Tompkins, eds. 2002. *Teaching aging: Syllabi, resources, & infusion materials for the social work curriculum.* Alexandria, VA: CSWE.

Kushner, H. 1991. *When bad things happen to good people.* New York: Schocken Books.

Lapp, D.C. 1995. *Don't forget! Easy exercises for a better memory.* Reading, MA: Addison-Wesley.

LeCroy, C.W. 1992. *Case studies in social work practice,* 186-197. Belmont, CA: Wadsworth Publishing Company.

Lichtenberg, P.A. ed. 1999. *Handbook of assessment in clinical gerontology.* New York: Wiley.

Lin, A.M.P. 1995. Mental health overview. *Encyclopedia of social work* (19th ed.). Washington, DC: National Association of Social Workers.

Linehan, M.M., J.L. Goldstein, S.L. Nielsen, and J.A. Chiles. 1983. Reasons for staying alive when you are thinking of killing yourself: The Reasons for Living Inventory. *Journal of Consulting and Clinical Psychology, 51*, 276-286.

Lonetto, R. and D.I. Templer. 1983. The nature of death anxiety. In C.D. Spielberger and J.N. Butcher, eds. *Advances in Personality Assessment,* (Vol. 3), 14-174. Hillsdale, NJ: Lawrence Erlbaum.

Mace, N.L. and P.V. Rabins. 1991. *The thirty-six hour day: A family guide for caring for persons with Alzheimer's Disease, related dementing illnesses, and memory loss in later life.* Baltimore: Johns Hopkins.

MacNeil, G. 1991. A short-form scale to measure alcohol abuse. *Research on Social Work Practice, 1, 68-75.*

McDonald, P. and M. Haney. *Counseling the older adult: A training manual in clinical gerontology* (2nd ed.). San Francisco: Jossey-Bass.

McDougall, G.J. 1993. Therapeutic issues with gay and lesbian elders. Special issue: The forgotten aged: Ethnic, psychiatric, and societal minorities. *Clinical Gerontologist, 14*(1), 45-57.

McMullin, R.E. and M. Gehlaar. 1990. *Thinking* and *drinking: An expose of drinkers' distorted beliefs.* Wheelers Hill, Victoria, Australia: Marlin Publications.

Mental Health Outreach Network. Mental health and older adults' video training series. Minneapolis, MN: Author.

Meyer, T. 1990. Development and validity of the Penn State worry scale. *Behaviour Research and Therapy, 28*, 487-495.

Meyers, C. and T.B. Jones. 1993. *Promoting active learning: Strategies for the college classroom.* San Francisco: Jossey-Bass.

Miers, T.C. and M.L. Raulin. 1985. The development of a scale to measure cognitive slippage. Paper presented at the eastern Psychological Association Convention, Boston, MA.

Moody, H.R. 1998. *Aging: Concepts and controversies* (3rd ed.). Thousand Oaks, CA: Pine Forge Press.

Morgan. J.P. 1994. Bereavement in older adults. *Journal of Mental Health Counseling, 16,* 318-327.

National Association of Social Workers. 1996. *Code of Ethics.* Washington, DC: Author. Available online: www.naswdc.org/pubs/code

National Center for Cost Containment. 1997. *Assessment of competency and capacity of the older adult: A practice guide for psychologists.* Washington DC: U.S. Department of Veterans Affairs.

Northwest Media, www.northwestmedia.com

Padgett, D. 1995. *Handbook on ethnicity, aging, and mental health.* Westport, CT: Greenwood Press.

Paggi, K. and B. Hayslip. 1999. Mental aerobics: Exercises for the mind in later life. *Educational Gerontology, 25*, 1-12.

Palmore, E.B. 1998. The facts on aging quizzes. New York: Springer Publishing Company.

Pearson, J.L and Y. Conwell, eds. 1996. *Suicide and Aging.* New York: Springer.

Quam, J.K., ed. 1997. *Social services for senior gay men and lesbians.* New York: Harrington Park Press.

Qualls, S.H. 2002. Defining mental health in later life. *Generations, 26* (1), 9-13.

Radloff, L.S. 1977. The CES-D scale: A self-report depression scale for research in the general population. *Applied Psychological Measurement, 1*, 385-401.

Richardson, V., ed. 2001. *Teaching gerontological social work: A compendium of model syllabi.* Alexandria, VA: Council on Social Work Education, Inc.

Rife, J. 1998. Use of life review techniques to assist older workers in coping with job loss and depression (pp. 77-78). *Clinical Gerontologist, 20*(1), 75-79.

Schaie, K.W., and S.L. Willis. 2002. *Adult development and aging* (5ᵗʰ ed.). Upper Saddle River, NJ: Prentice Hall.

Scharlach, A.E. and L.W. Kaye, eds. *Controversial issues in aging,* 92-102. Boston: Allyn and Bacon.

Scharlach, A., J. Damron-Rodriguez, B. Robinson, R. Feldman. 2000. *Journal of Social Work Education, 36*, 3, 521-538.

Schmidtke, C.R. 2000. Using a dramatic persona for a classroom life review. *Educational Gerontology, 26*, 447-465.

Schuldberg, D., D.M. Quinlan, H. Morgenstern, and W. Glazer. 1990. Positive and negative symptoms in chronic psychiatric outpatients: reliability, stability, and factor structure. *Psychological Assessment, 2,* 262-268.

Schwartz, G.E., R.J. Davidson, and D.J. Goleman. 1978. Patterning of cognitive and somatic processes in the self-regulation of anxiety: Effects of meditation versus exercise. *Psychosomatic Medicine, 40*, 321-328.

Scott-Maxwell, F. 1979. *The measure of my days.* New York: Penguin Books.

Shea, D.G. 2002. Parity and prescription: Policy developments and their implications for mental health in later life. *Generations, 26* (1), 83-89.

Smith, G. 1996. *Legal and healthcare ethics for the elderly.* Washington, DC: Taylor and Francis.

Smyer, M. and S. Qualls. 1999. *Aging and mental health.* Malden, MA: Blackwell.

Spitzer, R.L.1994. Utility of a new procedure for diagnosing mental disorders in primary care: The PRIME-MD 1000 study. *Journal of the American Medical Association, 272,* 1749-1756.

Strauss, P.J. and N.M. Lederman. 1996. *The elder law handbook: A legal and financial survival guide for caregivers and seniors.* New York: Facts on File.

Sundel, S.S. and M. Sundel. 1993. Behavior modification in the human services: A systematic introduction to concepts and applications (3rd ed.), 231-232. Newbury Park, CA: Sage Publications.

Tan, P.P., M.J. Hawkins, and E. Ryan. 2001. Baccalaureate student attitudes toward aging. *The Journal of Baccalaureate Social Work, 6,* 2, 45-56.

Teri, L. and R. Logsdon. 1991. Identifying pleasant activities for Alzheimer's disease patients: The Pleasant Events Schedule-AD. *The Gerontologist, 31,* 124-127.

Terra Nova Films, 9848 S. Winchester Ave., Chicago, IL 60643.

Thomas, W. H. 1999. *Learning from Hannah: Secrets for a life worth living.* Acton, MA: VanderWyk and Burnham.

Tice, C. and K. Perkins. 1996. Mental health and aging: Building on the strengths of older adults. Pacific Grove, CA: Brooks/Cole.

Tirrito, T., I. Nathanson, and N. Langer. 1996. Elder practice: A multidisciplinary approach to working with older adults in the community. Columbia, SC: University of South Carolina Press.

Toseland, R.W., M. Diehl, K. Freeman, T. Manzanares, M. Naleppa, and P. McCallion. 1997. The impact of validation group therapy on nursing home residents with dementia. *The Journal of Applied Gerontology, 16*(1), 31-50.

Turner, F. 1992. *Mental health and the elderly.* New York: Free Press.

Vandeputte, C. 1991. *Alcohol, medications, and older adults: A guide for families and other caregivers.* Minneapolis, MN: Johnson Institute.

Vincenzi, H. and F. Grabosky, F. 1987. Measuring the emotional/social aspects of loneliness and isolation. *Journal of Social Behavior and Personality, 2,* 257-270.

Wacker, R.R., K.A. Roberto, L.E. Piper. 1998. Community resources for older adults: Programs and services in an era of change, 227-228. Thousand Oaks, CA: Pine Forge Press.

Wechsler, D. 1981. Manual for the Wechsler Adult Intelligence Scale-Revised. San Antonio, TX: Psychological Corporation.

Weisberg, N. and R. Wilder, eds. 1985. *Creative arts with older adults: A sourcebook.* New York: Human Sciences Press, Inc.

Whitbourne-Krauss, S., ed. 2000. *Psychopathology in later adulthood.* New York: Wiley.

Wood, M.D. 2002. Books and short stories. In *Literature and Aging,* http://crab.rutgers.edu/~deppen/literature.htm

Worden, J.W. 1991. *Grief counseling and grief therapy: A handbook for the mental health practitioner* (2nd ed.). New York: Springer.

Yahnke, R.E. and R.M. Eastman. 1995. *Literature and gerontology: A research guide.*

Westport, CN: Greenwood Press. Online, *The poets of aging-a selected bibliography:* www.gen.umn.edu/faculty_staff/yahnke/poetry/poetry6.htm

Yeo, G. and N. Hikoyeda. 1993. *Differential assessment and treatment of mental health problems: African American, Latino, Filipino, and Chinese American elders.* Stanford, CA: Stanford Geriatric Education Center.

Yesavage, J.A. and T.L. Brink. 1983. Development and validation of a geriatric depression screening scale: A preliminary report. *Journal of Psychiatric Research, 17* (1), 37-49.

Zarit, S.H. and J.M. Zarit. 1998. *Mental disorders in older adults: Fundamentals of assessment and treatment.* New York: Guilford Press.

Zung, W.W.K. 1965. A self-rating depression scale. *Archives of General Psychiatry, 12,* 63-70.

Zung, W.W.K. 1971. A rating instrument for anxiety disorders. *Psychosomatics, 12,* 371- 379.

Editorial Commentary

ℰℭ

Nieli Langer & Terry Tirrito

Geriatric mental health is a growing field and it appears that a considerable portion of the work load of most public sector mental health professionals is allocated to care of the older adult. A recent survey indicates that a substantial minority of care providers have received no geriatric training while others have received some instruction; most of the respondents indicated an interest in learning more about dementia, depression, grief, substance abuse, legal and ethical issues, diagnosis, and anxiety. Most respondents requested a topic specific short workshop format or whole day workshops provided in a multiplicity of venues. These frontline professionals need to receive state-of-the-art knowledge, skills, and attitudes concerning this growing aging cohort. Training programs will have to be designed in order to address the diverse needs and schedules of the many discipline-specific professionals who practice with varied amounts of educational background in geriatric mental health (Molinari et al. 2002, 73).

Older adults can use religious expressions and orientation as effective coping mechanisms in dealing with the changes, problems, and challenges of life. Can religion be an effective coping mechanism for people suffering from mental impairments? For many older adults, the religious beliefs they developed in their early years are embedded in their memories which makes it possible for people who have even late-stage dementia to use religion as a coping mechanism. This information can be helpful to the professionals, lay persons, and family members who try to help older people deal with the realities of dementia, including Alzheimer's disease.

Whatever the progression of the disease, Alzheimer's has a devastating impact on the families of patients. It is often referred to as a family disease, because all members of the family are affected by it emotionally, financially, and socially. Social service professionals working with dementia clients and their families need to network with their religious community where they will often find strong allies. Religious worship is a safe and soothing activity for persons with Alzheimer's disease and related dementias. It enables them to respond to their faith and spiritual needs through long remembered rituals that connect past and present. Caregivers need to know that the congregation accepts their loved one and stands ready to reach out in assistance. The clergy is in a position to offer support and assistance to persons with dementia. They may be the first to recognize the problem, especially when there is a lot of denial in the family. The congregations that are most successful will probably have leaders who have a good awareness of the aging process, an understanding of changing demographics, and programs that are holistic and enabling. People with dementia might recognize a crucifix, a torah, a clerical collar, a hymn, even when they no longer know who they are and respond to little else. A man in Oklahoma, even as his dementia stripped away virtually all of his short-term memory, could recall 700 Bible verses he learned as a child.

In the synagogue of the Hebrew Home for the Aged in Riverdale, New York, the lucid residents attend their own separate Rosh Hashanah and Chanukah services. For residents with dementia, there is an abridged special service, more tactile and favors a higher ratio of music to words. The rules of conduct are understandably looser. "It doesn't mean you have to treat them like children and infantilize them," Rabbi Hirschhorn said. "But they live in a country with different rules. I have to go where they are" were the words of Rabbi Hirschhorn when interviewed in November, 2002 by N.R. Kleinfeld of the *New York Times*. Religious rituals for both the Alzheimer's patient and his/her family caregivers can be powerful ways of coping. They provide structure and comfort and make meaning out of life.

References

Albertson Owens, S.A., A.J. Berg, and R.L. Rhone. 1993. Religion, optimism, and health in older adults. Paper presented at the annual meeting of the Society for the Scientific Study of Religion. Raleigh, NC.

Molinari V., F.J. Kier, and M.E. Kunik. 2002. Obtaining age-related mental health competency: What is needed? *Educational Gerontology* 28: 73-82.

4

FAMILES AND AGING: ALZHEIMER'S DISEASE SPOUSAL CAREGIVER SUPPORT GROUP

ℬ

Gil Choi

Introduction

Alzheimer's disease (AD) is a neurological disease common in older populations that causes dementia. It results in a loss of intellectual capacities and impairs social, behavioral, and emotional functions. Loss of functional ability, development of behavioral disturbances, and dependency are the rule in patients with the disease. Once people develop Alzheimer's disease, their life expectancy is reduced; there is currently no known cure for the disease. People with Alzheimer's disease make up an amazingly large proportion in the old population. One out of ten older adults over 65 and nearly half of those older than 85 suffer from this disease (Evans 1990). Gruetzner (1992) has reported that the incidence of the disease is slightly higher in women than in men, but that this difference in incidence rate is likely to decrease as male life span increases.

It has been estimated that, for every American stricken with Alzheimer's and related dementia, three family members will be affected by the burden of caregiving (Weiler 1987). More than 7 out of 10 people with Alzheimer's disease live at home and are being cared for by family members (Wackerbarth 2002). Even though caring for a family member with Alzheimer's disease is stressful and challenging, many caregivers seem to draw immense satisfaction and existential meaning from their caregiving activities as some studies have shown (Rhoades and McFarland 1999). The authors report that caregivers derive three categories of caregiver meaning: other-directed-altruistic satisfaction, self-directed-self-actualization, and existential-purpose in life (Rhoades and McFarland 1999, 291).

Nonetheless, caring for the patient with Alzheimer's disease and related dementia has been described as one of the most demanding and extremely burdensome situations encountered (Rabins 1984; Tornatore and Grant 2002). The burdens imposed on family caregivers can often result in various physical, psychological, emotional, social, and financial problems during the course of the illness. Clinical depression is the most common emotional disorder detected in caregivers. The factors contributing to depression include social isolation, reduced control over their lives, fear of inadequacy, inappropriate guilt, and loss of a previously joyous relationship (Becker and Morrissey 1988; Morris, Morris and Britton 1988). High levels of psychological morbidity have been reported for caregivers regardless of whether the patient lives in the community, attends day center programs, or outpatient programs. Dura (1991) has reported that caregiver depression prevalence ranges from 14-47%. Caregivers report irritability, agitation, apathy, and delusions (Friedland 1993; Mega et al 1996). In addition, patient's physical violence, memory disturbance, incontinence, physical and emotional abuse, accusations, and suspiciousness are also identified as factors contributing to depression in caregivers (Rabins 1984). Physical problems associated with caregiving include sleeplessness, fatigue, back problems, and other somatic complaints.

There is also evidence to suggest that certain groups of caregivers are more vulnerable to psychological distress, depression or breakdown of the dyad relationship. These include wives rather than husbands, women rather than men, and spouses rather than adult children. Caregivers who are socially isolated and/or physically unwell themselves are also more vulnerable to caregiver morbidity (Brodaty 1996). A majority of caregivers are older adults themselves with one or more chronic health conditions (Bauer et al 2001). The burden of care-giving will also depend upon caregiver coping mechanisms, the ability of the caregiver to maintain the dyad relationship, supportive family and friends, professional support, and membership in a support group that provides general knowledge about the disease, anticipatory information and skills prior to each stage, and a neutral place to meet other caregivers to give and receive support.

An approach to improving the overall quality of life of caregivers and patients with AD has been the introduction of caregiver interventions that target psychological support, educational activities and developmental skills, and social support networks (Brodaty 1998). The purpose of this chapter is to propose a model psycho-educational AD spousal caregiver support program that provides a confidential environment for caregivers to meet in order to share their experiences, gain perspective, offer and receive advice, and feel the closeness and connection derived from being around others who know and empathize with their caregivers' burdens. The program will provide new information, teach and develop skills, and facilitate the enhancement of interpersonal relations and communication skills for AD caregivers. Therefore, it is caregiver needs that are primarily addressed and patient needs only incidentally. Therefore, caregivers are not only comforted but empowered. Particular emphasis is placed on how to develop and structure this model intervention session by session.

Program Development

Clarity of Purpose

Probably the single most important therapeutic force is clarity of purpose; that is, the facilitators and the group members clearly understand the program purpose. Not only should the facilitators be clear regarding the purpose, but the purpose must be relevant to all participants. In the current model, an educational support group is described. Facilitators will teach members information and skills. Concurrently, the leaders want to create a safe environment where members can share their ideas and concerns with the group. Trust, commitment, and genuine caring among members are the important affective dynamics that provide the foundation for this kind of educational support group. The Alzheimer's disease spousal caregiver intervention program will combine: (1) provision of new information; (2) development of therapeutic, problem-solving, and coping skills; and, (3) reduction of caregiver distress in a mutually supportive environment of camaraderie that empowers and comforts caregivers thereby enhancing caregivers' quality of life.

Aims

- To enable spousal caregivers to meet on a regular basis to provide mutual support and share feelings and exchange experiences.

- To provide caregivers with an opportunity to learn more about dementia and care provider coping skills.

Behavioral Objectives for Participants

1. Learn up-to-date information and ongoing education about dementia and caregiving skills.

2. Verbalize thoughts and feelings about caregiving experience.

3. Learn about methods of coping with the stress of caregiving.
   - A questionnaire at session one (pre-test) and at session twelve (post-test) will measure if coping skills have increased as a result of group participation.

4. Express and evaluate feelings about burdens of caregiving.
   - Care burden will be measured by pre- and post-test questionnaire.

Requirements for Participants

- Alzheimer's disease spousal caregiver 50 years of age or older.
- Spouse actively caring for partner with AD for at least one year.
- No reported elder abuse or neglect.

Group Composition and Duration

- Nine to eleven participants.
- Weekly meetings; 90-minute sessions.
- 12 sessions.
- Closed group.

- Two group facilitators (male and female).

Group Facilitators' Roles

- Ensure every one is given equal time to share.
- Avert group conflict.
- Keep discussions focused on agreed agenda.
- Start and end on time.
- Resolve relationship conflicts between participants.

Basic Rules

- All information about members and discussions remain confidential.
- Members of the group listen and support one another without criticism or being judgmental.
- Each member participates or not according to his/her motivations.
- Mutual respect for each member's situation.

Who is With the AD Patient?

- Another family member or friend provides relief.
- Supervised activities for AD patients in a room close to the meeting room.

Screening Intake

Co-therapists meet each prospective group member individually for an in-depth interview to assess: motivation, communication skills, personal background, and preparedness for the group experience. The purpose of the group and individual goals are discussed.

Education Support Group Structure

1. Sessions one through eight begin with a brief didactic presentation (five to ten minutes) by one or both of the facilitators. The presentation is based on the weekly theme. Specific group activities vary each session. They include handouts, questionnaires, and videos, disseminating information, or doing a creative activity. Sessions nine and ten are

unstructured with no planned themes. Group members will select the topics for these sessions. Sessions eleven and twelve address issues of termination.

    Session 1: Orientation
    Session 2: Characteristic problems of Alzheimer's disease
    Session 3: A guide to healthy coping skills
    Session 4: Caring for yourself: Recreational needs
    Session 5: Exploring feelings of care burden
    Session 6: Social support networks
    Session 7: Caring for yourself: Health care needs
    Session 8:   Institutionalized care
    Session 9:   Unstructured session
    Session 10: Unstructured session
    Session 11: Toward termination
    Session 12: Termination

2. Following the facilitators' greetings, members are asked how he/she has been doing/thinking/feeling since the previous session and if he/she has any questions or comments about the previous session. The check-in is a structured way of quickly assessing the state of each group member at the beginning of the group session. It also includes reviewing homework assigned at the end of the previous session.

3. After all members have checked in, the group discussion begins on the planned session theme.

4. Group closure is accomplished when members summarize their group experiences, help members leave the group on a positive note and facilitators provide homework assignments for group members to practice what they have learned in the session and compare and contrast with what they face in reality.

5. Newly implemented programs are likely to have some wrinkles to smooth out. The results of a program outcome evaluation are used to make decisions regarding whether a program is doing what it is designed to do and whether it is doing it consistently well. Results should not be feared. The results should be used to provide the staff and administrators with information that allows them to improve the program. This information helps staff to determine whether program

components should be continued, revised, expanded, or eliminated. *Formative evaluation* provides program personnel with feedback on whether that which was conceptualized on paper is consistent with expected outcomes. Formative evaluation results provide initial evidence of the program's ability to achieve success by identifying the strength of relationship between practices and outcomes (Shadis, Cook, and Leviton 1991). *Summative evaluation* should be conducted regularly in order to provide information about the program's performance over time. These results are relevant to program staff because results provide insight into the effectiveness of their work.

A number of measurement tools are used in this model to evaluate the outcomes of the treatment goals and group members' satisfaction with the program.

Program Implementation

Goals and Objectives

1. To assess suitability of client for group participation.

2. To respond to client's questions, concerns, and apprehensions about group experience.

3. To allow the client to become comfortable with the facilitators in meeting before the first session.

Intake Procedure

1. Approximately one hour for intake interview.

2. Explain the reason for the intake interview (to get background information and determine suitability for participation).

3. Demographics: Name, address, telephone number, occupation, educational background, martial status, number of children and ages, daily hours of caregiving; cumulative years of caregiving.

4. Group support experience:

     a. Have you previously participated in a group support intervention?

     b. If so, describe your experience.

     c. Are you currently participating in a support group?

5. Motivation for participation: What are some specific reasons that have now made you consider participation in a support group?

6. Current life situation:
     a. Are you currently employed outside the home?
     b. Are there financial burdens associated with your caregiver responsibilities?
     c. Do you currently have a network of friends and family that support your caregiving efforts?

7. Facilitator rules out abuse and neglect.
     a. Have you ever sought to harm your loved one?
     b. Have you ever sought to neglect his/her needs? If so, have you acted upon these inclinations?

8. Determining personal behavioral objectives of prospective member:
     a. How will group participation help change your knowledge, skills, and/or values about care responsibilities?
     b. How do you feel about sharing your thoughts and feelings in a group?
     c. What topics are you not comfortable discussing in a group setting?

9. Explain group format and expectations.

10. Client signs confidentiality and contract forms.

Group Sessions

Session 1

Purpose: Orientation

1. Welcome all members and restate the purpose of the educational support group.

2. Introduce group members and facilitators.

3. Identify similarities among members to create "we-are-in-the-same-boat" environment.

4. Explain that a support group helps people learn from the experiences of others.

5. Discuss individual and group expectations.

6. Establish ground rules with participants.

7. Facilitators and/or members share information about events that may be of interest to the group.

8. Introduce session topics and outline.

Activity:

1. Provide a bowl of sweets for the members.

2. Proceed with icebreaker activity: Ask each member to take a candy out of the bowl.

3. Once this is done ask the members to tell one thing about themselves for each piece of candy they take. Summarize activity purpose (members recognize that they have more in common besides their spousal caregiving responsibilities. When it is time for the meeting to end, the facilitator may ask members to share their thoughts regarding the session. The facilitator may summarize with his/her impressions and ask for feedback. The facilitator assigns homework.

Session 2

Purpose: Discussion of Alzheimer's disease characteristics

1. Teach information about the current knowledge of the disease.

2. Acknowledge AD caregiver burdens.

3. Teach effective caregiver skills.

4. Teach about what to expect and how to plan for future stages.

Materials:

Alzheimer's knowledge questionnaire, pens, chalkboard, markers, video about AD, and prepared handouts about Alzheimer's disease stages.

Procedure:

1. Welcome members back to this session and respond to questions and acknowledge feelings. Allow a few minutes for general discussions and relationship building. Briefly review the previous session and ask members if they have any comments or feelings about that session. Check and briefly discuss last session's homework assignment. Distribute the Alzheimer's knowledge questionnaire to each member. This is the pre-test. Allow ten minutes for completion. Discuss the questionnaire and ask members to comment on their responses.

2. Introduce the theme: Knowledge of Alzheimer's disease.
    a. Discuss the onset of the illness and how it changes the patient's cognitive, behavioral, and affective responses at various stages.
    b. Discuss how the patient's illness affects the spouse caregiver.
    c. Emphasize the importance of understanding the illness in order to be an effective caregiver.
    d. Using a lecture style format, provide group members with the following information: the disease's origin; symptoms; changes in brain function; disease progression leading to changes in behavioral, cognitive, and affective functions over time; statistics on current number of people diagnosed; and, advice to caregivers about patient management.
    e. Incorporate the following or similar questions to engage members: Can each of you identify with the pictures that this information generates? Can anyone suggest a patient management skill that they have found to be successful? At what stage is your care recipient at this time? Can you describe some of its manifestations?

3. Distribute the Alzheimer's questionnaire again to each group member (post-test). Allow five minutes to complete. Discuss the correct answers and have members grade the questionnaires. Solicit responses if members' scores increased and if so by how much. Ask members what they have learned and how this information can assist them in caring for their ill spouse.

4. Bring closure to the session; mention the topic for the next meeting; assign homework.

Session 3

Purpose: A guide to healthy coping skills

1. Help members recognize their current coping mechanisms.

2. Teach the risks associated with poor coping skills.

3. Determine which coping skills are detrimental and, therefore, need to be abandoned.

4. Identify the coping skills that need to be strengthened.

5. Introduce alternative healthy coping skills for members to implement.

Materials:

Healthy coping skills handout.

Procedure:

1. Welcome members back to this session.

2. Ask members to comment about their experiences of the past week and the feelings those experiences engendered. Briefly review the previous session and ask members if they have any comments or feelings about that session they would like to share. Review previous session's homework.

3. Introduce the theme of coping skills.

4. Discuss how healthy coping skills positively support daily life routines when caring for an Alzheimer's patient.

5. Distribute the handout on healthy coping skills.
    a. Encourage members to share their coping skills with one another.
    b. Discuss the suggested coping skills in the handout.
    c. The following are suggested questions to encourage discussion: Are there any coping skills in the handout that anyone can identify with? If so, which ones? Describe a coping skill that works for you. Are there any coping skills you would like to try out?

6. Bring closure to the session and assign homework.
    Homework: Ask group members to select at least one healthy coping skill from the handout that they are not currently using and implement it for the next session. Ask them to be prepared to discuss their success/failure with the skill at the next session.

7. Advise members of the theme for the next session. Request that members dress in comfortable clothes for the next meeting.

Session 4

Purpose: Caring for Yourself: Recreational Needs

1. Making members aware that they often deprive themselves while they over compensate to enhance the quality of life for their frail spouses.

2. Nurturing the needs of the care giver.

3. Reducing stress associated with caregiving by learning how to identify activities members' enjoy; learning to indulge themselves; and, relax and play.

Materials:

Kites, Frisbees, playing cards, checkers, bicycles, crossword puzzles, daily newspapers, and other recreational materials

Procedure:

1. Welcome members back to the new session.

2. Briefly review the previous session.

3. Encourage members to share their experiences with their newly learned coping skills.

4. Weather permitting, members will meet outside in a designated area, i.e., park.

5. Encourage members to select an activity (ies) and spend approximately 45 minutes "playing."

6. Lead a group discussion of the physical and emotional responses to "playing."

7. Leading questions: When was the last time you participated in an activity solely for recreation? Recreate the experience. What are some of the activities you would like to engage in if you could? What ways do you feel you could incorporate recreation back into your life?

8. Ask members to partake in a recreational activity during the week, record their feelings, and share the experience with other group members in the next session.

9. Summarize the session. Announce the topic for the next session.

Session 5

Purpose: Exploring Care Burden Feelings

1. Members will explore changes in family roles with the onset of AD.

2. The caregiver often feels: trapped, frustrated, angry, hopeless, helpless, confused, depressed, isolated, and anxious.

3. By giving members the opportunity to talk about these feelings and hear others describe comparable feelings, caregivers will realize these are valid feelings that are shared by many others in the same caregiving situation.

4. To increase the level of group support and disclosure.

Materials: The care burden inventory and pens.

Procedure:

1. Welcome members back to the new session.

2. Briefly review the previous session.

3. Ask members what recreational activities they engaged in, if any, since the previous session. Address changes in moods, thoughts, behaviors, and interactions with care recipient that they have noticed.

4. Introduce theme of exploring feelings of care burden .

5. Facilitate the group discussion by helping members talk about stress associated with caregiving and the impact of care burden on their psychological well-being.

6. Administer the care burden inventory.

7. Allow members 15 minutes to complete the questionnaire. Following the completion of the questionnaire, ask the members to give their definitions of care burden. The following questions might enhance group discussion: Was it difficult to answer the questionnaire honestly? Why? Inquire if members are experiencing other feelings that were not covered in the questionnaire. Discuss ways to manage and deal with these feelings in a healthy way.

8. Wrap-up the session; mention next week's theme, and give a homework assignment

Session 6

Purpose: Social Support Networks

1. Facilitators teach how to access information and referral to support care giving.

2. Members are encouraged to keep and/or develop an informal social network to ward off burnout.

3. Who to contact for what gives care providers the foundation and confidence to continue their caregiving duties.

Materials:

Directory of Local Resources for Alzheimer's Patient and Caregivers.

Procedure:

1. Welcome members back to this session and check upon their feelings.

2. Briefly review the previous session and ask members if they have comments or feelings they would like to share about the previous week's meeting. Provide time to review the homework.

3. Provide information about community resources for caregivers and Alzheimer's disease patients.

4. Discuss which resources members can/cannot avail themselves of.

5. To determine what types of support networks members have access to.

6. Encourage members to exchange resources and describe their experiences with each resource.

7. Lead the group in examining their support networks i.e. organizations, churches, family members, and friends who may be willing to help them with some of their caregiving duties. Distribute a directory of local resources to all members.

8. Summarize the session; mention next week's theme; assign homework.

Session 7

Purpose: Caring for Oneself: Health Care Needs.

1. Facilitators will emphasize that caregivers need to maintain their own health care needs if they, as sole care providers, are to be effective in their roles.

2. Facilitators will recommend and encourage that care providers seek evaluation of their physical health status.

3. If health care evaluation determines need, the spouse must seek help.

4. Welcome members back to this session and check upon their feelings.

5. Briefly review the previous session and ask members if they have comments or feelings they would like to share about the previous week's meeting. Provide time to review the homework.

6. Facilitators initiate group discussion about noted changes in the self evaluated health changes since initiation of caregiving. Once members identify specific changes, discussion should focus on how these have affected the care giver/frail patient in light of both physical and emotional toll.

7. In light of specific negative changes, how have members addressed them?

8. Summarize the session; mention next week's theme; assign homework.

Session 8

Purpose: Anticipating Institutionalization of the AD Patient

1. This session seeks to provide the knowledge and emotional support to help spousal caregivers determine when to seek institutionalized care and how to cope with the psychological impact of admission.

2. When to institutionalize? What is the procedure? Where to go for potential placement? How do I undertake this mission?

Materials:

Television, VCR, and video showing various types of institutional care such as assisted living, nursing homes, hospitals, etc.).

Procedure:

1. Welcome members back to this session and check upon their feelings.

2. Briefly review the previous session and ask members if they have comments or feelings they would like to share about the previous week's meeting. Provide time to review the homework.

3. Begin the group discussion with the fact that Alzheimer's disease is a progressive disease and each person progresses through the stages at varying rates. Share with members that some patients are able to be cared for at home for the entire duration of their illness while others may need a skilled nursing facility at some stage of their illness.

4. The group views the video and group discussion follows.

5. These are questions that could be raised during the discussion: What concerns do you have about your loved one's future? What are your feelings about institutionalized care? Have you had any experiences with institutionalized care? Considering your spouse's current stage, how do you think he/she will respond to nursing home placement? Do

you know other family members' views on the subject? Did your views about institutionalized care change after viewing the video? If so, how?

6. Remember to bring closure to this very emotional topic. Summarize the session; mention that next week's session is unstructured and that they should consider topics for discussion.

Sessions 9 and 10

Sessions 9 and 10 are unstructured. Allow the group members to determine what they wish to discuss for these sessions. The sessions will begin with the standard check in and then ask members for their suggestions on discussion topics. Then, allow the members to vote on the topics suggested.

Session 11

Purpose: Toward Termination

1. This session anticipates bringing closure to the program.

2. Members should be encouraged to address personal/collective unresolved feelings or issues.

3. Review the key points of previous sessions and summarize the group experiences and offer clarity if needed.

4. Address the topic of evaluation. Each member should make a determination if his/her individual goals as well as group goals were realized. If not, why not?

5. Members should be encouraged to seek further support if they are willing and/or able.

6. Emphasize that although this group as it exists is terminating its mission, remind members that they have created and can continue to rely on the supportive network of the group.

7. Welcome members back to this session. Briefly review the previous session and ask members if they have any comments or feelings about the session they would like to share.

8. Ask the members to reflect upon what their expectations were from the group and if they were met.

9. Ask the members to share what they have learned and what was most helpful to them.

10. Ask them how they have changed since joining the group and what they would do to maintain the changes? Encourage the members to continue to use the knowledge and skills that they have learned in the group.

Session 12

Purpose: Termination

1. To provide closure for group members who may find difficulty saying goodbye. It is important for the facilitators to acknowledge the feelings associated with termination.

2. To encourage members to see the amount of progress they have made.

3. To recognize the bonds of support that have been created and fostered; encourage members to remain in contact with one another.

4. To evaluate members' satisfaction with group experiences.

Material:

Certificates, healthy coping skills questionnaire, and group satisfaction scale.

Procedure:

1. Welcome the members back to the final session. Briefly review the previous session and ask members if they have any comments or feelings about the session they would like to share.

2. This final meeting is a celebration with refreshments and is somewhat unstructured. The facilitator(s) begins by expressing a number of positive thoughts and feelings that he/she has about the group and mentions a few memorable experiences. He/she continues and may say: "It is common for group members to have sad feelings about group termination especially when they have shared so much and have bonded. Each member may want to express thoughts/feelings…"

4. The following questions may be helpful for facilitators: How do you feel about this meeting being the final one in the series? Are you ready for the group to end? Is there any unfinished business that we should complete? Provide time for members to exchange phone numbers/e-mail addresses.

5. Administer the coping skills questionnaire (post-test) and group satisfaction scale.

6. Each member will be presented with a certification of completion to mark the completion of the program.

   The results of the post-test will be compared with the questionnaire that was completed earlier to note improvement in coping skills. Members will fill out a questionnaire measuring their level of satisfaction with the group experiences.

   In an educational support group, individuals facing common eldercare challenges can come together in a confidential environment to share their experiences, offer and receive advice, and gain strength from being surrounded by people who share comparable burdens. The laughter, tears, and companionship experienced in group sessions help banish feelings of isolation. Support groups are energizing and empowering since they help caregivers, who in turn, are strengthened to continue their caregiving duties in behalf of their loved ones.

Appendix

Alzheimer's Knowledge Questionnaire

In the following spaces place a T before true statement, and an F before the false statement.

_____ 1. Alzheimer's disease is a form of dementia.

_____ 2. Alzheimer's is a disease that slowly kills nerve cells in the brain.

_____ 3. Personality change is uncommon with Alzheimer's patients.

_____ 4. More men are diagnosed with Alzheimer's disease than women.

_____ 5. The disease affects the frontal lobe more severely than any other part of the brain.

_____ 6. High concentrations of aluminum are commonly found in brain tissue of individuals with Alzheimer's disease.

_____ 7. Seizures typically occur during the middle stage of the disease.

_____ 8. Alzheimer's patients often become confused about eating, personal hygiene, and coordination.

_____ 9. Long-term memory is often most affected by the disease.

_____ 10. Doctors can predict when an individual will experience the onset of a new stage in the disease.

Answers: 1-T, 2-T, 3-F, 4-F, 5-F, 6-T, 7-F, 8-T, 9- F, 10-F

Source: The questionnaire was developed from the content of the following book: Gruetzner, H. 1992. *Alzheimer's: A caregiver's guide and sourcebook*. New York: John Wiley and Sons, Inc.

Careburden Inventory

Respond to the following statements by placing an A for Agree or D for Disagree before each statement.

_____ 1. I feel resentful of other relatives who could but do not do things for my loved one.

_____ 2. I feel that my loved one makes requests that I think are beyond his/her needs.

_____ 3. Because of my involvement with my loved one, I don't have enough time for myself.

_____ 4. I feel stressed between trying to take care of my spouse as well as attending to other family responsibilities, job, etc.

_____ 5. I feel embarrassed over my loved one's behavior.

_____ 6. I feel guilty about my interaction with my loved one.

_____ 7. I feel that I don't do as much for my loved one as I could or should.

_____ 8. I feel angry about my interactions with my loved one.

_____ 9. I feel that in the past I haven't done as much for my loved one as I could or should have.

_____ 10. I feel nervous or depressed about my interactions with my spouse.

_____ 11. I feel that my loved one currently affects my relationship with other family members and friends in a negative way.

_____ 12. I feel resentful about my interaction with my loved one.

_____ 13. I am afraid of what the future holds for my loved one.

_____   14. I feel pleased about my interactions with my loved one.

_____   15. It's painful to watch my loved one suffer and age.

_____   16. I feel useful in my interaction with my loved one.

_____   17. I feel my loved one is dependent.

_____   18. I feel strained in my interactions with my loved one.

_____   19. I feel that my health has suffered because of my involvement with my loved one.

_____   20. I feel that the present situation with my loved one doesn't allow me as much privacy as I'd like.

_____   21. I feel that my social life has suffered because of my involvement with my loved one.

_____   22. I wish that my loved one and I had a better relationship.

_____   23. I feel that my loved one doesn't appreciate what I do for him/her as much as I would like.

_____   24. I feel uncomfortable when I have friends over.

_____   25. I feel that my loved one tries to manipulate me.

_____   26. I feel that my loved one seems to expect me to take care of him/her as if I were the only one he/she can depend on.

_____   27. I feel that I don't have enough money to support my loved one considering all of our expenses.

_____   28. I feel that I would like to be able to provide more money to support my loved one than I am currently able to do.

Source: Zarit, S.H., K.E. Reever, and J.M. Bach-Peterson. 1980. Relatives of the Impaired Elderly: Correlates of feelings of burden. *The Gerontologist* 20, 649-655.

Group Satisfaction Scale

Circle the response that reflects your feelings.

1. Overall, how helpful was this group for you?

    Very much   Somewhat   Not at all

2. To what extent did you accomplish what you expected when you joined the group?

    Very much   Somewhat   Not at all

3. To what extent did this group teach you new ways of caring for yourself?

    Very much   Somewhat   Not at all

4. To what extent did participation in the group help you learn to recognize your personal, emotional, and physical needs?

    Very much   Somewhat   Not at all

5. Do you feel the group accomplished its goals?

    Very much   Somewhat   Not at all

6. Comments:

    _____

    _____

    _____

    _____

    _____

    _____

References

Bauer, M., M. Maddox, L. Kirk, T. Burns, and M. Kuskowski. 2001. Progressive dementia: Personal and relational impact on care giving wives. *American Journal of Alzheimer's Disease and Other Dementias,* 16, 6, 329-334.

Becker, J. and E. Morrissey. 1988. Difficulties in assessing depressive-like reactions to chronic severe external stress as exemplified by spouse caregivers of Alzheimer patients. *Psychology of Aging,* 3, 300-306.

Brodaty H. 1996. Caregivers and behavioral disturbances: Effects and interventions. *Int Psychogeriatr* 8: 455-458.

Brodaty, H. 1998. Outline of a dementia caregivers' training program. In: B. Vellas, ed., *Research and practice in Alzheimer's Disease weight loss and eating behavior in Alzheimer's patients.* New York: Springer Publishing.

Dura, J.R. 1991. Anxiety and depressive disorders in adult children caring for demented patients. *Psychol Aging 6: 467-473.*

Evans, D. 1990. Estimated prevalence of Alzheimer's disease in the United States. *Milbank Quarterly,* 68, 267-289.

Friedland, R. 1993. Alzheimer's disease: Clinical features and differential diagnosis. *Neurology,* 43 (suppl. 4), s45-s51.

Gruetzner, H. 1992. *Alzheimer's: A caregiver's guide and sources book.* New York, NY: John Wiley and Sons.

Mega, M., J. Cummings., and J. Gorbein. 1996. The spectrum of behavior changes in Alzheimer's disease. *Neurology,* 46, 130-135.

Morris, R., L. Morris, and P. Britton. 1988. Factors affecting the emotional well-being of the caregivers of dementia sufferers. *British Journal of Psychiatry,* 153, 147-156.

Rabins, P. 1984. Management of dementia in the family context. *Psychosomatics,* 25, 369-375.

Rhoades, D. and K. McFarland. 1999. Caregiver meaning: A study of caregivers of individuals with mental illness. *Health and Social Work,* 24, 4, 291-302.

Shadis, W.R. T.D. Cook, and L.C. Levitton. 1991. *Foundations of program evaluation.* Newbuty Park, CA: Sage Publications.

Tornatore, J. and L.Grant. 2002. Burden among family caregivers of persons with Alzheimer's disease in nursing homes. *The Gerontologist,* 42, 4, 497-506.

Wackerbarth, S. 2002. The Alzheimer's family caregiver as decision maker: A typology of decision styles. *The Journal of Applied Gerontology*, 21, 3, 313-332.

Weiler, P. 1987. The public health impact of Alzheimer's disease. *American Journal of Public Health*, 77, 1157-1158.

Zarit, S.H., K.E. Reever, and J.M. Bach-Peterson. Relatives of the Impaired Elderly: Correlates of feelings of burden. *The Gerontologist* 20, 649-655, 1980.

Editorial Commentary

ഇ൦ഷ

Nieli Langer & Terry Tirrito

A *journal* is a record of thoughts and events recorded over time. A journal is helpful in recording successive stages of understanding or wondering, and in keeping track of where one has been intellectually and emotionally. To the learner, it can give a sense of accomplishment, a chance to raise questions to be pondered, a place to think on paper about answers and more questions, a way to locate misconceptions and work out better understandings. For the instructor, the learner's journal can be a way of getting inside the thought processes of the learner, to check for misconceptions, to find ways to present information so that it is meaningful to the learner, and provide the foundation for dialogue. Journaling has been a productive strategy when students are enrolled in internships. It may also be an effective strategy when primary caregivers need to transfer their loved one to a nursing home.

Nursing home placement of a frail parent for whom the family has cared for until now triggers emotional alarm that they may be "dumping" their family member. Researchers have consistently found that children go to great lengths to support their elderly parents. Nevertheless, the emotional alarm nursing home tales trigger and the fact that the myth of the nursing home as a dumping ground has persisted, are causative factors for the guilt experienced by some children. Failure to adequately explain to the family what they are experiencing and why, and helping them work through the conflicts, may mean the difference between family reintegration and adaptation or long-term morbid family grief reaction.

One constructive means for meeting the family's needs in the transition to a nursing home is teaching family members how to use a variation of journaling. After intake, the patient's social worker may initiate a dialogue with the daughter, who, as the former primary care provider, may now be feeling like an "outsider" after nursing home placement of her parent. The social worker may suggest and explain the concept of journaling. After agreeing to try this strategy, the social worker asks her to factually record her experiences during and after the placement on half of the page and then on the opposite side to relate her feelings about those experiences. Reflection about experiences can also be stimulated by having the daughter ponder and respond to such questions as: How long can this go on? What are the possibilities? Can he get better? What are heroics? Who keeps track of information and how is it processed? How do decisions get made? Why does staff do what they do? What are my new roles? Used in this setting, journals can provide a neutral, stressless forum to rehearse one's thinking, including emotional aspects like indignation, confusion or joy, as well as more reasoned judgments. The journal provides the foundation for constructive dialogues with the social worker on the needs of the parent for optimal care, and personal freedom and expression balanced with institutional demands for efficacy, cost-effectiveness, and uniformity. Not all social workers are created equal, nor are they immune to the myths surrounding disability and long-term care. Not all former primary care givers are willing and/or able to successfully use journaling and/or are interested in any form of professional counseling. However, if this is a mutually viable strategy, changing certain thought patterns and behaviors can help the spouse or adult child manage difficult situations and stress. Journaling will give him/her the opportunity to check assumptions, share expectations, receive validation, and communicate feelings.

5

AN APPROACH TO TEACHING
SPIRITUALITY FOR PRACTICE
WITH THE OLDER ADULT

℘

Larry Ortiz & Milissa B. Littlefield

T he roots of the helping professions, social work, in particular, are
clearly established within the moral dictates of religious teaching,
even though during the twentieth century the profession moved away from
its historical roots. There are several reasons for this. One, as social work
identified with the development of the social sciences, it embraced an
epistemological approach based on scientific methods of investigation that
minimized the role of the spiritual. Frequently, it also adapted such over
simplistic apocryphal views of religion associated with theorists such as
Marx and Freud. Two, politically, the rise of the religious right that
embraced politicians like Jerry Falwell, Pat Robertson, Ronald Reagan,
Newt Gindrich, and the Bush administrations, with its assaults on the civil
rights of women, minorities, the poor, and gays and lesbians, further
distanced the profession from its roots. Social work as a value based
profession with its commitments to social and economic justice was
antagonistic to such draconian policies and beliefs as promoted by these
religious and political fundamentalists (Ortiz 2003). Three, the tendency to
view religion as a personal issue that enhanced psychological well being

while not attending to greater macro concerns left spirituality and religion irrelevant to social change efforts (Ai 2002).

These concerns have made acceptance of teaching material on spirituality and religion somewhat controversial in social work education. Where to place it in the curriculum? What is the epistemological foundation for the material? And, how do we instruct students/practitioners on balancing the variance of spiritual and religious expressions without imposing alternative or dominant views on others (Ai 2002)? Although these are reasonable questions, answers to them require thoughtful and well founded responses. However, the questions raised are not sufficient cause to omit teaching this very important content in our curriculum. The growing body of literature that links various levels of well being with spirituality and religion suggests that this material is essential in any social work or human service curriculum. The approach to teaching this content requires both humility and openness. Humility because our knowledge base on this material is formative and growing, and openness because the wide range of spiritual expressions may be as diverse as there are people.

In recent years, the social work and allied health professions have attempted to take a more holistic approach to service delivery by giving increased attention to religiosity and spirituality in client care. In this expanding model, spirituality and religion are regarded for their contributions to primary prevention, an indicator of health and well being, a source of emotional and instrumental support, and healing. Although this focus has spanned all ages and health issues, a significant amount of attention has been directed at the elderly due to the significance of religion and spirituality during the later stages of life. Speculation abounds as to why. Perhaps it is because as people age they have more time to reflect on the existential as opposed to the temporal, or perhaps some of the answers to the complexities of life begin to emerge in the values and beliefs of one's spirituality, or perhaps concerns about the afterlife are more pronounced during this period. No matter how one decides to answer this question, religion and spirituality ought not to be dismissed as an important aspect of working with the aging person since this appears to be a developmental feature of this phase of life.

In this chapter we discuss the relationship of religion and spirituality to elder well being and review important concepts and terms as they are used in the literature. Concluding the literature and conceptual review, we submit a spirituality "mini assessment" protocol that is based on broad conceptual aspects of spirituality and requires the practitioner to tailor his or her own questions to the client. An underlying assumption of the protocol is that helping professionals are better situated to provide effective care if they have an understanding of the client's meaning perspective vis-à-vis the presenting problem. The protocol is intended to establish dialogue between practitioners and clients regarding the attended presence of these factors in the clients' lives rather than to measure their levels of spirituality or religiosity. Various approaches to using this protocol are offered in conclusion.

Religion and Spirituality and the Elderly

Researchers have identified several aspects of aging that appear to be mediated by religion and spirituality. In summary, elder well being is associated with higher levels of religiosity/spirituality because of its social integrating power (Abramowitz 1993; Black 1999; Brunk 1996; Hooyman and Kayak 1993; Husaini, Blasi, and Miller 1999; Koenig, Kvale, and Ferrel 1988; Koenig, George, and Ziegler 1988; McFadden 1999; Markides 1983; Musick et al. 2000; Levine, Taylor, and Chatters 1994; Neill and Kahn 1999; Sasson 2001; Young and Dowling 1987). This seems especially true for seniors of color due to the historic role of the church as a social institution providing instrumental and affective support (Husaini, Blasi, and Miller 1999; Markides 1983; Ortega, Crutchfield and Rushing 1983; Sasson 2001; Taylor and Chatters 1986; and Wilson-Ford 1992). From a Durkheimian perspective, involvement in the communal aspects of religion and spirituality have a very positive impact on several dimensions of life, primarily social and instrumental support, that lead to higher levels of well being in its various forms of measurement.

Positive associations with good health, preventive and protective health factors, and health decision making in the elderly have also been found (Arcury, Quandt, and Bell 2001; Levine and Chatters 1998; Fesher and Maly 1999; Gregory 2001; Husaini, Blasi, and Miller 1999; Levine 1994; McAuley, Pecchioni, and Grant 2000; Magily et al. 2000; Musick et al. 2000; O' Connell 1994; Wilson-Ford 1992). Spirituality and religion are reported linked to several health related variables. For example, in the face of declining health, the elderly reportedly find solace in their sense of religion or in their spirituality. Further, it is not uncommon that aging persons report instances of healing after they have prayed or engaged with others in various forms of intercessory prayer or meditation. Another aspect of health prevention is spiritual or religious living and behaving in ways that promote good health. Many devotedly religious people follow prescribed patterns of eating and abstaining that indeed make good health sense. And, the elderly often report that they use prayer, meditation or spiritual consultation when faced with making decisions about their health and health care.

Religion/spirituality is also important for reflection, life review, and meaning making in old age (Baker and Nussbaum 1997; Fry 2000; Moody 1994; McFadden 1995; Newman and Newman 1996; Musick et al. 2000; O'Connell 1994). Jung quite aptly summarized this aspect of aging when he stated, "[a] human being would certainly not grow old if longevity had no meaning for the species. The afternoon of life must have a significance of its own and cannot be merely a pitiful appendage to life's morning" (Moody 1994, 411). Spirituality and religion both provide the overarching plausibility structure for finding meaning, fitting the pieces of one's life together through reflection, and providing solace in the unanswered questions and mysteries of life.

However, despite the mounting evidence of positive associations, religion and spirituality should not be viewed as a panacea for what may ail the elderly or the simple answer to well being. There is some emerging evidence that religion and spirituality may actually have a negative impact on some aging people in several different ways, i.e., being unduly restrictive and controlling leading to feelings of guilt and despair regarding past transgressions, attitudes or inadequacies (Pargament, Koenig, and Perez 2000). Or, for those whose prayers are not answered regarding health or other welfare issues, they may feel angry, embarrassed, or guilty wondering if they are to blame for a lack of faith resulting in prolonged distress. These feelings can lead to depression and impact negatively on elder well being (Hays et al. 2001; Husaini, Blasi, and Miller 1999). The consequence is that a source of hope rooted in the basis for life meaning can be quite disempowering for some. Although most studies report positive indictors between religion/spirituality and outcomes of well being, there remain several unanswered questions regarding whether there are varying amounts of religious intensity, prior history, and participation that may have negative impact on elder well being. Illumination of these questions is likely viewed with respect to demographic variations by region, gender, and ethnicity (Hays et al. 2001; Pargament, Koenig, and Perez 2001) underscoring the importance of considering the personal experiences and meanings associated with spirituality and religion.

Spirituality and Religion:
Variances in Use of Terms

An important issue in this discussion is the use of concepts and terms, religion and spirituality. The literature on this topic has historically focused on religion. However, more contemporary literature, especially in social work, has begun to use the term spirituality. A review of the literature (Ortiz and Langer 2002) suggests that these terms have been used interchangeably with some problematic results. Both terms have conceptual properties of the other, thus resulting in a confounding of the variables in the measurement and assessment process (Ortiz 2003; Ortiz and Langer 2002; Ortiz and Smith 1999). Consequently, a major problem in the research literature has been whether the measurement of spirituality can be delineated from measurement of religion without creating threats to internal validity. Since concepts, like objects, are reified, the terms gain meaning in one's experiences. For some, therefore, religion and spirituality are the same concepts and they interpret the concepts accordingly. While for others, religion strikes images of denominational dogma and conjures up negative thoughts and feelings to be avoided. At the same time, people of this latter group are quite spiritual and often express it in non-religious ways or in a manner not completely consistent with religious doctrines. Personal understanding of the terms religion and spirituality are clearly based on individual interpretations. Therefore, in using such terms and concepts, practitioners need to consider these interpretations and account for them accordingly. Age and culture appear to account for the variance in the use and understanding of these terms. For example, the elderly and ethnic minorities are more inclined to reference the term religion over spirituality (McFadden 1999; Baker and Nussbaum 1997; Musick et al. 2000). This is especially true of elderly African Americans (Johnson 1995; Taylor and Chatters 1986) and Latinos (Goizueta 1995; San Diego State University Center for Aging 1997).

Due to their important role in well-being for many people as they age, we suggest that practitioners routinely assess for religion and spirituality as part of a larger treatment plan. The spirituality protocol developed by Ortiz and Langer (2002), presented in this chapter, is designed to assess for religion and spirituality and ascertain their meaning in the terms and ideas of the client. The questions can be asked about spiritual concepts and answered in religious or non-religious terms thereby allowing the client to respond in whatever direction that is comfortable for him/her.

However, development of this protocol required some differentiation of terms and a conceptualization of spirituality as the meta variable and religion as a concept nestled within. The assessment tool the authors use in this chapter to identify and facilitate spirituality with clients is based on the assumption that spirituality is a larger conceptual category with several dimensions. These dimensions, derived from the works of others in social work and the health-allied professionals, include several themes. These include interconnectedness between self, others, and a sense of ultimacy; generativity; and inner meaning (Berggren-Thomas and Griss 1995; Canda 1990; Derezotes 1995; Hungelmann et al.1996; Joseph 1988; Miller 2001; Pargament, Koenig, and Perez 2000; Post, Puchalski, and Larson 2000; Simmons 1998; Waldfogel 1997; Young and Dowling 1987). From these characteristics, Ortiz (2003) and Ortiz and Langer (2002) identified five specific dimensions of spirituality: relationship with a transcendent force, interconnectedness, power for living, meaning making, and behavioral expressions within a plausibility structure . Relationship with a transcendent force refers to a link that connects one with a source that is larger than life and not bound by physical or material existence. In monotheistic cultures this concept is conceptualized as God, who is all-powerful, ultimate, supreme, and ubiquitous. Interconnectedness refers to the relationship one has with the transcendent force and others in community. Although spirituality is very personal, it is mostly experienced in commune with others and in nature. The essence of interconnectedness is living in triadic peace and harmony with others, nature and the ultimate force. An outcome of these relationships is power to be courageous, resilient, determined, and hopeful even in the bleakest of situations. Through spirituality one develops a sense of meaning, a "making sense of it all". In this capacity, one is able to develop a sense of reason, purpose, and direction in the absence of clarity. And, behavioral expressions refer to the private or public activities that reflect the religious context or social code of the spiritual. Often experienced as religion, spirituality at this level becomes codified into a set of doctrines, beliefs, and guides to live by. It is the social cultural congruence of the spiritual.

Regardless of whether one conceptualizes this aspect of life as spirituality or religion, it is clear that it has relevance for well-being, particularly in the later stages of life. Therefore, we suggest the spiritual assessment protocol described in the following section as a tool for discerning the ways in which these concepts bring meaning to the client's life and consequently how they shape the client's understanding of the presenting problem, help-seeking behavior, and treatment options. The following seven-question protocol is based on the conceptualization of spirituality and religion discussed above, in-depth interviews with older people, and discussions with social workers and gerontologists.

Spiritual Assessment Protocol

The Spiritual Assessment Protocol (Ortiz and Langer 2002, 47) was designed to be incorporated into a general bio-psycho-social-spiritual assessment for older clients. The purpose of the protocol is to ascertain sources of power and meaning in clients' lives and their view of the ultimate; it is, therefore, not concerned with the degree of spirituality or religiosity a person possesses or with their doctrine of beliefs per se. Rather, the questions are designed to aid the helping professional uncover older clients' beliefs regarding patterns for living and approaches to coping with problems and barriers normally associated with this stage of development. Failure to consider the client's worldview may thwart the establishment of a viable helping relationship, and may suppress important client strengths.

The protocol is essentially an interviewing tool that can be used cross culturally and for clients with or without a particular religious orientation. The wording can be adapted to fit various programs or clients, as the tool is primarily designed to open rather than constrain discussion. Therefore, the wording is not prescriptive, but designed for the practitioner to develop their own questions tailored to the person or group. The questions seek methods of spiritual and religious integration in the clients' lives, and address spiritual implications at the personal, community, and social levels. Answers to the questions can offer insight into the ways in which the clients' sources of spirituality and personal power serve as a basis for self-identity and connection with others; for example, how they are used to cope with crisis, stress, and loss, and to promote psychological resilience. It is important to note that professionals are not required to share the clients' spiritual or existential orientation, but they should be open to clients' views and be supportive of them. That being said, when the practitioner values the clients' spirituality, clients are likely to be more open about their views on life and to be empowered to use their inherent spiritual coping mechanisms. One limitation for the use of this protocol might be its use with the cognitively impaired; however, questions can be adapted to inquire of caretakers their recollections of the person's life at an earlier time (Ortiz and Langer 2002).

Questions

1. When talking with others, what common beliefs do you share with them that bring you a sense of comfort and belonging?

2. Can you identify a spiritual force that brings you a sense of comfort and belonging?

3. Do you have family or friends that you depend upon to give you strength for living and energy to overcome obstacles? If so, what is it about this relationship that gives you this strength or energy?

4. Can you identify spiritual resources from which you gain strength and energy to overcome life's obstacles?

5. Do you have a belief system that helps give your life meaning or purpose? Can you give examples of how this meaning or purpose is reinforced in your life?

6. As you are able, do you attend religious or other social meetings that give purpose to your life?

7. Privately, what rituals or practices do you engage in that are renewing or comforting?

Teaching the Spiritual Assessment Protocol

The andragogical (adult learning) method described for teaching the protocol to students and practitioners is designed to achieve the following learning objectives. Learners will be able to:

1. Define key concepts related to spirituality and religiosity.

2   Develop awareness of their own personal spiritual resources and identify the personal religious values and beliefs that may impact upon their professional practice.

3. Apply the Spiritual Assessment Protocol to specific populations.

This section outlines a three part method that employs active learning strategies to teach adult learners how to use the Spiritual Assessment Protocol. Instructional strategies for face-to-face and online class settings are provided. The online strategies employ Blackboard™, a commonly used e-learning software program. Blackboard™ integrates various online features including email and discussion board, and makes them relatively simple for even inexperienced students/practitioners to access and use. It also allows the class to be subdivided to facilitate small group activities online. This software is similar to other programs that are now widely available (e.g. WebCT), especially on college campuses, so the strategies should be transferable with only slight modifications, if any.

Teaching Key Concepts on Spirituality and Religion

The initial focus is on teaching key concepts related to spirituality and religion and reviewing the background and context that support the Spiritual Assessment Protocol, per learning objective 1. Students are assigned readings that synthesize the relevant literature in this area. The present chapter identifies and defines key concepts and provides an overview of these topics including an extensive reference section, and may be used to this end. Specific topics to be covered in the reference section include the following:

■   Defining and differentiating the concepts of spirituality and religion;

■   The importance of the sociohistoric context in defining spirituality for a particular age cohort;

■   The role of spirituality in the well-being of the aged, including similarities and differences for various ethnic groups; for example, its role in help seeking behavior, definition of health, mental health, or the problem(s) in living for which it is being sought, and the possible influences on treatment options and compliance behavior.

After completing background reading, students should be actively engaged in discussing the concepts to develop a level of personal understanding that has meaning vis-à-vis their own professional needs and experiences. The instructor can assign concepts or discussion questions to small groups of students to discuss and construct their own definitions, examples, and applications for the professional setting. Definitions and examples may not be verbatim or closely paraphrased from the readings.

Following the small group session, sheets of newsprint or clipboards with one concept or discussion question written at the top of each page can be stationed around the classroom. Each group then reports to a station and writes its definition, examples, and application of the concept or response to the discussion question on the corresponding sheet. Groups then rotate to the next sheet where they can clarify, modify, and even challenge definitions or responses provided by the previous groups and add their examples and applications. Groups continue to rotate until each group has had a chance to respond to each concept or question. Once all responses are in, the instructor reviews the concept sheets and provides feedback and corrections as well as additional information, examples, and insights in an open class discussion.

A modified version of this activity may be accomplished online using the discussion board. Instructors can organize students into small groups online using the Group Pages feature, and provide each group with the concepts or discussion questions. Groups can use their group discussion board feature for their deliberations. Instructors should provide a deadline by which this phase of the process is to be completed, as well as guidelines for the interaction, since this is likely to be a new way of working for most students. Instructors might suggest the following to groups to facilitate their online process:

1. Develop a timeline for initial comments to the discussion board by each member and follow up responses, including feedback on the final statement that will be going forth to the class from the group.

2. Designate a member to synthesize the comments into a cogent response and present the group response to other members for review, feedback, and final approval. This person will also make the final edits and submit the response on behalf of the group.

Once students have devised their responses, the instructor can create a discussion board for each concept or discussion question and have each group of students post its response. Once all responses are in, the instructor provides feedback for each concept on the discussion board. Students may be allowed to comment or pose questions after the instructor has provided feedback until they feel comfortable in their comprehension of the concepts.

Self Awareness of Spirituality and Religion

This step addresses learning objective 2. It involves students in developing self-awareness of their spirituality and the religious beliefs and values they hold that can potentially affect their professional practice. This step is important in the learning process because, despite their critical role, the manifestations of spirituality and religion tend to be transparent to people in their everyday transactions within their social environments, particularly if one is of the dominant religious persuasion in a particular community. Students need to become aware of their own values in order to prevent them from imposing them on their clients or patients and to avoid pitfalls and ethical violations. This is especially true given prior discussion on generational differences in viewing spirituality and religion.

Students are required to write a five to seven page essay using the Spirituality Assessment Protocol as a guide to assess the role of spirituality and religion in their own lives. In addition, they must also address how their beliefs may affect their professional practice in terms of being a source of strength or resilience as well as the pitfalls or challenges they may face in implementing their professional code of ethics as a result of these beliefs. Upon completion of their essays, students are paired with other students to share their personal discoveries and to discuss the process of writing the paper. They are asked to discuss whether the paper was easy or hard for them to do, what challenges they experienced in responding to the questions, what feelings were evoked in completing the assignment, whether conflicts between their personal and professional values surfaced, and how they would want a helping professional to engage them in an interview of this nature. The paired discussion can take place during class time in face-to-face meetings, or via email between the student pairs in online settings. Instructors may want to require a minimum number of posts for online students to promote a back and forth discussion versus merely a one time statement of each person's point of view.

Protocol Application

The final step in this educational strategy provides students with an opportunity to practice applying the protocol with others. Students are divided into small even numbered groups (to the extent possible). Half of each group is assigned to develop a brief client or patient profile. These profiles might reflect the types of clients that are typical to the experiences of the class and possibly some extremely atypical types of clients that might present. The other members of the groups are assigned to tailor the Spiritual Assessment Protocol questions to the specific profile developed by their colleagues, keeping in mind that protocol questions are intended to provide conceptual guidance for specific population appropriate inquiries. Next, each question writer pairs up with a profile writer in the same group and interviews that person using the questions he or she has developed. The profile writers role play the person portrayed in the profile and respond to the tailored assessment questions. Upon completion of the interviews, the entire class is re-divided into profilers/interviewees and question writers/interviewers. Each group is now asked to generate suggestions or considerations for administering the protocol. The profiler group suggests considerations from a client perspective and the interviewer group suggests considerations from a professional perspective. This discussion may also be extended to address how the information ascertained using the protocol might be incorporated into a treatment plan.

In an online setting, instructors can set up small groups. It may be more pragmatic to construct an even number of groups with an even number of members (to the extent possible; some may have to double up on an interview). Half of the groups can write profiles and have a designated member email them to the instructor. The instructor can email a profile to each of the remaining groups, and have them generate tailored questions and email them back to the instructor. The instructor can then pair students from the profile writer groups with students from the question writer groups for an online interview via email or a real time feature such as instant messaging if it is available. Following the interviews, the instructor can set up a discussion board for the discussion of suggestions or considerations for implementing the protocol. As in step 2, instructors may want to provide guidelines for this discussion, including a minimum number of posts by each student to the full-class discussion and a time frame in which to post all responses.

Conclusion

In this chapter we have argued that the spiritual component of life, whether it is understood as religion or some other notion of spirituality, may be an important part of a treatment plan, particularly for clients or patients who are aging or elderly. We have offered a Spiritual Assessment Protocol as a tool with which practitioners can engage clients in discourse about the ways in which religious and spiritual meaning impact their worldview and lifestyle, and how these meanings may in turn affect the client's view of the presenting problem and the viability of various intervention options. We have also provided an andragogical method for instructors to assist students/practitioners in grasping the concepts we have presented, increase their self-awareness of the ways in which religion or spirituality bring meaning to their own lives, and apply the protocol for specific target groups. This method relies on active learning strategies to allow students to more fully engage with the material during the training period and receive feedback from peers as well as the instructor. It also allows students to view the material in relation to their real life practice experiences and make it relevant to their practice settings. The proposed method may be incorporated into a professional practice course as a learning unit, or offered as a continuing education course or seminar.

References

Abramowitz, L. 1993. Prayer as therapy among the frail Jewish elderly. *Journal of Gerontological Social Work,* 19, ¾, 69-75.

Ai, A. 2002. Integrating spirituality into professional education: A challenging but feasible task. *Journal of Teaching in Social Work,* 22 (1/2), 103-130.

Arcury, T., S. Quandt, and R.Bell. 2001. Staying healthy: The salience and meaning of health maintenance behaviors among rural older adults in North Carolina. *Social Science and Medicine, 53,* 1541—1556.

Baker, D. and P. Nussbaum. 1997. Religious practice and spirituality—then and now: A retrospective study of spiritual dimensions of residents residing at a continuing care retirement community. *Journal of Religious Gerontology, 10, #3,* 33—51.

Berggren-Thomas, P. and M.Griggs. 1995. Spiritual need or spiritual journey? *Journal of Gerontological Nursing,* 5-9.

Black, H. 1999. Life as a gift: Spiritual narratives of elderly African American women living in poverty. *Journal of Aging Studies, 13,* #4, 441—455.

Brunk, D. 1996. Power of faith. *Contemporary Long Term Care, 19,* #5, 40—44.

Canda, E.R. 1990. After word: Spirituality reexamined. *Spirituality and Social Work Communicator,* 1(1), 13-14.

Derezotes, D. 1995. Spirituality and religiosity: Neglected factors in social work practice. *Arete, 20*(1), 1-15.

Fesher, S. and R. Maly. 1999. Coping with breast cancer in later life: The role of religious faith. *Psycho-oncology, 8,* 408—416.

Fry, P. 2000. Religious involvement: Spirituality and personal meaning for life: Existential predictors of psychological well being in community residing and institutional care elders. *Aging and Mental Health, 4,* 375—387.

Goizueta, R. 1995. *Caminemos con Jesus: Toward a Hispanic/Latino Theology of Accompaniment.* Maryknoll, New York: Orbis Books.

Gregory, F. 2001. Racial differences in the association between religiosity and psychological distress. *Dissertation Abstracts International: Section B: The sciences and Engineering. 62(2-B).*

Hooyman, N. and H.A. Kiyak.1993. *Social Gerontology,* 3rd ed. Boston: Allyn and Bacon.

Hungelmann, J., E. Kenkel-Rossi, L. Klassen, and R. Stollenwerk.1996. Focus on spiritual well-being: Harmonious interconnectedness of mind-body-spirit use of the JAREL Spiritual Well Being Scale. *Geriatric Nursing, 17,* #6, 262—266.

Husaini, B., A. Blasi, and O. Miller. 1999. Does public and private religiosity have a moderating effect on depression? A bi-racial study of elders in the American south. *International Journal of Aging and Human Development, 48.* 63—72.

Joseph, M.V. 1987. The religious and spiritual aspects of clinical practice: A neglected dimension of social work. *Social Thought, 39,* (2), 12-23.

Koenig, H., L.George, and C. Siegler. 1988. The use of religion and other emotion regulating coping strategies among older adults. *The Gerontologist, 28,* 303-310.

Koenig, H., J.N. Kvale, and C. Ferrel. 1988. Religion and well being in later life. *The Gerontologist, 28,* 1, 18 - 28.

Levine, J., R. Taylor, and L. Chatters. 1994. Race and gender differences in religiosity among older adults: Findings from four national studies. *Journal of Gerontology: Social Sciences, 29,* #3, S137—S145.

Levine, J. and L. Chatters. 1998. Religion, health, and psychological well-being in older adults: Findings from three national surveys. *Journal of Aging and Health, 10,* #4, 504—531.

Magily, J., J. Congdon, R. Martinez, R. Davis, and J.Averill. 2000. Caring for our own: Health care experiences of rural Hispanic elders. *Journal of Aging Studies, 13,* #4, 441—455.

Markides, K. 1983. Aging, religion, and adjustment. A longitudinal analysis. *Journal of Gerontology,* 38, 5, 621-25.

Mc Auley, W., L. Pecchioni, and J. Grant. 2000. Personal accounts of the role of God in health and illness among older rural African American and white residents. *Journal of Cross Cultural Gerontology, 15,* 13—25.

McFadden, S. 1995. Religion and well being in aging persons in an aging society. *Journal of Social Issues, 51.* 161—175.

McFadden, S. 1999. Religion, personality, and aging: A life span perspective. *Journal of Personality, 67,* 6, 1081—1104.

Miller, D.W. 2001. Programs in social work embrace the teaching of spirituality. *The Chronicle of Higher Education, 47,* 36, A12-A13.

Moody, H.R. 1994. *Aging concepts and controversies.* Thousand Oaks, California: Pine Forge Press.

Musick, M., J. Traphagen, H. Koenig, and D. Larson. 2000. Spirituality in physical health and aging. *Journal of Adult Development, 7,* 73—86.

Newman, B. and P. Newman. 1996. *Development through life,* 6th edition. Pacific Grove, California: Brooks/Cole.

Neill, C. and A. Kahn. 1999. Role of personal spirituality and religious activity on the life satisfaction of older widowed women. *Sex Roles, 40,* #3-4, 319—329.

O'Connell, L.J. 1994. The role of religion in health related decision making for elderly patients. *Generations.* 18(4): 27-30.

Ortega, S., R. Crutchfield, and W. Rushing. 1983. Race differences in elderly personal well being. *Research on Aging* 5 (1), 101-118.

Ortiz, L. and G. Smith. 1999. The role of spirituality in empowerment practice. Shera, W. and Wells, L, (Eds.), *Empowerment Practice in Social Work.* Toronto, CA: Canadian Scholar's Press, 307—319.

Ortiz, L. and N. Langer. 2002. Assessment of spirituality and religion in later life: Acknowledging clients' needs and personal resources. *Journal of Gerontological Social Work.* 37(2):5-21.

Ortiz, L. 2003. Religiosity and spirituality. Tirrito, T. and Cascio, T.,eds. *Religious organizations in community services: A social work perspective.* New York: Springer.

Pargement, K., H. Koenig, and L. Perez. 2000. The many methods of religious coping: Development and initial validation of the RCOPE. *Journal of Clinical Psychology, 56,* 4, 519—543.

Post, S., C. Puchalski, D. Larson. 2000. Physician and patient spirituality: Professional boundaries, competency, and ethics. *Annals of Internal Medicine, 132,* #7, 578—583.

San Diego State University, University Center on Aging. 1996. *Older Mexican Immigrants: Who Cares?* San Diego, CA: University Center on Aging, College of Health and Human Services, San Diego State University.

Sasson, S. 2001. Religiosity as a factor affecting adjustment of minority elderly to a nursing home. *Social Thought, 20,* 70—96.

Simmons, H. 1998. Spirituality and community in the last stage of life. *Journal of Gerontological Social Work, 29,* #2-3, 73—91.

Taylor, R. and L. Chatters. 1986. Patterns of informal support to elderly black adults: Family, friends and the church. *Social Work,* 432-438.

Waldfogel, S. 1997. Contemporary and alternative therapies in primary care: Spirituality in medicine. *Primary Care: Clinics in Office Practice, 24,* #4, 963—976.

Wilson-Ford, V 1992. Health-protective behaviors of rural black elderly women. *Health and Social Work, 17(*1) 28-36.

Young, G. and W. Dowling, W. 1987. Dimensions of religiosity in old age: Accounting for variation in types of participation. *Journal of Gerontology 42(*4) 376-380.

Editorial Commentary

℘℃ℛ

Nieli Langer & Terry Tirrito

While many older people lead fulfilling lives, others feel a loss of meaning and purpose. DeVogler and Ebersole 1980; Fiske and Chiriboga 1991; Hedlund and Birren 1984; and, Thurner 1975 all describe themes as the underlying aims, goals, and commitments that collectively provide an orientation to an individual's life, i.e., his compass or identity. They cite prominent themes such as family relationships, interpersonal relationships, specific hobbies or interests, maintenance of health and independence, and maintaining the integrity of one's home. However, in light of each person's experiences that may include a crisis or loss, they have maintained their life themes, although in an altered hierarchy. It is during times of crisis and loss when life loses its old compass that people of necessity have to reinterpret, reconfigure, and prioritize the components of their personal meaning-making compass. Whereby family relationships may currently be a prime life theme and a major life compass, work roles and outside interests previously contributed greater weight to their identity. Prager's study of personal meaning in later life (1997) revealed that life themes of older male respondents did not appreciably change through the life course. These older men continued to reveal consistency in their identities. In addition, the data revealed that the life themes of these aging individuals were not significantly different than those of younger subjects (Prager 1997). "If we can find the sources of meaning held by the elderly and see how individuals put it together, we will go a long way toward appreciating the complexity of human aging, and the ultimate reality of coming to terms with one's whole life" (Kaufman 1987, 65).

In light of the above, the editors offer an alternative assessment instrument that focuses more specifically on the concept of life themes as the key to an individual's identity. This instrument can be used by practitioners in the same way that the Ortiz and Langer (2002) assessment protocol is used. The questions include the following:

1. What are the most important themes (sources of meaning and purpose) in your life that you value the most? Name them.

2. Have these themes remained the same throughout your life? Explain.

3. How have these themes given your life meaning and/or purpose?

4. How have they helped you to cope during difficult times as you got older?

5. What activities continue to give meaning and/or purpose to your life? (Langer 2000).

It is a great irony that modern society has made it possible for larger numbers of people to live a significant portion of their lives in old age than ever before, while at the same time often ignoring the exploration of the spiritual or meaning-making values that have provided significance and purpose to these longer-lived lives. The use of these assessment instruments (Langer 2000; Ortiz and Langer 2002) that incorporate spirituality into the whole person model no longer ignores nor isolates this very important aspect of humanity.

Old age may be detracting, yet older people are often happy with themselves and their circumstances. Older individuals may not feel that their age is a prominent trait, even though most human service profession- als think it is a highly relevant factor. An elderhood turned constructively toward the world, whether inspired by religious institutions or through a spiritual disposition, becomes an art of living the final phase of life. Some of the world's great artists such as Titian and Michelangelo, stand, in old age, as models for others in turning suffering and the temptation to despair into creative endeavors for posterity. Although most of us do not possess the creative genius of great artists, from them we can learn an attitude and a vitality that keeps elderhood and the products of their creative genius alive for the world. Elderhood, therefore, is not a time to withdraw from the world but rather to make an effort to persevere since the need for the unique contributions that the elderly can make to younger and to future generations is immense (Bianchi 1982, 220).

References

Bianchi, E.C. 1982. *Aging as a Spiritual Journey*, New York: Crossroad Publishing.

DeVogler, K.L., and P. Ebersole. 1980. Categorization of college students' meaning of life. *Psychological Reports*, 46, 387-390.

Fiske, M. and D.A. Chiriboga. 1991. *Change and continuity in adult life*. San Francisco, CA: Jossey-Bass.

Hedlund, B. and J.E. Birren. 1984, November. *Distribution of types of meaning in life across women*. Paper presented at the Annual Meeting of the Gerontological Society of America, San Antonio, Texas.

Kaufman, S.R. 1987. *The ageless self: Sources of meaning in late life*. Madison: University of Wisconsin Press.

Langer, N. 2000. The importance of spirituality in later life. *Gerontology and Geriatrics Education 20(3): 41-50.*

Prager, E.1997. Meaning in later life: An organizing theme for gerontological curriculum design. *Educational Gerontology*, 23, 1-13.

Thurner, M. 1975. Continuities and discontinuities in value orientation. In M.F. Lowenthal, M. Thurner, and D.Chiriboga, eds. *Four stages of life: A comparative study of women and men facing transition*. San Francisco, CA: Jossey-Bass.

6

EDUCATION ABOUT DYING, DEATH, GRIEF & LOSS PRINCIPLES & STRATEGIES

℘ℭ

Kenneth Doka

Introduction

E ducation about loss, grief, dying and death is a critically, often overlooked facet of gerontological education. It is critical for two reasons. First, death is a significant developmental issue in later life. Many of the major conceptual frameworks for later life such as life review (Butler 1963), awareness of finitude (Marshall 1980), ego integrity (Erickson 1963), or disengagement theory (Cumming and Henry 1963), are based upon the premise that the acknowledgement of a limited lifespan is tied to the psychological development of older persons.

Second, as persons experience longer life, they encounter a host of tangible and intangible losses. They may face the deaths of family members and friends. Older persons may relinquish significant roles. Abilities may diminish and cherished activities may be curtailed. In short, grief is evermore a companion in later life.

Yet, education about death, dying, loss and grief was often neglected in gerontology curriculums. In many ways this was a reaction to the ageism of contemporary society. Gerontologists, both implicitly and explicitly, wanted to emphasize that aging and death were not synonymous terms. They emphasized that older persons were vital, healthy and active. In the rush to discount prevalent negative images of later life, the study of loss, grief and death was neglected. There was also a dearth of materials, even of research. Many thanatologists entered that emerging field with a clinical or personal focus on "out-of-order" or sudden traumatic losses. They paid scant attention to death and loss in later life.

Yet, education about death, dying, loss and grief is a critical aspect of gerontological education. The question remains: How is it best accomplished? This chapter explores that question. It begins by reviewing critical principles that are basic to death education. It then offers an assessment and illustrates varied strategies to assist adult learners encounter dying, death, grief and loss.

Principles of Death Education

Prior to discussing strategies, it is critical to review some basic principles that should frame the choice of learning activities in this area.

Develop Intentional Goals and Objectives

One criticism that might be made of early experiences in death education was that there was often a rush to develop and utilize activities with little thought to their dangers, limitations, or applications. Effective education always begins with careful assessment of the audience—their needs and experiences. This analysis frames the goals and learning objectives for any module, training course, or curriculum. Strategies are just that—strategies or tools to assist the prospective students and practitioners to attain these objectives.

Embrace Diversity

There are significant cultural variations in the ways individuals deal with dying, death, loss and grief (Doka and Davidson 1998). Content and strategies should be respectful of different cultural beliefs and practices. In planning strategies, it is essential to ask two questions. Is the exercise sensitive to cultural diversity? Is it a good cultural fit with this audience?

Understand That Education about Dying, Death, Loss and Grief is Emotionally and Personally Charged

By the time they are adults, most students—even if they have never experienced the death of a family member—likely have had some encounters with dying and loss. In fact, there is some early evidence that significant exposures to death may predispose a student to register for a dying and death course (Doka 1981).

In developing strategies, it is important to remember that this topic is emotionally and personally charged. For example, a colleague once shared how he led students through a simulation exercise where they imagined receiving "bad news." He was unaware that one of his students had just taken an HIV test after being informed that a sexual partner was infected with HIV.

The fact that the context is so emotionally and personally charged may influence strategies in a number of ways. Certain exercises may be done responsibly in the context of a course experience where instructors are readily accessible and where there is ample opportunity for continued assessment and discussion of the experience. The same exercise may be problematic in a one-day training workshop. The climate can influence decisions on timing. Is this strategy better earlier or later in the experience? Has requisite trust been developed? Is there sufficient time for debriefing? In some activities, there may be value in co-facilitators—one to run the exercise and another to be available for any participants in need. Since education about dying, death, loss and grief can trigger the consideration of earlier unresolved issues, it may be helpful to know local resources for referral. As exercises become more intense, allow students options. For example, on less intense exercises such as an expressive activity, students may have a choice whether or not to share their product with the larger group. In more intense exercises such as a simulation, informed consent is essential. In some exercises, the instructor may find it helpful to indicate any conditions such as a recent loss that cautions participation.

A vital part of any exercise or simulation is the debriefing period at the end of game play. This discussion allows participants to express feelings about their experiences and permits them to draw parallels with real-world situations. The debriefing enables participants to ventilate their reactions to the material covered and to achieve closure for themselves. Professional and paraprofessional participants presently working with older clients have the opportunity to consider what experiences were relevant to them and what knowledge, skills, and attitudes they have acquired that may have implications for their own practice.

Be Current

A survey of nursing education about dying and death showed the continued prevalence of the work of Kubler-Ross. While Kubler-Ross' (1969) book *On dying and death* is a classic work (Corr 1993), it is now also considerably dated. Educators always retain a responsibility to ascertain that they are using the most current models (Corr and Doka 1994).

Strategies for Death Educators

There are a number of distinct strategies that can be useful in educating persons about dying, death, grief, and loss. Again, exercises and technologies of teaching follow goals and objectives rather then simply divert shock or entertain. Such activities should always be sensitive to the needs of the target audiences, sensitive to diverse values and beliefs, and designed with attention to any student vulnerabilities that may arise.

Lecture / Discussion Exercises

The body of thanatological literature has increased considerably in the past forty years (Corr and Doka 1994). An examination of the two major introductory texts (DeSpelder and Strickland 2002; and Corr, Nase, and Corr 2003) impress with their breadth and depth. Lecture and discussion remain the most efficient ways to convey information. Yet, even in lecture and discussion, appropriate exercises can amplify critical learning objectives and involve students. The following is an example of an exercise that can be used after a lecture or discussion of the needs of dying patients.

Exercise: What Does a Dying Person Need? Following a discussion or lecture on this topic, the instructor writes the question "What does a dying person need?" on the board. Students are encouraged to brainstorm, composing a list without evaluation or extensive comment. Students will call out responses such as "love," "respect," "honesty," "humor," or "touch". When responses slow, the instructor can add some additional needs. When a considerable list has been generated, the instructor erases the word "dying," replacing it with the word "living". The needs, of course, remain the same reinforcing the fact that dying persons retain basic human needs that remain even as their condition and definition changes.

Value Clarification

Value clarification allows students to examine their underlying assumptions and attitudes. Since these exercises do involve a certain amount of self-disclosure, they are best used after the group has had an opportunity to interact and some level of trust has been developed. Such activities are especially critical in the education of a wide range of clinicians as these activities assist them in acknowledging and confronting their own attitudes and values. Some early exercises such as "bomb shelter" or "life boat" asked participants to either exclude or remove individuals in a life threatening situation such as a nuclear attack or sinking ship. This often caused some degrees of anxiety, often leading to discussion of morality that diverted from the task. I have preferred exercises that ask participants to prioritize individuals for a life-enhancing operation such as a kidney transplant. This often seems more realistic since there is a clear recognition that health resources have to be rationed. In addition, it seems to cause less anxiety or conversations about the morality of rationing (although that can always evolve into an outcome).

Exercise: Kidney Transplant. Participants are given information and then a rating sheet where they are asked to prioritize individuals for access to a rationed health resource such as a kidney transplant. Individuals should first examine materials and rank their own chances. This is important since it notably minimizes the influence of others. Individuals are more likely to defend their initial choices, allowing later group discussion. After a time, depending on size, small groups, and then the class, collectively prioritize. The material presented can vary depending on needs and available time. It can include a continuum from brief descriptions such as "a 21 year-old male with developmental disabilities" or a "36-year-old female leader of a 'white supremacy group'" or even "photographs" (an excellent way to unearth biases relating to physical attractiveness) to more extensive "files". The descriptors can vary depending on what biases—age, political stance, race, ethnicity, and gender that one wishes to examine.

Expressive Activities

Any of the expressive arts can be used in a range of ways to assist thanatological education. Expressive activities allow discussion as well as offer students and practitioners opportunities for catharsis, reflection, and even projection. Again, since they are powerful tools for self-disclosure, they should be used after a level of trust has been established.

Exercise: Draw "Death." Provide ample art supplies such as crayons or markers. With no other comment, ask students to draw "death," "before birth," and "after death." Provide opportunity for students who wish to share and discuss their examples with the class. I often begin with my own drawings. This seems to reinforce a sense of safety. Drawings often may reflect religious beliefs as well as experiences on death. For example, students who came from more violence prone neighborhoods tended to draw death as intrusive and frightening.

Guest Speakers and Site Visits

Since the topic of death has a sense of the taboo attached to it, a legitimate goal is to demystify the processes associated with death. There may be value in visiting a cemetery, funeral home or have a speaker such as a funeral director, grief counselor, health care worker or even, if appropriate, a person living with a life-threatening illness. In arranging speakers, be clear about goals, objectives, and theme. It also helps that you have heard someone speak before a group. Speaking before a group of students can be anxiety provoking. Not everyone does it well even if they are articulate in an individual setting. Allow ample time for questions. I often remind students that the only foolish question is the one not asked. In site visits, three things are helpful—information, options, and support. For example, a visit to a funeral home can be frightening to students who have never been in one. Explain at each step what students will see and allow them options. Recognize and be available should students need support. Of course, allow class time for debriefing.

Films

Films are a wonderful way to illustrate a point and evoke discussion. A range of films has been produced primarily for education about dying, death, grief and loss. These have ranged from dramatizations of children's books on death such as *My Grandson Lew,* to cinematic treatments that accurately depict death. These are more didactic and instructional pieces, protective and evocative films designed to encourage speculation and discussion. For example in one such film, *The Death of a Peasant,* there is an ambiguous conclusion as a partisan breaks free from an execution pursued by a Nazi patrol. These films are regularly reviewed in thanatological journals such as *Omega and Death Studies,* both major texts. Corr, Nabe, and Corr (2003) and DeSpelder and Strickland (2003) include recommendations in their instructor manuals. In addition, many commercial films may have scenes that could offer useful material for discussion. For example, the film *Terms of Endearment* includes a powerful scene where a terminally ill mother meets with both her angry preadolescent and adolescent sons.

As with any activity, it is important to assess one's goals and audience in seeing a film as well as any copyright issues that might arise either in duplication or presentation. There may be other criteria as well. Is the film's appearance dated? The otherwise excellent *My Grandson Lew* has a clear 1970's feel both in the décor of the home and the appearance of the actors that may distract viewers. Does the film reflect cultural diversity? While not every film could conceivably portray every ethnicity, films that reflect only white suburbia will disenfranchise students. How does the time fit? A film that takes a great deal of class time may not offer much opportunity for discussion and debriefing.

Case Studies

Case studies, too, are excellent ways to encounter issues in education about dying, death, grief and loss. They are particularly well suited to education about ethics and counseling. An interesting variation of the case study is to give a group two related case studies or to vary a case study among the groups in the class. For example, one can develop a case study of a 78-year-old man with osteogenic sarcoma (bone cancer). While the prognosis is good, the man, though competent, declines the standard treatment or an amputation. An interesting variation of this case would be to modify the age of the client to a 16 year old. It should be noted that films, too, are excellent sources for case studies.

Role-Play

A critical advantage of role-play is that it draws more direct involvement of a group of students. Role-plays can offer students opportunities to "take the role of the other," that is, to understand something of the differences that another can face, engaging insight and empathy as well as practicing skills. While simple role-plays can be used as icebreakers, more extensive role-plays, especially those that practice skills, are better designed later in the course experience when students have developed a greater sense of competence, confidence, and trust. Again, one has to know one's audience. In a professional audience, the group may already be comfortable and competent.

Illustrative Exercise: First Responder.

Cast: Two police officers and the parents of a 16-year-old boy.

Plot: As police, you have been dispatched to inform the parents that their 16-year-old son has been involved in a fatal accident. At least one parent needs to come to identify the body. As parents, your 16-year-old son has recently received his license. Due to the poor weather, a heavy rainfall, you were reluctant to let him have the car tonight, but he eventually prevailed. In developing a role-play, often less is better. This can allow participants to create their own dynamic, determining their own interpretation of their roles. For example, in this role-play, what police officer will break the news, what parent will blame the other?

Debriefing: As with other exercises, one needs adequate time to debrief. This debriefing should include both the emotions evoked as well as an examination of the responses and reactions of the players. The goal is to generate a dialogue between the players and the other participants. As facilitator, it is important to insure that the dialogue remains supportive on the players and final comments should focus on their major contributions to the experience.

A Variation: *Directed Role Play*. A more advanced version of this learning experience is called "directed role play". Here any participant can become involved, changing the course of interaction by merely placing a hand on a role player's shoulder and then replaying a scene. For example, if the mother responded to the death by blaming her husband, another participant might place a hand on her shoulder and say instead "I feel so guilty, I never should have given him the car". This technique keeps the dynamic moving, allowing participants to change the direction of the role-play as well as to experiment with different helping responses.

Imaging and Simulation

Imaging and simulation remain popular staples in education about dying, death, grief and loss. Yet, such exercises need to be used carefully. Imagery attempts to engage the power of imagination to evoke insight or empathy. Some popular techniques that have used imagery include such exercises as writing one's own obituary or death notice or a directed imagery in envisioning a life threatening illness that begins with evoking a terminal prognosis.

Yet, these popular exercises demonstrate the danger in using such methods. I recommend against using personalized exercises. There are a few reasons for this. First, one never really knows the experiences or anxieties of participants. In one directed imagery, envisioning a life threatening illness, I realized I was sitting next to a colleague who had just received a cancer diagnosis. The danger is that such exercises can evoke strong anxieties. Second, imaging as a technique arises from a theoretical basis that emphasizes a strong mind-body connection. If positive imagery can help heal, it stands to reason that negative imagery can also have an effect. Respect for the mind-body connection suggests caution in using overly personal imagery. This does not mean that imaging cannot be used but simply that it should allow a distance.

Simulations are techniques that allow participants to engage in an experience indirectly. In simulation, a participant engages in an activity or exercise that evokes reactions that might be experienced in another context. For example, a common simulation in aging is to have a classmate feed another classmate who is blindfolded and has earplugs—simulating an experience of helplessness that some older nursing residents may experience. Like imagery, they offer powerful opportunities for insight and understanding. Since they allow an indirect encounter, they often can offer a therapeutic distance for participants. Nonetheless, they are powerful exercises that can uncover significant affect; leaders should offer any appropriate cautions. For example, in the sudden loss simulation provided as an illustration here, I warn individuals who have experienced a significant sudden loss within the past year that they may wish to take an observer role.

Sudden Death Experiential Workshop: *Caution*: In introducing the simulation, offer some individuals the possibility of being observers—especially those grieving a sudden loss.

Materials: Crayons or magic markers; soft music; use pieces of paper cut in the shape of neckties.

Process: Give each participant a tie.

1. With music playing in the background, ask each participant to think about his or her family ties.

2. At this point students should be asked to draw their family "tie," that is, illustrate their paper necktie so that it symbolizes their "family ties."

3. Have participants mingle for about 5 minutes—discussing what they see in the family ties of others.

4. Ask students to sit down in pairs to explain their ties to one another.

5. The facilitator then cuts one partner's tie in each dyad. Allow the participants an opportunity to process that experience as they remain in pairs.

Debriefing:

1. Group those with cut ties in an inner circle; the persons with whole ties should sit in the outer circle. This amplifies the unique experiences of each group—one as victims, the other group as survivors.

2. Process reactions and feelings of both groups.

3. Focus on unfinished business (allow participants to redraw or tape their ties). Remind them that their true family ties remain in tact. Encourage them to consider ways they might wish to strengthen those ties as they are reminded of how quickly ties can be severed.

Conclusion

Education about dying, death, grief, and loss is a critical part of gerontology. Yet, it is not one that should be handled lightly. It is healthy that taboos about death are lifting—in gernotological education and society as a whole. Nonetheless, educators in thanatology need to respect not only the beliefs and values of students, but their fears and experiences. The end of a taboo should not result in careless license.

Resources

The following manuals include a range of activities and exercises that might be useful in teaching. The activities here do not always adhere to the philosophy and principles suggested in this chapter. Facilitators are cautioned to use their own judgments as to appropriate exercises for a given audience.

Knott, J.G., M.C. Ribar, B. Duson, and M.R. King. 1982. *Thanatopics: A manual of structured learning experiences for death education.* Kingston, RI: SLE Productions.
Straub, S.H. 2002. *Death 101: A workbook for educating and healing.* Amityville, NY: Baywood Publishing Company.
Welch, D., R. Zamistoski, and D. Smart. 1991. *Encountering death: Structured activities for death awareness.* Muncie, IN.: Accelerated Development.

References

Butler, R. 1963. The life review: An interpretation of reminiscence in the aged. *Psychiatry*, 26, 65-76.
Corr, C. 1993. Coping with dying: Lessons that we should and should not learn from the work of Elizabeth Kubler-Ross. *Death Studies*, 19, 59-83.

Corr, C. and K.J. Doka. 1994. Current models of death, dying, and bereavement. *Critical Care Nursing Clinics of North America*, 6, 545-552.

Corr, C., C. Nase and D. Corr. 2003. *Death and dying: Life and living.* 4th Ed. Belmont, CA.: Wadsworth.

Cumming, E. and W.E. Henry. 1961. *Growing old.* New York: Basic Books.

DeSpelder, L.A. and A. Strickland. 2002. *The last dance: Encountering death and dying.* 6th Ed. N.Y.: McGraw Hill.

Doka, K.J. 1981. Recent bereavement and registration for death studies course. *Omega,* 12, 51-60.

Doka, K.J. and J. Davidson. 1998. *Living with grief: Who we are, how we grieve.* Washington, D.C.: Hospice Foundation of America.

Ericksen, E. 1963. *Childhood and society.* New York: Norton.

Kubler-Ross, E. 1969. *On death and dying.* New York: Macmillan.

Marshal, V. 1980. *Last chapters: Sociology of aging and dying.* Monterrey, CA: Brooks / Cole.

The author wishes to acknowledge Therese A. Rando and Edie Stark. They taught me much about experiential learning.

Editorial Commentary

ഔഈ

Nieli Langer & Terry Tirrito

There is evidence that health and social service providers feel poorly prepared to effectively care for persons who are dying because programs of professional and paraprofessional education do not adequately prepare them for the task (Ross et al. 2002). In addition, there is paucity of resources for the educators of health and social service providers who are charged with teaching and role modeling end-of-life care for the elderly. A major reason contributing to this lack of awareness is that dying, which was once viewed as natural and expected, has become medicalized into an unwelcome part of medical care; it has become medicine's enemy.

Palliative care is referred to as "good end-of-life" care. It does not try to cure people of disease, but to do everything possible to make them comfortable and promote quality of life, however short. Palliative care relieves physical symptoms and provides emotional and spiritual support to patients and family members. Although it is true that palliative care has gained greater credence both within the medical community and among the lay public, Americans remain a deeply divided nation when it comes to issues of death and dying. We remain a death-defying culture focused on individual notions of control and a deep-seated belief in the almost limitless possibilities of medical technology. Therefore, practitioners are having difficulty in providing skilled and sensitive care to those who are dying, especially for seniors who are dying from chronic and progressive diseases. As more seniors demand care that relates to the naturalness of dying and death in later life, there needs to be an increased public and professional awareness of end-of-life issues for seniors. The challenge to healthcare systems is to commit resources that support care to elders in their last months or years of life and to educate consumers to request and expect excellence in end-of-life care.

Academic institutions that educate nurses, social workers, and physicians must give increased attention to end-of-life care and pain and symptom management, and, through faculty practice and continuing education, to assisting practitioners and family members as they provide this care. Curricular development for practitioners should include: respect for values; technical proficiency; and, effective communication skills that respect preferences and beliefs. In addition, healthcare workers need to become culturally competent, i.e., know how to thoughtfully apply a client's cultural data into practice.

Physicians and other healthcare workers who have been raised in the United States, trained in Western medical ethics conventions, and practicing under U.S. law must reconcile their personal beliefs and obligations with those of their patients who may not share those beliefs and values. The effectiveness of Western medical ethics may be limited in the face of issues that are closely linked to different cultural perspectives. All of us, regardless of our ethnic backgrounds or professions, are likely to become dependent on the healthcare system to some degree as we age. Improved communication, mutual understanding, and negotiation may help both healthcare workers and their clients/patients receive treatment at the end of life in a manner that reflects respect and tolerance of diversity.

Ross, M.M., M.J. MacLean, and R. Fisher. 2002. End-of-life care for seniors: Public and professional awareness. *Educational Gerontology* 28(5): 353-366.

7

Act III:
Maximizing Choices
in Retirement

୬ୠ

Nieli Langer

We are what we do. It is how people know us. Lynn was a dental hygienist for 35 years; George owned an automobile repair shop and was respected as an honest mechanic in his town. Regardless of how these people arrived at their respective job titles, they were identified by these roles until they retired. As the first generation to fully experience retirement, Baby Boomers are embarking upon unchartered territory that will give them the freedom to do and not be defined by what we do. The expectation of retirement has become a feature of the adult life course that we take for granted. We can make the Third Act and us anything we want it to be. The message is that this Third Act is a new interpretation of retirement. Retirees will be redefining it as they go along and as they pursue their goals they must be aware that they can have a great deal of influence over how they age. In the United Sates, retirement is much less prescribed than in other Western countries. Therefore, we must seize this time so that it is transformed into an opportunity and not a burden.

The concept of retirement as we've known it is obsolete. Our ideas about old age are archaic, based on outdated models. The combined effect of the senior boom and the birth dearth in America is creating a senior population of retirees who, with the gift of longevity and the added years it brings, will be redefining the style and purpose of those later years of life for themselves. We cannot anticipate the changes that will be brought about by population aging and retirement by looking backward because these concepts are unprecedented in human history. The rules of aging have been forever altered as the lifestyles and life cycles of the older population are continuously being reinvented. The concept of reinventing yourself postretirement is a groundbreaking one. It requires throwing away the negative stereotypes and myths of aging that have been accepted until now. If given the opportunity, the trick is to create a Third Act that provides meaning, structure, and purpose rather than acceptance, ossification, and withdrawal. People appear to thrive better when they are positioned to make their own choices. When job and child rearing responsibilities are no longer pressing concerns, men and women will have more opportunities to pursue activities of their choice. Most of today's retirees are leading full, vibrant lives, unimpaired by poor health or frailty. With the aging of the population and the attention being paid to geriatric medicine and other health specialties, we can be assured that this trend toward active, healthy senior years will continue.

The central focus of this chapter is on retirement as a life stage and as a process of separation from employment. There is no agreement about how to measure retirement status. However, two criteria are generally part of most definitions: receipt of a public or private pension and reduced activity in the job market at some advanced age (Gendell and Siegel 1992). In addition, retirement has become more transitional as a life stage since people, especially those in middle and upper income levels tend to phase into retirement (Mutchler et al. 1997). Some older people are using phased retirement programs in career jobs, while many others are moving into bridge jobs that ease the transition from fulltime career employment into retirement.

Retirement is a time of change and it has many faces. It is now generally accepted as an appropriate stage of the adult life cycle and is seen in Western culture as a legitimate, earned privilege (Atchley 2000, 229). Retirement comes in all shapes and sizes, strengths and weaknesses, personalities and behavior patterns. The hallmark of the Baby Boom is its diversity and the increased diversity it will bring to "getting older." Not only is there age diversity in the Baby Boom, but also diversity in lifestyle choices, timing of life events, economic status, and racial/ethnic composition. Many Baby Boomer cohorts followed traditional patterns of marriage, employment, and childbearing while the timing of life events for other Baby Boomers has varied widely. They have been instrumental in the dissolution of the traditional linear life plan. In its place they have opted for a much more flexible arrangement, known as the "cyclic life plan." Longer life has eliminated the rigid correlations between age and the various roles and activities and challenges of adult life. Time spent in education has pushed back the timing of childbearing so that women, not just men, can extend the timing of child rearing well into mature decades of life. Whereas education has been primarily geared to preparing for lifetime careers, we are now coming to think of learning as an ongoing, lifelong process. Baby Boomers have been retrained and retooled many times throughout their lives. With the cyclic life plan, most people will have more years of adult life after the children have grown and have left home than they had when they were raising them. Lifetimes of financial security will probably translate into comparable lifestyles for some, while persistent poverty will doubtless be the lot for others in these large and diverse cohorts. A final component of Baby Boomer diversity is the large immigration from Hispanic and Asian populations. The Baby Boom cohorts have been differentiated from the current older cohorts by greater racial/ethnic diversity. In general, ordinary aging Americans have broken free of the traditional expectations of age to shape new and rewarding cyclic lives for themselves (Dychtwald 1990, 92-100).

While many retirees can expect a long healthy retirement with adequate financial resources, retirement can have its difficulties. The majority of employer-sponsored retirement seminars spend little or no time on family adjustment issues, educational opportunities for adult learners, housing choices in retirement, mental health issues, the role of religion, and quality-of-life concerns in the later years (Brady et al. 1996). Moody (1988) expressed the hope that culture, spirituality, and education—quality-of-life factors, would not take second place to materialistic issues in retirement; he deems all late life issues worthy of serious consideration.

Persons who retire from productive employment are faced with several important adjustments to loss: the job itself, the work role, personal and social associations that work provided, and income. If events such as declining health or the loss of a spouse closely coincide with retirement, adjustment to retirement can be stressful and difficult, and for some, even impossible.

Many retirement planning programs reach the more educated and financially secure older adults and tend to disregard the needs of the poor and minority elderly. Even as the definition of retirement changes, questions remain whether retirement has ever been a meaningful life transition for minority, disadvantaged, and female workers, who often have experienced discontinuous labor force histories and more often continue employment into old age because of financial necessity (Calasanti 1996). Each of these populations could benefit from education about benefits and entitlements for which they may be eligible and could benefit from guidance in structuring the non-working years of their lives. Providing information tends to be more effective than counseling for retirees.

The retirement educator will need to determine the meaning of retirement from the perspective of the older client. He/she will need to determine how clients conceptualize retirement: how they feel about it, what it symbolizes to them, and how it affects their feelings about themselves, their families, and their friends. Social and environmental forces will determine how the retiree views retirement. Teaching retirement education/counseling in aging studies programs can bridge the gap that currently exists in the provision of these services to seniors. Preparing practitioners represents an effort to address the specific needs of the current cohort of retirees and the lack of available professionals trained to address their needs.

Suggested objectives in a retirement counseling course could include the need to:

1. Address the evolution of retirement from an exclusively man-centered focus to one that includes transition for women and minorities.

2. Increase awareness of the social and economic issues that arise prior to and following retirement.

3. Learn how to use intervention strategies with clients for resolution of issues related to retirement.

4. Adopt an approach to retirement counseling that respects individual client and/or couple needs as it relates to gender, ethnicity, life and work experiences, and personal agenda.

As the instructor, you will make the determination of which topics to include in your syllabus. I will highlight several topics that my experience has shown to be essential in the discussion of retirement for current and/or future retirees.

Topics

"Money Makes the World Go 'Round..."

Who is responsible for retirement planning? Each of us is. Even the individual who seeks no more than the base income provided by Social Security needs to plan as the age of full benefits under Social Security rises, the level of inflation adjustment is redefined downward, and Medicare premiums are increased and its benefits reduced. The age of candor, myth breaking, and individual responsibility is upon us. Any individual who hopes to live above the safety net needs to plan for his/her retirement.

Retirement planning has always been the responsibility of the individual and the family. However, the sources of income to fulfill the plan have always differed across society and will continue to do so. One of the major issues facing retirees, pre and post retirement, is the availability of money. As a non-minority working male, the opportunities to plan ahead for retirement are numerous. The retirement outlook for them is significantly better than for other groups of individuals. As white males have historically had the highest earnings potential of any work group, they are the group that is most likely to be prepared for retirement.

"The Queen Was in the Parlor, Eating Bread and Honey..."

Historically, low wages have caused many women to be shortchanged when it comes to collecting their Social Security benefits. Pension entitlement is the single largest gender difference in retirement. To date, women's discontinuous work histories and higher likelihood of part-time employment decreased the probability that they would become entitled to adequate retirement pensions (O'Grady-LeShane 1996, 103-109). Retiring female Baby Boomers with a more consistent work history will conceivably fare much better.

"The Maid Was in the Garden,
Hanging Out the Clothes..."

For a large segment of society, retirement focuses on leisure, enhanced quality of life, and maintaining financial resources. For people of color and many women, questions about whether they will have sufficient money for retirement are a major factor associated with retirement decisions. The primary reason for retirement among this group is likely to be poor health, not adequacy of saving, pensions, or assets (SPRY 1999). A disproportion-ate number of older people of color, women, and gays and lesbians do not have a reasonable opportunity to achieve a version of the "retirement dream." The unskilled workers and minority workers often suffer the greatest financial hardships upon retirement. Many of these workers have limited education and maintained low job status while employed. This inability to earn high wages kept many of these employees at or near the poverty level, despite the long work histories. This low wage history becomes detrimental upon retirement. As their Social Security is based on averages of past wages, their benefits are extremely limited. Though many workers of these groups have contributed to the Social Security system, many more have worked in non-contributing jobs, i.e., field laborers, etc. These employees will not have any entitlements at all under the current federal system. Strong family ties and informal support networks often provide the majority of resources to minority workers upon retirement. Many opt to be "disabled" rather than "retired" (Barrow 1996). The lack of financial means available to minority and unskilled laborers places undue stress upon these individuals who, without Social Security benefits, are left to rely on other nominal resources.

Regardless of ethnicity, gender, or socio-economic status of an employee, retirement voids all boundaries. The main economic objective will be to determine a level of financial comfort and security that is possible with the resources available to the individual/couple upon retirement.

"Humpty Dumpty Sat on a Wall..."
"Humpty Dumpty Had a Great Fall..."

Unfortunately, we do not have the capability of predicting our healthcare needs. Nor do we have the power to ward off any illness or diseases that may come our way. Heredity and other involuntary forces can have as much of an impact on overall health as one's direct actions (Rowe and Kahn 1998). However, the evolving healthcare system now provides a menu of options that will generally provide for most healthcare needs. In addition to the standard Medicare and Medicaid, there are standard medical plans, health maintenance organizations or preferred provider organizations.

We define, describe, diagnose, and treat illness using a medical model, i.e., attempting to solve the problems of ill health but disregarding maintenance and enhancement of physical, psychosocial, and spiritual well-being. The medical model addresses acute illness while the aging population's greatest health care need is maintenance of current chronic conditions. In addition, health care for older people in the United States is fragmented and biased towards institutional care rather than a community care model. Even if policy makers and lobby groups were in agreement that a well financed, integrated, and accessible system of health care was our goal, the fundamental problem would still remain, i.e., how do we pay for it? Difficult decisions face us in the very near future as we prepare for the aging of the Baby Boomers.

"Eenie, Meenie, Miney, Moe…" or *"How Will I Spend My Time?"*

The range of activities that occupy man's time and attention are boundless. Atchley (2000, 269-270) has written about the significance that activity has for different people. He describes activities as sources of personal identity and/or development, prestige or status, feelings of accomplishment, or, joy and pleasure. The activity, such as volunteering may be goal oriented. The activity can be assessed in terms of how much meaning the individual attaches to its performance. The activity and the accompanying significance that the individual attaches to it help determine how that activity contributes to the person's life goals.

Employment: Retirement should not be confused with stopping to work. Healthy men and women may stop working toward economically motivated goals in the workplace but they do not stop working, i.e., they continue to pursue personal goals. For some, a personal goal may, in fact, mean a return to the workplace.

The decision to return to the workforce post-retirement depends on several factors. Not only must there be an opportunity for gainful employment but the person must want to work. The need to supplement insufficient income, to regain the role and status that the job provided, and to maintain the associations with others that the work place provided are the major incentives to seek out post-retirement employment. One of the hardest roadblocks for a retired individual is gainful employment post-retirement. Jobs are tough to come by in later life and age discrimination in employment is common. The majority of retirees do not seek out gainful employment after age 70 (Atchley 2000, 276).

There are retirees who pursue new and sometimes multiple careers often related to hobbies or activities they have engaged in or never had an opportunity to pursue. Retirees sometimes find their hobbies turning into "second careers" as their interest in these endeavors intensifies. They are able to focus on these activities without the pressures of job related expectations.

Education: Retirement provides the opportunity for people to pursue learning. Some people are interested in personal issues such as fitness or finance; others may be seeking job placement and training; still others want to keep their knowledge current on a broad variety of issues such as technology or current events. Retirees are able to take courses as well as pursue degrees and professional certification at many private and public institutions of higher learning.

Elderhostel is the fastest growing educational program designed for adults 55 or over. It is a national nonprofit corporation that coordinates short-term programs (usually a week) at college campuses that provide the classrooms, dormitories, college dining facilities and usually the recreational facilities. Courses are not for credit and there are no exams or grades; no prior knowledge of the topic is expected or required. *Elderhostel* is a unique concept that appeals to the individualism and humanism of the current cohort of retirees and their lifestyles (Atchley 2000, 282).

Volunteer Work: The roles and responsibilities that accompany volunteer efforts provide the "purpose" that some retirees seek once they have left the workplace. However, Fischer et al. (1991) found that almost 60 percent of retirees provided assistance to their children and grandchildren and approximately 40 percent provided help such as transportation and visiting to their neighbors. This is a form of volunteerism even if it is not sponsored by a formal organization. The 52 percent of retirees who volunteered in mostly church organizations were more likely to have higher incomes, be better educated, in generally good health and married. Volunteering at any level provides the individual with an opportunity to reciprocate and thereby maintain a certain level of social responsibility in his/her lifestyle.

Activities provide structure to people's lives yet families, academicians, and practitioners cannot impose their notions of which activities should be pursued by retirees. Activity patterns are highly individualized and highly stable over the life course. People will often continue to pursue activity and social patterns unless limited in later life by physical, financial, and/or transportation factors.

Given the daunting human-resource shortages that exist all across the nonprofit and public-service sectors, engaging these individuals to fill critical gaps in our workforce might well produce a windfall for American communities in the twenty-first century. We may also bring opportunities for greater fulfillment and purpose to the later years and transform what it means to age in this country. While many worry about the fiscal implications of the Baby Boom's mass retirement, what may outweigh these worries are the potential economic and civic contributions of a large pool of healthy and publicly minded older Americans.

"There Was an Old Woman Who Lived in a Shoe..."

Fortunately, she had retired and the children had long since moved away and started their own families. As she grew older, she realized that aging had changed her housing needs in a variety of ways. She could respond to these changes by aging in place or by relocating. She will probably have to compromise between security and autonomy. In order to get the security she needs for personal care, she may have to give up at least some measure of autonomy. She will have to consider her income level, marital status, and functional status in her decision-making. If she remains in relatively good physical and financial health, the housing opportunities are limited only by her needs and desires.

There is a continuum of care in the United States today in which most financial and social/health care needs will meet consumer demands. This menu of housing options include living with relatives, home sharing, foster care, accessory apartments, congregate housing, board and care homes, assisted living or community residential care facilities, continuing care communities and nursing home placement.

"Diddle, Diddle Dumpling, My Son John..."

No amount of planning regarding an estate and the legal considerations of growing older should be overlooked, regardless of the size of an estate. The two major areas of legal and estate planning will concern the standard measures of making the decisions regarding how the estate will be handled after a person is gone, and having the appropriate documentation of his/her wishes in the event of incapacitation. It is imperative that arrangements for the disbursement of assets be made prior to the reality of such a chore. Once a person becomes incapacitated, or even deceased, it is too late for him/her, the spouse and/or family to correct the matters that only he/she has the power to do. Never before have people been so vulnerable to the statutes that govern the assets that people leave behind. Failure to prepare adequately can lead to negligence on behalf of the estate when the time comes to allocate its contents.

Living will and durable powers of attorney, known collectively as advance directives, are widely acknowledged to be increasingly important in medical decision making. The durable power of attorney for health care allows a person to name any willing person, empowering them to make health care decisions, in particular with respect to withholding or withdrawal of life sustaining treatment. The agent must act consistently with the patient's wishes as stated in the document.

Guardianship or conservatorship is the "legal tool of last resort" (Sabatino 1998). A court will appoint a guardian for the incapacitated person if he/she can no longer care for him/herself, manage property or their personal affairs, and has failed to leave an advanced directive.

"Will You Still Need Me; Will You Still Feed Me, When I'm 64?"

"And they lived happily ever after...What was their marriage like? As the years passed, did the prince undergo a mid-life crisis and the princess a hysterectomy? Did she decide to color her golden hair and he to take up jogging along the palace walls?" OR... "Did she want no one but him? And did they spend their days walking hand in hand in the palace gardens waiting for sunset?" (Silverstone and Hyman 1992, 2-3).

Most elderly couples today have grown old together. Because more people are living longer, their marriages have a chance to live longer, too. Although the starring roles are portrayed by couples, how each partner interprets their own personal aging is an individual process. Jessie Bernard has described every marriage as possibly three marriages—his marriage, her marriage, and "our" marriage, the one the couple jointly presents to the outside world and even to one another. If asked, each partner would recite a very different tale about the same relationship and each would undoubtedly interpret late life according to his/her own personal timetable, life experiences and emotions (Silverstone and Hyman 1992, 13).

Couplehood is the generally accepted desired lifestyle. Most older couples report that their marriages are happy, and there is evidence from many studies that marital satisfaction in later life tends to be quite high. The overall quality of those marriages does not seem to be appreciably affected by retirement. One pattern that emerges clearly is that older couples are no different from couples of any other age, their views are equally diverse and their problems just as pronounced (Atchley 2000, 195).

Limited attention has been given to the needs of minority elderly in our population; even less is directed toward identifying and understanding the needs of lesbian and gay elders.

> Joe has one year until retirement. He had always thought it would be a joyful year in preparation for the many trips he and Paul planned. Paul started showing signs of forgetfulness a few years ago shortly after his own retirement. Now he needs almost constant supervision, and Paul wants to be with him. How can he explain this at his job? The Family Medical Leave Act doesn't apply to gay families, and he certainly hasn't been "out" at work. (Schneider et al. 2000, 343)

Recognition of needs and issues relevant to this "invisible" minority as they approach retirement is critical to improving their lives and quality of care.

The role of couplehood in adjustment to late life changes cannot be diminished. As our population continues to age, the role of couplehood in sharing age-related issues such as health, financial stability, leisure vs. work, and choices of where and what type of housing to select looms very large. Marital intervention for retirees is seldom a topic that is discussed in retirement counseling (Richardson 1993). It is often left to the retiring spouse to seek help in dealing with the changes that occur during most marriages while one of the spouses is contemplating, or initiating, retirement. Some of these couple-related issues may include: recognition of the emotional support of the relationship; the role of family ties not only for help in times of trouble but for pleasure and companionship; facing illness and disability; and, "till death do us part..." issues (Langer 1998, 73-80).

Activities and Strategies

Activity: The Case Study

One major reason for using case studies is to let learners use abstract information in safe situations that are similar to what they will encounter in their occupations. This approach is process-centered rather than content-centered. It is well suited to higher cognitive objectives such as analysis and synthesis of ideas. In general, the reflection on and discussion of complex reality with peers and an informed facilitator often results in various interpretations and suggestions for resolution. Having one's experience and decisions challenged in a supportive learning environment can help refine thinking processes. Case studies can also be valuable in evaluating what has been learned by a group of participants. The analysis performed by each individual should reflect how well previously taught concepts have been integrated into that person's behavior. The following suggestions for teaching students/practitioners the process of analysis are proposed and can be used for analysis of the case study that follows.

1. Develop an overview of the situation and the prospective role of each person involved.

2. Identify the real issues facing each of the players.

3. Organize the material that has been presented to you and anticipate how you will begin to assign roles and responsibilities to each person.

4. Develop a plan as well as realistic alternatives.

5. Make a determination if the recommended actions are feasible and conducive to problem resolution.

6. Develop criteria for evaluating each option as well as outcomes.

Retirement will include many stages and events and the problems encountered during these times will change in scope and intensity. It is difficult to imagine a system in which only one professional manages the broad spectrum of potential needs of a client. Therefore, becoming aware of, and developing in-class programs will be invaluable to the case manager(s) involved as well as future clients. The following activity is an example of the team approach in solving the problems experienced by someone already retired whose needs have changed and the services of more than one professional are needed. In this case study, the primary players are the geriatric case manager and a financial planner. Also of import will be the woman's son and daughter. Despite the importance of financial resources in determining an appropriate care plan, geriatric practitioners are sometimes uncomfortable with the financial aspects of the assessment process, especially compared to areas in which they are clinically trained. The focus of this case study will be in abstracting the division of responsibility of each participant. Having a clear understanding of who does what and when precludes redundant tasks and costs and enhances the energies available for creative problem solving. Despite the different professional framework (case manager and financial planner) from which the problem will be approached, the cooperative experience should prove mutually beneficial to both professionals and ultimately for the client and her family (Tacchino and Thomas 1997).

Case Study: Lenora Greene

Lenora Greene, 78, is a retired Chicago school teacher. A few years before her retirement at age 63, she sold her home and moved into a rent-controlled apartment on Chicago's East Side. About ten years after retirement, she had a mild heart attack, so she moved to New Mexico to live with her son.

For the past five years, Mrs. Greene has lived a moderately active and fairly independent life. She has what amounts to a small apartment in her 54-year old bachelor son's home, with her own bedroom, bathroom and kitchenette, and even her own entrance. Her rooms adjoin the main house's family room, so she is integrated into the household but also perceives herself as independent.

Her son is a sales representative for a middle-sized computer hardware manufacturer and has responsibility for the southwest region of the United States. Consequently, although he has some control over his travel schedule, he often has to be away from home for days at a time.
Mrs. Greene's daughter, a housewife, lives in Texas with her husband, a policeman, and their two college-age children. Mrs. Greene and her daughter are estranged and have not spoken to one another in over fourteen years.

Mrs. Greene has a $21,000 annual pension from her teachers' retirement fund, but the pension does not include cost-of-living adjustments. She also receives $8,000 per year from Social Security. In addition, she has financial assets of about $130,000, which are invested conservatively. She is a member of a health maintenance organization and is covered by Medicare, but she has no long-term care insurance.

At the present time, Mrs. Greene complains a lot about being sick, although her physical health is reasonably good. In addition to her cardiac history, her chronic problems include high blood pressure and late-onset diabetes. All of these problems have been well under control, through a complex pharmaceutical regimen, until recently. For the past two years Mrs. Greene has exhibited symptoms of depression. Five times over the past six months she completely confused her medication schedule and had to be taken to the emergency room by ambulance.

Her son thought her complaints about depression and her failure to properly comply with her pharmaceutical schedule were a play for attention because of his difficult travel schedule, but it has become increasingly apparent that Mrs. Greene's memory and cognitive capacities are in fact declining at what appears to be a more rapid than average pace. A recent magazine cover story about Alzheimer's disease suggested to the son that his mother may not be able to live in her quasi-independent status in his house for much longer. He is unsure about how to evaluate appropriate nursing homes, but believes that Medicare will help with the expenses.

*Casestudy reprinted with permission from Tacchino, K. and N.D.Thomas 1997 Summer. Why financial practitioners and geriatric care managers must talk to each other, *Generations*, 21:2, 41-44. © 1997, American Society on Aging, San Francisco, CA. www.asaging.org.

Activity: Team Planning

Two class members are selected as team managers who will lead their groups in the creation and presentation of alternative designs for the following staff training. Each group works as a team and presents the results of their discussions in oral presentation. As a coordinator for staff training (team manager), you realize that the staff of your agency needs a series of training sessions on working with gay and lesbian elders. The project will incorporate a series of activities designed to achieve a specific outcome within a set budget and time frame. However promising and desirable a project may seem, always carefully examine whether it is the right time to initiate it. To achieve the desired outcome, this project must have *defined* and *approved goals*, a *committed team*, a *viable plan of action* that can be altered to accommodate change, and a system in place to *evaluate attitude and performance outcomes.*

Activity: "Break a leg..."

Shakespeare told stories that taught life's lessons. Even though Shakespeare taught without Powerpoint or videoconferencing, his audience remembered those lessons and sometimes applied them to their own lives. The use of theater in the classroom both to teach subjects and to develop personal skills in students is well documented, but seldom observed.

The power of theater lies in its capacity to arouse, to clarify, and to evaluate. It is an innovative and entertaining strategy to realizing many educational objectives, regardless of the topic. Educators can help adult learners and practitioners use playacting to disprove the many myths about aging and help to positively shape society's concepts of what it means to grow old.

There are many books that have been compiled with scenes, monologues, and short plays that depict topics relevant to aging. The plays can be staged in class or in larger venues with participants either reading or memorizing their lines. It is always more useful for the players to receive the script and rehearse instead of giving an impromptu presentation. By answering the following questions, each player can portray his/her character with intelligence and imagination:

1. What does your character want to achieve? If you don't know what your character wants to achieve, then your acting will be vague, and lacking in clarity. Theater is about passion, not about indetermination. Dig deeply to discover your character's primary motivations.

2. What obstacles keep your character from achieving the objective?

3. What actions does your character take to overcome the obstacles?

4. What stakes are involved and what is your character willing to give up in order to achieve the objective?

Remind your students that theater, whether serious or comic is about conditions of discomfort and desperation and about people who no longer want to remain in those situations. Theater is a lot like life: no pain, no gain (McDonough and Brown 2000).

Activity: Concept Mapping

A concept map is a diagram that shows pieces of information and their relations to each other. A concept map can be used by the learner to build understanding and clarify relationships during the learning process. It can be an aid in note-taking and in review of notes. The instructor can ask the learner to produce and explain a concept map in order to know how the learner constructs certain knowledge, what relationships may not yet be clear to the learner, what pieces of information have not found their way into the learner's construction. A well-developed concept will be illustrated by a complex map that shows numerous relationships and probably some hierarchy among pieces of information. There should be less emphasis on whether a map is "correct" and more on what it shows about how the person organizes the information. Concept maps provide a summary of what we say, believe, think, feel, or value at a particular point in time. An example of a concept map (Figure 1) was drawn by a participant in a pre-retirement course who was undecided about where to retire. His initial list of concepts included weather, income, freedom and independence, cost of housing, and rural life-style. As he constructed the map, additional concepts emerged that were more personal and, therefore, raised new criteria for what would constitute a wise decision. This shift of values evolved into a revised concept map of choices for retirement location (Figure 2) (Deschler 1990, 341-2).

Figure 1: Concept Map on Choice of Retirement Location.

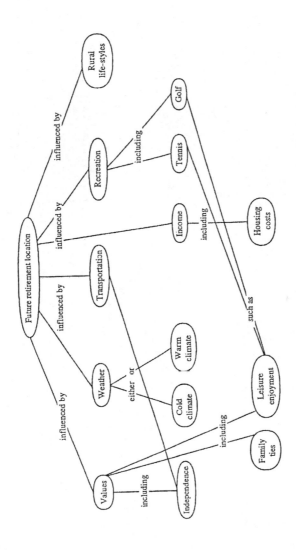

Figure 2: Reconstructed Concept Map on Choice of Retirement Location.

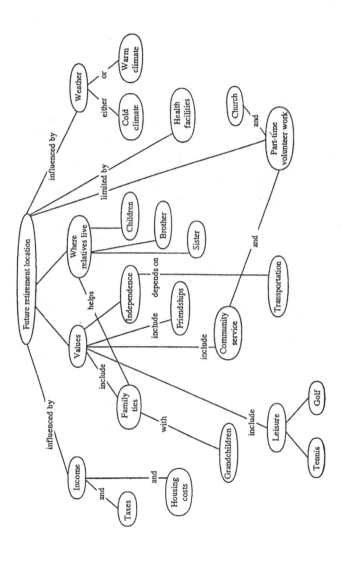

Permission granted by WILEY to reprint: Deschler, D. 1990. Conceptual mapping: drawing charts of the mind. In: *Fostering Critical Reflection in Adulthood: a Guide to Transformative and Emancipatory Learning.* J. Mezirow (Ed.) San Francisco: Jossey-Bass.

References

Atchley, R.C. 2000. *Social forces and aging*; ninth edition, Belmot, CA: Wadsworth.

Barrow, G.M. 1996. *Aging, the individual and society.* New York: West Publishing Company.

Brady, M.E., A. Leighton, R.H. Fortinsky, E. Crocker, and E. Fowler.1996. Preretirement education models and concepts: A New England study. *Educational Gerontology* 22(4), 329-339.

Calasanti, T. 1996. Gender and life satisfaction in retirement: An assessment of the male model. *Journal of Gerontology: Social Sciences* 51B (1): S18-S29.

Deschler, D. 1990. Conceptual mapping: drawing charts of the mind. In: *Fostering critical reflection in adulthood: A guide to transformative and emancipatory learning.* J. Mezirow (Ed.) San Francisco: Jossey-Bass.

Dychtwald, K. 1990. *Age Wave.* New York: Bantam Books.

Fischer, L.R., D.P. Mueller, and P.W. Cooper. 1991. Older volunteers: A discussion of the Minnesota Senior Study. *The Gerontologist* 31(2):183-94.

Gendell, M. and J. Seigel. 1992. Trends in retirement age by sex, 1950-2005. *Monthly Labor Review* 115(7): 22-29.

Langer, N. 1998. Grow old along with me, the best is yet to be!?! *Our Changing Culture* . Lampe, P.E. and R. Barnes (Eds.). San Antonio, Texas: University of the Incarnate Word Press.

McDonough, A. and K.R. Brown. 2000. *A grand entrance: Scenes and monologues for mature actors.* Woodstock, Illinois: Dramatic Publishing.

Moody, H.R. 1988. *The abundance of life: Human development policies for an aging society.* New York: Columbia University Press.

Mutchler, J., J.A. Burr, A.M. Pienta, and M.P. Massagli.1997. Pathways to labor force exit: Work transitions and work instability. *Journal of Gerontology: Social Sciences* 52B (1): S4-S12.

O'Grade-LeShane, R. 1996. Older women workers. In W.H. Crown (Ed.) *Handbook on employment and the elderly.* Westport, CT: Greenwood Press.

Richardson, V.1993. *Retirement counseling: A Handbook for gerontology practitioners.* New York: Springer Publishing.

Rowe, J. and R. Kahn.1998. *Successful aging.* New York: Pantheon Books.

Sabatino, C. 1998. *American Bar Association: Legal Guide for Older Americans.* American Bar Association, New York: Times Books.

Schneider, R.L., N.P. Kropf, and A.J. Kisor. 2000. *Gerontological social work.* Second Edition. United States: Brooks/Cole.

Silverstone B. and K.H. Hyman. 1992. *Growing older together.* New York: Pantheon.

SPRY Foundation and National Committee to Preserve Social Security and Medicare (April 1999). *Redefining retirement: Research directions for America's diverse seniors.* Washington, D.C.: SPRY Foundation and National Committee to Preserve Social Security and Medicare.

Tacchino, K. and N.D. Thomas.1997. Why financial practitioners and geriatric managers must talk to each other. *Generations.* 21(2):41- 45).

Editorial Commentary

ℬℭ

Terry Tirrito

The Baby Boom generation can be defined by its place in history. All were born into the post-World War II society, with its revolution in social values and customs. This cohort is sandwiched between two smaller cohorts. As a result of its enormous size and vast racial and ethnic diversity, it has commanded attention at every stage of its life course. The world inhabited by this cohort can be characterized by greater sexual freedom, increased empowerment of women and minorities, an antiauthoritarianism which extends to all professions, especially health care and social service providers, and which is counterbalanced by the evolution of a strong self-help movement. As in the 1960s when school systems were forced to react to the soaring enrollments of the baby boomers, social institutions that serve the older population will be challenged to reexamine current aging policies and services that will affect the baby boom cohort as they contemplate retirement.

Barbara Silverstone (1996) talks about the cohort effect of self-confidence exhibited by this enormous population for being members of the powerful generations that changed American society in the '60s and '70s. She contends that this cohort will be far more confident about being old—a confidence derived from being part of the largest cohort group in the history of humankind which has enjoyed huge strides in education and technology. This cohort will not tolerate ageism and will, therefore, refuse to be harassed or intimidated. The effect of the feminist revolution coupled with the sheer number of well educated confident women who are socialized to the workplace will greatly influence their lives in retirement. They will feel far freer than today's old to enter nontraditional intimate relationships—an advantage for women where the risk of isolation in late life is greater. Having espoused self-help networks, the Baby Boom women will be far better able to negotiate the perils of old age, and they will not do it alone, but within supportive peer networks.

An older, well educated Baby Boomer, used to practicing preventive health care, will seek more control over his/her physical and mental health, and will not tolerate paternalism. This cohort will be more confident about aging and better prepared to tackle the predictable challenges of late life in a world of potentially diminishing financial, medical, and social service supports. However, there is no reason to expect that the demands on the provision of social services for the elderly will diminish. Sheer numbers alone suggest they will only increase. The high employment rate of women and the lower birth rate of their children will translate into potentially fewer primary care providers. However, even frail elderly clients, educated to be proactive, will take more aggressive charge of their care. Clinical skills will have to accommodate a client who will expect to be a partner with the care provider who has been used to the role of case manager. Clinical assessment and community organization skills will have to be enhanced especially in the area of cultural competence, i.e., the thoughtful application of cultural data to practice. Ethnocultural diversity in value preferences, perceptions of illness, health beliefs, and communication style requires that human service and health care providers are knowledgeable about the older minority population they serve. Such information is critical to determining the likelihood of patients following through with therapy, engaging in self-care activities, and successfully adapting to serious illness. As social service and health care providers we need to be aware of the growing numbers of older people stalked by poverty into a late life which offers few reprieves. Creative solutions, experiental learning, and innovative models of service will stimulate the development of appropriate policy, education and practice, and research endeavors to adequately meet the retirement needs of Baby Boomers.

...And do academics go gently into their retirement years? In *The sun still shone: Professors talk about retirement,* Lorraine Dorfman (1997) explores the difficulties and rewards experienced by academicians as they near retirement. Unlike most occupational groups, they often have the opportunity to continue some aspects of their work duties after retiring; their scholarly pursuits keep them professionally and personally engaged. This status is institutionalized at most institutions of higher learning in the rank of emeritus professor. The book uses direct transcription from more than 400 interviews of American and British professors over a ten year span. This group represents professors who were hired during the 1960s to educate the Baby Boomers who were then entering college. Many of these academicians expect to retire in the next ten tears. She recommends a phased retirement if at all possible because she acknowledges that people do better with transitions.

References

Dorfman, L.T. 1997. *The sun still shone: Professors talk about retirement.* Iowa City: University of Iowa Press.
Silverstone, B. 1996. Older people of tomorrow: A psychosocial profile. *The Gerontologist.* 36 (1); 27-32).

8

SENIOR VOLUNTEERS: STAYING CONNECTED WITH THE COMMUNITY

ℰℭℛℴℭ

Nina Dubler Katz

Introduction

In this chapter we will explore the world of volunteerism and its importance for older people by addressing:

- Why people choose to spend their time at unpaid work.

- Who recruiters encourage/discourage to become volunteers.

- How professional recruiters assist potential volunteers to make appropriate choices.

- Older adults as candidates for volunteerism .

- Responsibilities of the volunteer.

- Available opportunities for volunteering and how prospective volunteers locate them.

- Choosing between volunteer opportunities.

- The principles of adult education theory and how they support the orientation and integration of new volunteers.

Why Do People Choose to Spend Their Time Doing Unpaid Work?

In a society such as ours where pursuit of monetary gain and the accumulation of personal wealth appear to be primary motivators, the existence of a substantial body of voluntary unpaid workers seems to be an anomaly. Yet, in the United States and Canada there are multitudes of thriving volunteer organizations and workers. No compensation? Of course, there is no earned income accrued from volunteer work. However, volunteers widely report a wealth of payback from their activities, benefits, tangible and intangible, that express in concrete terms their personal values and their sense of self-worth. We seek to give students and practitioners insight into the various motivations for and benefits of volunteering. Armed with this understanding, professionals can choose to motivate and prepare clients to pursue volunteer activities.

There is no single profile of the contemporary volunteer. Volunteers are young, old, of all descriptions and backgrounds. Individuals of all ages are active today in a wide range of public and private volunteer positions. In this chapter we will focus on recruiting and working with the older person who is already retired or who is contemplating semi-retirement. This group is the largest growing segment of our population today, and represents a vast potential volunteer workforce which can not only benefit society in myriad ways, but which can also remain an active contributing force within the community for years beyond their formal retirement. The rapid social and demographic changes in Western society are, and will continue to have far-reaching implications for the size and quality of the pool of skilled and semiskilled men and women who reach retirement age.

Today's older population is healthier, better educated, and more affluent than previous cohorts. Professionals can encourage retirees to remain vibrant and productive individuals who can ward off loneliness and boredom through ongoing learning and commitment through volunteerism. A higher level of well-being in retirement will often occur when individuals substitute one role for another. A retired lawyer recently wrote his advice to older adults in an article in the January 5, 2003 *New York Times* Westchester Section entitled "A New Volunteer's Confession". "Recognize that you've acquired wisdom and life experiences worth sharing...put your wisdom and experience to good use...helping nonprofit organizations help others. You'll be at the top of the list of beneficiaries."

The decision to volunteer one's time usually begins with an individual's compassion, empathy for an individual's need or for an organization's mission. The motivation is generally focused on benefitting others. Yet, it has been noted in scientific studies as well as anecdotally, that consistent volunteer activity can have measurable positive effects on the volunteer as well. Dr. Neena Chappell, gerontologist and director of the Centre on Aging at the University of Victoria, Canada, enumerated some of the benefits, both physical and psychological, that volunteers can derive from their altruistic endeavors. New social networks and structure bring opportunities to continue to grow and learn, and seniors have reported increased mental and physical vigor, and positive outlook. Dr. Chappell asserts that by taking on volunteer responsibilities seniors will benefit by being able to:

- meet new people
- gain new experiences
- take on new challenges
- feel good and build self-esteem
- fulfill the need to be needed
- take pride in sharing knowledge and abilities
- keep the mind actively engaged
- keep the body active
- and have fun...increased self-confidence, self-worth and empowerment

Dr. Chappell's research affirms that "volunteers derive health benefits from volunteering," in no small part due to their increased sense of continued self worth. By making meaningful contributions to organizations or to individuals, as formal or informal volunteers, they experience a "...tremendously positive impact on their health and overall sense of well-being." In a limited study, senior volunteers were shown to exhibit:

- improved immune system functioning and nervous system performance
- decreased blood pressure and improved mental alertness
- increased vitality and longevity

  It appears that there are at least two sources of this benefit: the idea
  of belonging to something larger than oneself and the social support
  derived from others who are also involved or from those served. Volunteering, then, is a win/win situation - good for those who receive your
  services and good for you! (Chappell 2001)

Confirmation of these findings is provided by a University of Michigan
research project (Woolston 1994) which found a link between volunteer
work and longevity. The researchers surveyed 1,211 adults over 65 (mostly
retirees) in 1986 and reassessed their activities again in 1994. The subjects
who continued to volunteer at least 40 hours each year to a single cause
were 40 percent more likely than non-volunteers to be alive at the end of
the study. These findings are supported by studies by the American
Administration on Aging (AOA) (1999) which confirm that older people
who participate in productive activities and consider themselves contributing members of society live longer and healthier lives. Furthermore, these
studies concluded that..."there are 14,000,000 seniors who would be
willing to volunteer their time if asked, and 4,000,000 current volunteers
would be willing to give more of their time (AOA 1999)."

Seniors, surveys have found, "want to be productive, intellectually
stimulated, to have something significant to do, and to stay physically
active...they believe volunteering will produce a better, happier fuller life"
(Kleyman 2003). "The studies attest to the accuracy of this assessment,
finding that "people who volunteer are more optimistic...feel more
productive...feel more empowered to improve the lives of others in their
communities...and they're likelier to feel healthier and more involved"
(Kleyman 2003).

Recruiting and Encouraging Senior Volunteers

We thus have confirmation that being a volunteer is good not only for
the community but also for the individual volunteer. This is true for
volunteers of all ages, but especially for older adults who have retired or
who are contemplating retirement. Today's seniors can look forward to
longer and healthier life expectancy than previous generations. Conse-

quently, as they move from full time employment to retirement, they have potentially more productive time to fill. Professionals who work with seniors can focus their clients' attention on the creative and dynamic opportunities available to them if they become volunteers. Many may never have considered volunteerism as an outlet for their time, energy, and talents. They may be unaware of the variety of available possibilities for volunteering and how they themselves might benefit as well as contribute. Professionals, therefore, need to be concerned with opening this avenue to their clients and helping them identify volunteer activities which will be meaningful to them.

Ice-Breaker and Energizer Activity

The Human Flow Chart is an introductory interactive strategy that explores the process of a new retiree's decision to become a volunteer.

1. Prepare a set of ten cards, each containing one of the statements:
   a. I've heard that my neighbor works as a volunteer and enjoys it.
   b. I've signed up for a volunteer position.
   c. I don't feel useful anymore.
   d. I feel useful and connected to other people again.
   e. I have no special talent. What could I possibly do as a volunteer?
   f. I'm so bored.
   g. Finally, I don't have to go to work anymore.
   h. I'm going to a volunteer recruiting program today.
   i. I can't wait to retire and sit back and relax.
   j. How much time could I give to volunteering? One day a week? One week a month? Weekends?

2. Select ten participants to come to the front of the room. Each one receives a card with one of the statements. Distribute the cards randomly. (The correct sequence for the ten statements can be found at the end of the Chapter).

3. The task is for the participants to line themselves up, from left to right at the front of the room, in the sequential order they think the statements, inquiries, and decisions would have been made by a potential volunteer. The participants need to circulate among themselves and decide which of them represents the first, second, etc., state-

ment/inquiry/decision in the process. They will thus become a Human Flow-Chart. When the order is agreed upon, participants take turns, from left to right, stating the rationale for their position in the decision-making process. The facilitator should encourage discussion among participants and elicit responses from the non-participant observers.

Who Should Volunteer?

Despite the potential benefits, not all retirees are appropriate candidates for volunteer positions. And, some may be suitable in certain situations but not in others. Before suggesting the possibility of a volunteer position to an individual, the practitioner needs to view the individual through a volunteer administrator's lens. For example, does he/she have the skills necessary for the assignment? Will he/she be willing and/or able to maintain a required schedule of attendance? The objective is to create the "best fit" between the volunteer and the organization or mission. Although recruiters do not want to deny a willing and able candidate the opportunity to volunteer, it is possible to minimize embarrassment and hurt feelings if an individual's suitability is taken into account in advance of approaching an organization.

Volunteering "Professionally"

It may seem a contradiction in terms to speak of a volunteer in terms of professionalism. However, a potential volunteer needs to understand that the commitment to a volunteer job is indeed a professional and serious commitment and that it deserves to be fulfilled in the best, most professional manner possible. A large measure of success for both the volunteer and the recipient individual or organization will often be the result of the attitude that the volunteer brings to the fulfillment of an assignment. An individual who considers a volunteer position to be a time filler of no intrinsic value will treat the experience as a worthless chore that is only minimally worthy of respect. The volunteer would consequently see him/herself in a similarly negative light and positive outcomes become more unlikely. However, when an individual assumes a professional attitude, no matter how menial the task might seem, there is enhanced likelihood for constructive personal/organizational effects. Stuffing envelopes is a simple chore that can be understood as a key to important fundraising and outreach organizational efforts. It can also become an important social outlet for the volunteer and an introduction into an organization that may provide more stimulating activities over time.

It is crucial that the potential volunteer understand and accept that the duties of a volunteer position are in fact responsibilities. Schedules need to be met and appointments kept. Standards need to be supported and maintained and assignments appropriately completed. It is important from the outset that the volunteer assume only as much responsibility as he/she can realistically fulfill after considering personal schedules and preferences. The possibility of a volunteer commitment should be discussed with family and partners. Will one's social network be supportive or resent time spent away from home? Could they, too, be encouraged to commit to a volunteer position? Will established plans be interrupted? For example, a "snowbird" with seasonal commitments should not apply for an assignment with year-round responsibilities. A seasonal option to volunteer is probably a more responsible choice. A potential volunteer still grieving a recent personal loss i.e., a loved one's death from cancer, may still be too emotionally vulnerable to volunteer in a hospital with patients and families. However, he/she may be able, instead, to pursue meaningful volunteer work by doing fund raising for research to combat the disease.

Role Play

This exercise demonstrates the importance of appropriate placement of potential volunteers. It provides the adult learner with the opportunity to role play a would-be volunteer who is motivated for personal gain, or not prepared to volunteer responsibly.

Roles

The volunteer recruiter at an adult day care center is interviewing prospective volunteers. He/she is focusing on the mission of the organization, the center's stated programs, and the needs of its professional staff such as social workers and nurses for assistance in: (1) transportation of clients/patients to on-site doctors' offices; (2) overseeing recreational activities such as bingo.

Prospective Volunteers: (1) a semi-retired business person who has the idea that the day care population or their families could represent a new outlet for a particular product or service that he is promoting; (2.) an executive who has just retired and is unfamiliar with volunteer work; (3.) students create their own "uninformed" potential volunteers who interact with the recruiter. Prospective volunteers are interviewed by the recruiter and they, as well as non-participant observers, are encouraged to respond to the role play.

Group Activity and Discussion: The outcome will be a wide variety of potential personal/organizational benefits derived from the volunteer experience.

1. Prepare a set of cards, each of which contains the job description of a volunteer position.

2. Distribute a card to each individual or small group.

3. Each participant or group is responsible for compiling two lists of potential benefits, one for the individual and one for the organization. The benefits for the individual can be tangible or intangible- e.g. status, a uniform/badge, a sense of belonging, feelings of usefulness, (free) lunch, personal recognition, organized lifestyle, etc. What concrete/subtle benefits accrue to the organization?

4. As each group reports their list of benefits, the facilitator records them on the chalk board, noting duplications.

5. Follow with discussion: Any surprises? Which benefits were repeated most often? How might a selected benefit appeal to a particular senior (e.g., fulfilling need for companionship or recognition?) Are there any negative effects of volunteering?

Helping Seniors Make Appropriate Choices

Once the recruiter has determined that a client would be a suitable volunteer, it is important to consider how to maximize the potential for this volunteer's efforts and job satisfaction. The recruiter needs to adhere to the same basic guidelines that all job seekers are given: consider the fit of job and jobseeker by matching the values/abilities/preferences of a worker to those of the job and of the organization. The greater the congruence, the greater is the potential for a successful match. Choosing where to expend one's volunteer time and energy can be as easy as responding to a friend's invitation to join a local group, setting a schedule for reading to a sight-impaired neighbor, or driving a friend to medical appointments. The decision to volunteer and then making the determination of how and where often involves a considerable amount of thought and research in order to arrive at a decision which can yield the most successful and positive result. Choosing a volunteer venue and activity is in a very real sense a career choice. As such, it requires the same forethought and planning that all career choices demand. The professional can assist the client in making thoughtful choices by following the standard guidelines followed by career counselors who guide job seekers to locate the most promising opportunities.

Just as in salaried work, it is important to seek congruence in job placement, good employer/employee "fit." To that end, the employee, in our case, the potential volunteer, needs to identify personal interests and abilities. This individual also needs to acknowledge personal limitations and priorities. Good volunteer job "fit" requires the volunteer's knowledge of self as well as of the targeted organization, its mission, and the opportunities it presents. Self-assessment either informal or formal, guided by the professional, can help ensure as positive an outcome as possible. To make this a less stressful experience, the professional should be sure to emphasize that these assessments, whether formal or informal, written or oral, are not tests! Responses are solicited in order to form an accurate volunteer profile of the individual. Providing candid responses enhances the "matching" process. Areas to be explored should include:

- What are the individual's personality preferences? Is the client a leader, an educator, a planner, a technical whiz, an organizer, a motivator, a line man?

- What skills and abilities does the client wish to use: talent in art, reading, writing, patience for care taking, medical knowledge and skills, communication skills (appropriate in teaching, public speaking, fund raising, etc.)?

- What are the time considerations and required availability: is the client available for full days, several hours weekly, consistently year-round, seasonally, on-call, etc.?

- Is reliable transportation readily available? Is handicap-accessibility an issue?

- Does the volunteer need to appear in person or can he/she operate a telephone hotline or volunteer from home online as a cyber-volunteer?

- Which environment appeals most: indoors, outdoors, school, healthcare/social service, office?

- What working relationships exist at a site? Is there a preference for working by oneself or in a group, need for a leadership or supportive role, working with familiar people or meeting the public?

Individuals need to assess the requirements of the potential position:

- What skills are required? Is there on-the-job training?
- What are the physical and emotional demands of the job?
- What kind of commitment of time is there? How many hours/days?
- How much supervision will there be?

Neither the individual nor the organization should assume that the prospective volunteer will want to stay within the bounds of previous work experiences. Volunteering can be a perfect opportunity for individuals of all ages to explore and develop new skills and become familiar with new settings. In interviewing clients, recruiters need to encourage volunteers to be open to the possibilities of continuing in established modes of work, as well as to, perhaps, actualizing undeveloped or underdeveloped career goals. Professionals can guide their clients by using the conventional job-search literature such as the popular series, *What color is your parachute? (Bolles 2003)*.

Charting Activity

Charting Activity demonstrates the preferences that a potential volunteer should consider in advance of applying or even contemplating a volunteer job. Participants draw up a chart and fill the boxes either with numbers to denote importance, or with words to describe preferences. Blank rows should be included in order to accommodate the specific needs of a client.

Requirements	WANT: Very Important	WANT: Important	Not Important	DO NOT WANT: Important	DO NOT WANT: Very Important
time availability day/night/ seasonal/ single event					
indoor /outdoor					
kind of work					
kind of venue or organization					
transportation availability					
work with friends					
administrative					
routine work					
identification badge or uniform					
group activities					
leadership role					
supportive role					
physical or manual dexterity					

Workshop Experience

Workshop Experience develops a practical understanding of how individual profiles can help determine appropriate volunteer placement.

Part I:

1. Each participant describes a hypothetical potential older adult volunteer by listing at least 10 character traits. Alternately, the facilitator can choose to list a fixed set of traits for all participants to consider. These can include: gender, approximate age, physical attributes/abilities and/or impediments if any, marital status and/or living situation, personality: e.g., optimistic/pessimistic, cheerful/grouchy, introverted/ extroverted, quiet/loud, sensitive, clumsy, thoughtful, gruff, etc., previous occupation(s), special talents, interests, and/or abilities, level of education/intellectual ability, losses/honors, pertinent information relevant to a person's life: recent relocation, recent widow/widower, lives with children and has childcare responsibilities, etc.

2. Participants exchange cards and consider the hypothetical individual described on that card. Participants should address the following questions: Is volunteer placement a viable option for this person? What kind of placement would impose an improper fit?

3. Each participant introduces his "client" to the group and presents a set of recommendations and the rationale for a suitable volunteer placement for that individual.

4. The group discusses these findings and related questions such as: Does the use of walkers or canes disqualify a would-be volunteer? What post, if any, can a partially sighted or hearing impaired volunteer fill?"

Job Research

Volunteer Job Research on the World Wide Web develops and enhances skills for internet searches and exploration in pursuit of a volunteer position.
1. Retaining these hypothetical individual profiles, continue this volunteer placement activity by searching the Web. Consult the list of Web sites

at the end of this chapter and choose one or two which you think might apply to your hypothetical client. Search the sites and report both your positive and negative findings.

2.   The Web is constantly expanding. Search out sites and search engines that are not listed here. Report and share with the group.

Finding the Possibilities

Applying for a volunteer position in an organization which has volunteer opportunities can seem daunting to a potential volunteer, especially the individual who has been feeling disconnected from the community. The professional can be instrumental in helping individuals find this information and in preparing them to apply for volunteer status. Older adults should be encouraged to network with friends, local professionals, and clergy who can provide information about opportunities that are close by and perhaps in organizations where the individual is already affiliated. Such accessible resources as the listing for "Social Services Organizations" in the Yellow Pages, stories and ads in local newspapers, and websites on the Internet contain listings and postings by volunteer organizations. Agencies such as United Way act as clearinghouses for volunteer opportunities and have listings of organizational needs and job descriptions. (See Resource List of internet sites below). A multitude of opportunities to get involved exist. Many organizations have volunteer programs which are in need of all levels of volunteer assistance, from secretarial support to strategic planning.

Finding a fulfilling volunteer position often requires an interview. The amount of preparation and advice by a recruiter will be dependent upon the potential volunteer's lifetime work experience and time away from the workforce. For some, the volunteer opportunity may be a continuation of previous work. A retired teacher may wish to teach. A retired businessman may enjoy volunteering with a group of similarly experienced people who mentor inexperienced entrepreneurs. This can also be the perfect time for individuals to develop new skills and express unexplored interests. The teacher might enjoy working in the hospital thrift shop and the businessman might find great satisfaction holding an infant in a neo-natal unit.

Considering the Possibilities

What follows is a compilation of a wide variety of volunteer positions based, but not limited to positions that are currently being filled and publicized on Voluntary Action Center U.S. Department of Labor websites (www.volunteertoledo.org/volunteer.cfm;www.metrounitedway.org/Volun teer; Opportunities.cfm;www.metrounit edway,.org/Volunteer/Volunteer Connection.cfm; http://verity.doleta.gov)

Time commitments include: year-round: daily, weekly, weekends; on-call; pre-holiday and holiday times. Volunteer sites might include:

Health care:

- hospitals and nursing homes providing friendly visiting, patient advocacy, conducting religious services or recreational games, gift shop clerking
- daycare center providing aide support for children and adults
- soup kitchen activities involving cooking, serving, hosting
- Meals-on-Wheels providing cooking, delivery, organizational services
- assisting agencies devoted to mental health, or helping the blind or deaf

Political Activism:

- working for social change
- voter registration, campaigning
- manning polls
- Medicare Fraud Patrol, The National Hispanic Council On Aging

Educational Venues (Schools and Libraries):

- nursery and elementary teaching aides
- literacy programs training adults
- tutoring and mentoring children and adolescents
- storytelling and reading

Informal settings:

- respite care and support services to a caregiver of a handicapped or frail care recipient

The arts (theater, museum, symphony):

- fund-raising
- ticket selling, mailings, ushering, tour guiding
- docent presentations

Animal care:

- local shelter or zoo support

Environment and Parks:

- tourist guide
- park/beach maintenance
- promotion of environmental issues

Visualization and Storytelling

Visualization and Storytelling are creative activities which can assist potential volunteers explore options. Older adults who are resistant or ambivalent about entering the realm of volunteerism can investigate and explore the possibilities safely in this way. They can be encouraged to view possibilities and favorable outcomes by linking the possibilities of the future with past successes and reawakening old aspirations. Someone who could not pursue a medical career because of previous economic constraints might see volunteering as a friendly visitor in a nursing home or hospital as a way of fulfilling that goal. Someone who would have liked a career on the stage might enjoy volunteering in a local dramatic club or after school program. An individual who once dreamed of a large extended family but is now alone might seek out an intergenerational program.

1. **Storytelling:** Encouraging seniors to speak about their careers, life experiences, and past/current successes, provides a positive asset search which could suggest continued areas of interest that they might still be able to pursue. Confirming their successes and validating their talents and interests may open them to the possibilities of achieving fulfillment as volunteers in related activities.

2. **Visualizing**: Set the mood with lowered lights and chairs drawn in a circle. Invite the group to close their eyes and see themselves in a situation where they were successful. What was it that made them happy or proud? Alternately, have them recall early career aspirations. Were these hopes fulfilled?

How Do the Principles of Adult Educational Theory Help Orient and Integrate New Volunteers into this Role?

The workshop-type experiential exercises included in this chapter are formulated according to the principles of contemporary adult educational theory. They are designed to be interactive and interesting, promoting learning through doing. They are also practical rather than theoretical, and are meant to be used as presented or adapted creatively to the specific needs and interests of a group. They are models to be exploited freely but always positively, emphasizing participants' skills and ideas, not their deficits or errors.

We have modeled:

- role play
- small buzz group discussion and reporting
- large group discussion
- human flow-chart
- visualization and storytelling
- charting
- workshop activity

Some additional effective instructional models not included in the chapter are:
- brainstorming... an open forum for a flow of spontaneous ideas which are initially unhampered by prejudgment, and only later analyzed and evaluated

- case study... a group analysis of hypothetical or actual situations and their resolution

- field trip... a planned and focused visit to the proposed volunteer environment with attention given to observation and analysis

- neighbor discussions... brief, timed discussions, as pairs deal with a specific question or problem and then report back to the group

- peer-assisted learning... advanced learners train others in specific skills

(Langevin Learning Services: *Train –The-Trainer*, www.langevin.com/success)

Program Assessment

Adult learners need to be engaged by a creative presentation format that utilizes a variety of presentation techniques. They also need to understand the importance of what they are learning as it relates to the end goal of their learning. To monitor and ensure the ongoing progress of a program for adult participants, it is crucial to solicit feedback on a regular basis, and to remain flexible enough to react to constructive suggestions. Formal or informal assessments are useful. Questions about course content, structure and validity should be asked. Whether in individual conversations or by written checklists, an ongoing evaluation process will support what is going well and will help identify what improvements, if any, need to be made. It will also assure the adult learners that their needs and concerns are being addressed and that their views and suggestions are contemplated for future inclusion in the course/seminar, etc. In this way, the educator acts as a significant role model, demonstrating that self-evaluation and reflection are important professional attributes to be emulated.

Summary

Volunteers perform vital services in a great variety of community settings. Their activities enrich their own lives in as great a measure as they benefit the lives of the recipients of their actions. If professionals and educators who work with older adults recognize this bilateral benefit, they can begin to improve their clients' outlook through the introduction of worthwhile activity and the regular social contact of volunteer work. For older adults, in particular, volunteer experiences can provide important opportunities for developing new skills, meeting new people, and generally feeling productive and connected to the community at large. Volunteering is not for every senior. Nor is every volunteer position appropriate for every willing senior. How can we ensure or at least maximize the potential for volunteer job satisfaction? A successful volunteer experience depends in large part on the proper fit of person and assignment. Attention must be given to the needs of the recipient organization as well as to the availability, skills, and preferences of the volunteer. A thoughtful match can yield multiple benefits and provide a meaningful way in which a senior can connect and reconnect with the community. "Volunteering is a people-to-people business, being in touch with others and having an impact on their lives." (Chappell, N. Laurushealth.com/healthtopics/july01).

Answer to Ice-Breaker quiz: i, g, f, c, a, e, j, h, b, d

References

Bolles, R.N. 2003. *What color is your parachute?* Berkeley, California: Ten Speed Press.

Chappell, N. 2001 August. Volunteering and Healthy Aging: What We Know [online]. *Stride Magazine,* Available from the World Wide Web: www.stridemagazine.com/2001_Aug.

Chappell, N. 2001. Laurushealth.com/healthtopics/july01.

Kleyman, P. 2003 January. Study Shows How Older-Volunteer Force in U.S. Could Double [online]. *Aging Today*. Available from the World Wide Web: http: www.asaging.org.

U.S. Administration on Aging (1999) [online] Available from the World Wide Web: LaurusHealth.com/Healthy Living.'

Woolston, C. 1994. *Seniors and Volunteering: A Whole New Life* [online]. BluePrint for Health. Available from the World Wide Web: www. blueprint.bluecrossmn.com.

Resources

Most volunteers learn about opportunities to offer their services through friends, having an existing contact with an organization or by responding to advertisements and publicity. As older volunteers become more computer literate, they may scan the Internet for web sites that will help them get started in their search.

Volunteer Match—www.volunteermatch.org connects volunteers with more than 22,000 nonprofit and public sector organizations.

Idealist.Org—www.idealist.org connects volunteers with more than 30,000 nonprofit and community organizations in over 150 countries.

City Cares—www.citycares.org provides links to affiliates in over 30 cities for local volunteer opportunities for community service projects and events.

Interaction—www.interaction.org is a coalition of over 160 U.S.-based development and humanitarian nongovernmental organizations.

Service Leader—www.serviceleader.org is a comprehensive site with everything you need to know about volunteering.

Action Without Borders http:// www.idealist.org

Advice for Volunteers http://www.serviceleader.org/advice/

American Association of Retired Persons http://AARP.org

American Society on Aging http://www.asaging.com

Association for Research on Nonprofit Organizations and Volunteer Associations (ARNOVA) http://www.arnov.org

Association for Volunteer Administration (AVA) http:www.avaintl.org Associations with Volunteerism Resources http://www.volunteertoledo.org/volunteer

BluePrint for Health, from BlueCross http://www.blueprint.bluecross mn.com

Career Information via AOL and Monster Board http://aolsvc.careerfinder.aol.com/career_guide

CON-NECT to Volunteer http://www.metrounitedway.org/Volunteer/Opportunities.cfm

Corporation for National Service, AmeriCorps/Vista, Learn and Serve America, and National Senior Service Corps http://cns.gov/news/factsheets/faithbased.html

ERIC: Clearinghouse on Adult, Career, and Vocational Education http:ericacve.org

FCS International Long Term Care Specialists http://www.stridemagazine.com/2001Aug

Independent Sector Volunteering http://www.independentsector.org.prog

Internet NonProfit Center http://www.nonprofits.org/

Points of Light Foundation: is a non-partisan, non-profit foundation to promote volunteerism, formerly National Volunteer Center. http://www.pointsoflightfoundation.org

Promoting community involvement http://www.impactonline.org

RSVP Retired and Senior Volunteer Program of community service volunteers http://www.rsvp.org

SCORE, volunteer retired executives http://www.score.org

Senior Care Web http:/www2./seniorcareweb.com
Senior Corps is a national organization that connects seniors with local organizations http://www.fostergrandparents.org

National Hispanic Council on Aging www.nhcoa.org/smfp.htm

United Way, citizens/organization for volunteerism http://www.unitedway cg.com

U.S. Administration on Aging http://www.aol.gov

U.S. Department of Labor http: //wdsc.doleta.gov/seniors

VHA's health and volunteer information http://www.LaurusHealth.com

Volunteers of America http://www.voa.org

Volunteer Canada http://www.volunteer.ca

Volunteerism information from Senator Rick Santorum

http://www.santorum.senate.gov.Issues/Sen

Workshops for professional trainers, Ogdensburg, Nyhttp://www.lange vin.com

Editorial Commentary

℘℃ℛ

Nieli Langer & Terry Tirrito

Aging, in and of itself has no predictable effect on overall participation in volunteer activities. It is the changes and losses such as poor health, inadequate income, and problems with transportation that occur during participation that may affect continuation of these activities. However, the possibilities for volunteering on the part of older people are endless. Society is waking up to the enormous potential of older people and organizations are concerned with increasing and enhancing opportunities for third age volunteers with the time, interest, and ability to volunteer their services. Matching the talents of a better educated and healthier cohort to unmet and/or under met needs is the key. In 1840, Alexis de Tocqueville observed the pervasiveness of volunteer activities in the United States which remains a country of volunteers. Between the government and the private sector, there is a large third sector of unpaid individuals working with and for others. Volunteering is an organized way of being a good neighbor.

Atkinson and Birch (1978) have explained that the need for achievement and affiliation are motives that affect behavior. Achievement motives will influence our pride in accomplishment and a pursuit of excellence. An affiliation motive affects our concern to be part of something bigger than ourselves. Achievement and affiliation are significant determinants of performance in work as well as in volunteering. The interpersonal rewards such as creating meaningful relationships and the satisfaction resulting from feeling that one is achieving a valuable goal are the principal incentives for volunteerism (Maehr and Braskamp 1986).

The use of the able aged as volunteers with their frail, less advantaged peers is an area that has been explored as providing enhanced role and task satisfaction as well as worthwhile service. Writing on retirement roles, Garms-Homolva (1988) proposed that socio-gerontological research is an area in which the special experiences and qualities of older people are required. The author has found that volunteers gain insight into the research process and into the way scientific knowledge is produced while they are involved in the learning process. Gerontology as a discipline seeks measures that will improve the living conditions of older people. It is logical to assume that those who are the intended beneficiaries of such research should be involved in its design and implementation. In Israel, Bar Ilan University has offered a program in applied gerontology that was designed for retirement-age students (average age of 70). These students conducted interviews of their octogenarian and nonagenarian classmates on issues related to life-styles, adjustment patterns, living arrangements, intergenerational relations, perceptions of independence, sexual functioning, and life long learning as reported by *Hadashot Daily Newspaper* in March of 1992. In another study, applied-gerontology students interviewed over 450 middle-aged family caregivers with respect to the incidence of elder abuse within their family. These are examples of the active involvement of older learners in applied research projects targeting pressing social issues involving their peers (Prager 1995). The Israel National Insurance Law several years ago provided for partial to full payment for both in-home and day-care services for the frailest aged residing in the community. The law required a massive effort to identify the thousands of aged who might qualify for the law's cash provisions to defray the costs of services, as well as the identification of those who did not qualify but whose physical/mental well-being might be of concern to professional care providers. A pilot demonstration was designed to determine whether able aged volunteers could identify aged persons at risk as well as establish the credibility and efficiency of these volunteers as field interviewers. The average age of the volunteers was 73; most of the volunteers had completed high school but none of them had previously been employed in healthcare or social services or had previous training in research design. The interviewers were introduced to the conceptual framework of the research and were provided hands-on interviewing experiences. This group of 11 volunteers evolved into a focus group, identifying possible trouble spots in wording, timing, and explanatory introductions so that the survey respondents would be able to comprehend what was being asked of them. So that basic performance information could be obtained on the volunteers, graduate social work students were trained concurrently in the interviewing skills. Reliability over time within each group of interviewers was similarly high and significant for both groups. The older interviewers proved themselves to be no less capable than the younger graduate students of accurately reporting on respondents' situations. The older interviewers proved to be more effective than student interviewers in reporting substantive and research design issues. The work of the older volunteers also provided more extensive and multidimensional portraits of the respondents. The success of this project paved the way for additional older volunteer research projects by the National Insurance Institute because the pilot project illuminated the experience, tact, and competence of older volunteers to successfully carry out their assignments (Prager 1995).

When social service and healthcare agencies expand services to the growing number of aged consumers, they would do well to enlist the untapped potential of older volunteers waiting to be engaged in direct service roles or research-related activities for their peers. Professionals would be getting an invaluable human resource while providing opportunities for "generative participation" (Prager 1995). Researchers have found that this sense of purpose, or generativity, is an important developmental need well into later life. Older adults should be given opportunities to make a significant contribution to society, help to attain a valued goal, or gain the feeling that they are contributing to some purpose. Satisfying motives and rewarding older adults with meaningful incentives will be critical in recruiting and retaining older adult volunteers.

References

Atkinson, K.W. and D. Birch. 1978. *Introduction to motivation.* New York: D. Van Nostrand.

Garms-Homolva, V. 1988. Retirement roles: volunteers in gerontological research. In S. Bergman, G. Nagels, and W. Tokarski, eds., *Early retirement approaches and variations—an international perspective,* 137-149. Jerusalem: JDC-Brookdale.

Maehr, M and L. Braskamp.1986. *The motivation factor.* Lexington,
     Massachusetts: Lexington Books.
Prager, E. 1995. The older volunteer as research colleague: Toward
     "generative participation" for older adults. *Educational Gerontology,*
     21: 209-218.

9

ELDER ABUSE: POLICY & TRAINING OF LAW ENFORCEMENT PERSONNEL

ഇൻരു

Nieli Langer & Tan Kirby-Davis

History and Definitions

Most authorities agree that the concept of elder abuse has a long history. Shakespeare addressed it through "King Lear" around 1600; Jonathon Swift described it in "Gulliver's Travels" in 1726. The first reference in the medical literature is attributed to Burston in 1975 in a letter to the editor of the *British Medical Journal* (Burston 1975). Elder abuse encompasses a diverse and unsavory backdrop to human degradation: confidence schemes, physical battery, deplorable living conditions, abandonment, neglect, sexual assault, and unreasonable confinement. Elder abuse in domestic settings is a serious problem, affecting hundreds of thousands of elderly people across the country. The problem is largely hidden under the shroud of family secrecy. Since the signs of elder abuse are not uniformly recognized, it has led to gross under-reporting of the problem. About two decades ago, it was described as a "hidden family problem"; it has since emerged as an important area of policy development, research, and training not only for adult protective services but also for law enforcement personnel. The research, along with reporting laws, has helped create social awareness of the problems faced by abused and neglected older adults. This awareness has been very valuable in documenting unacceptable events and circumstances in the lives of victims.

Elder abuse was initially focused on family violence, including physical, sexual, psychological abuse, and caregiver neglect of an older adult by others. There is some belief that elder abuse should be viewed more from the perspective of power and control and thus treated as a criminal matter whereas neglect may need to be viewed as a crisis in caregiving and therefore a health and social issue. The two phenomena are distinctly different. Abuse implies assault and battery, while neglect implies withholding of services. The roots of elder mistreatment are the ability of the perpetrator to misuse power and control over the victim. He/she may use coercion and threats, promising to hurt or abandon them, threatening to move them into a nursing home, and not allowing them to see their grandchildren. They may use intimidation by making victims afraid by action, gestures, or looks, i.e., raising arms as if to strike them or abusing pets. By intimating that the victim is crazy and/or humiliating them, making them feel guilty because of real or imagined actions, saying they have caused the abusive behavior or denying the existence of the abuse, the perpetrators are engaging in emotional abuse. Disregarding the care recipient's thoughts or rights and overriding their decisions are additional forms of coercion and emotional abuse. Enforcing isolation of the older adult may include: hiding personal mail, preventing access to family and friends or limiting the use of the telephone, hiding a walker or cane, and exaggerating physical/mental limitations. Neglect on the part of the caregiver may take the form of withholding medication, inadequate provision of food, ignoring physical needs, and not allowing medical/ social services to become involved in the victim's care (Wisconsin Coalition Against Domestic Violence [WCADV] 1998).

The definition of elder abuse was broadened to include financial elder abuse, sometimes referred to as "victimization." Financial abuse by a family member may have the following characteristics: preventing the older adult from getting or keeping money, forcing the victim to ask for money, giving them an allowance, or actually taking all sources of income. Financial abuse refers to exploitation by family and close associates as well as larger well-organized efforts such as telemarketing fraud, home repair scams, and investment schemes (WCADV 1998).

Findings from a National Survey of States conducted by the National Association of Adult Protective Services Administrators (NAAPSA) on behalf of the National Center on Elder Abuse (Otto 2002) indicated that twenty-nine states had received almost 50,000 reports of financial exploitation—an increase of more than 61% since 1994. Financial abuse of the elderly covers an expansive array of issues. These include misuse of durable powers of attorney and bank accounts and the misuse or neglect of authority by a guardian or conservator. It also includes failure to transfer funds or real estate; excessive charges for goods and services for which one is paid; using fraud or undue influence to gain control of money or property. Some swindles have cheated people out of their property and taken thousands of dollars in sham investments by slick talkers who make friends with victims over the phone. Many of the victims have been widows, lonely and inexperienced in handling the family finances. Older people fall prey to swindlers offering moneymaking offers because they fear inflation will erode their savings or they want to leave a nest egg for their children. These schemes are so pervasive that some lawyers now specialize in what is called elder financial abuse, and work to regain stolen real estate or undo fraudulent loans. All these devices, including home-improvement deals where the work never gets done and the bills grow higher; itinerant workers "passing through" who offer to mend the roof; and, expensive home-equity loans are examples of financial chicanery. Predatory lending, telemarketing schemes, and sweepstakes fraud are all included under the rubric of financial abuse.

Focusing on organizational forms of abuse, AARP examined telemarketing and charity fraud in 1996. They found skilled and well trained perpetrators defrauding victims who had difficulty recognizing the deceptive practices. In many instances of financial abuse, loneliness and a desire to be engaged in any "exciting" transaction or experience have made older persons victims. Another victim of financial abuse is one who suffers some level of mild mental impairment which makes them easy marks due to their inability to make sound judgments (Gross 1999). However, in evaluating the results of their investigation, AARP realized that it was mostly educated, middle-aged and older Americans who were being duped. Most of those surveyed weren't socially isolated but were educated, held jobs, went to church and had family and friends. They were aware of the dangers of fraud but as described by an older middle class victim in an article in the *New York Times* in March of 2003 ..." it was hard to spot when it was happening to me." AARP concluded that simple awareness of the problem of fraud was not enough. The organization changed its theme to emphasize that fraudulent telemarketers are criminals and that what was happening to victims was not their foolishness or cause for embarrassment but a crime. AARP continuously disseminates material on the internet, i.e. www.aarp.org/confacts/heealth/avoidabuse.html to educate consumers.

Adult Protective Services (APS) is the principal public source of response to reports and cases of vulnerable adult abuse, neglect, and exploitation. States and local communities have empowered APS to investigate reports of abuse, neglect, and financial exploitation of the elderly. Whereas in the past APS intervention has focused primarily on cases of self-neglect, APS has been instrumental in discovering cases of financial exploitation and bringing it to the attention of law enforcement agencies. It is often the APS worker who is the first to suspect financial exploitation. Given this suspicion, it is the APS case worker who gathers and makes sense of countless documents (unpaid bills, check stubs, financial statements, property deeds, powers of attorney, etc.) as well as eliciting evidence from reluctant sources. The victim is often confused or ill; the suspected perpetrator is anxious to hide or destroy evidence; financial institutions may not always cooperate in providing financial records; law enforcement officers are indisposed to assume financial investigations on the behalf of victims who are often unwilling and/or unable to cooperate; and, the courts are often reluctant to intervene in these cases since the victims, who may be poor witnesses, may not be able to provide the reliable evidence that will lead to prosecution.

Another major category of elder abuse is self-neglect. It is the most common form of abuse; the goal is to protect the older adult from himself. Quinn and Tomita (1998) have defined it as the inability of an adult to perform essential self-care activities including provision of food, shelter, administration of medications, and general safety. It is characterized by filthy living conditions and lack of insight that there is a problem. Although many researchers have insisted that self-neglect is not a form of abuse, "adult protective services practitioners know that self-neglecting adults make up the majority of their caseloads" (The Public Policy and Aging Report 2002). APS professionals have argued with researchers that failure to categorize self neglect as a form of elder abuse further reduces attention and limited resources for service delivery to these older adults.

Often the categories that constitute elder abuse have been ambiguous and evolving as, too, have been the definitions and means to measure within categories. Cross cultural variation as to what constitutes abuse also exacerbates the issues. Studies have found that some cultural groups are more tolerant of certain forms of abuse than others. This finding suggests that in ethnic minority communities, strategies that address both general components of elder abuse and culture-specific prevention and treatment will probably prove more effective to the victim (Moon 2000). In addition, rather than concentrating solely on ethnicity, researchers should consider acculturation level when assessing reasons for elder abuse. Acculturation would include place of birth, age at immigration to the United States, number of years of U.S. residency, English proficiency, and awareness of health care and social service delivery systems. Failure to address income, educational level, socioeconomic factors, living arrangements, and social network may mislead researchers and practitioners who may assess minority clients solely through a culturally "appropriate" prism (Moon 2000).

There has, to date, been no national policy developed on elder abuse. It has been the states that have individually determined standards for definition of terms and categories, identification of abuse situations, and training to protect the victims. Therefore, what constitutes elder abuse in one state my not be considered abuse in another (Wolf 2000).

Who are the Victims?

Authors of a comprehensive longitudinal study have suggested that gender per see is not a risk factor but that functional and/or cognitive impairment may be more indicative of vulnerability to abuse (Lachs et al. 1997). Wilber and McNeilly (2001) have suggested that frail older women have a greater likelihood of suffering the most serious forms of abuse and are more likely to come to the attention of adult protective services. In a study by Comijs et al. (1998), the authors found that the majority of abused adults were able to manage the problem themselves. This finding may suggest the possibility of creating enhanced services whereby the victim can receive needed outside intervention.

Wilber and McNeilly (2001) have suggested that the extent of the abuse, depending on what categories of abuse are included, is approximately 1 million individuals 65 years of age or older. Studies vary on what type of abuse is most prevalent. However, researchers believe that psychological and financial abuse appears to be more prevalent than physical abuse and caregiver neglect. There is general agreement, too, that self-neglect has the highest prevalence rates in studies where it is included in the definition of abuse. Self-neglecting elders may present themselves in antisocial and life-threatening situations. Self-neglect is often manifested by a disregard of the needs of both oneself and the environment. This form of abuse results from physical and/or mental impairments that reduce the elder's ability to perform essential life tasks. Sometimes self-neglecters become embroiled with the police, wander into emergency rooms, and cause disturbances in social service agencies. Important ethical questions arise when the desire to guarantee a victim's personal safety is pitted against that person's right to self-determination. Wilber and McNeilly (2001) also suggest that older persons may simultaneously be victims of more than one type of abuse.

Who are the Perpetrators?

Several causes have been identified as contributors to elder abuse. Among these are caregiver stress, lack of adequate services and support, family violence, and abuser psychopathology (mental disorders, and substance abuse). Spouses and adult children are the most frequent abusers and, therefore, elder abuse has been characterized as a family problem. Approximately 90% of abuse is committed by family members (NCEA 1998). A highly stressed caregiver caring for a dependent family member has continuously been the explanation for abuse. However, research has failed to support this idea and instead has identified a different type of abuser. Wolf and Pillemer (1989) have demonstrated that caregiver (abuser) financial dependency on the victim was an important risk factor for abuse. This hypothesis suggests that the older adult may in fact be both the caregiver and the victim. In their screening instrument to identify risk for elder abuse, Reis and Nahmiash (1998) have demonstrated that the single most significant factor was pathology of the abuser (mental health disorders and substance abuse). When frail elderly are the sole support for mentally disabled adult children and spouses, providing adequate mental health services for the perpetrators may then become a priority for remediation of this situation. Work by Paveza et al. (1992) suggests that much of the physical and psychological abuse that occurs is perpetrated by the care receiver when he/she suffers from some forms of dementia.

Ramsey-Klawsnik (2000) offers a typology of offenders to explain the dynamics operating when people mistreat older adults. *Overwhelmed offenders* are generally well-intentioned and both willing and able to provide adequate care. However, they become stressed and overwhelmed and experience shame and remorse after committing any form of abuse. Their actions are episodic and not chronic. In addition, when confronted regarding their actions, they may deny allegations or defend themselves in light of their stress and burden of care giving. Many will express remorse and a desire to improve their caregiving behavior.

Impaired offenders are well-intentioned care providers who have their own impairments such as frailty, physical and/or mental illness, and developmental disabilities. They are often unable to recognize the inappropriateness of their actions and may themselves be in need of support services. They are often neglectful of care recipients and mismanage the older adult's finances. They may use psychological or physical abuse to coerce a victim.

Narcissistic offenders become involved with older adults for personal gain. The most common types of maltreatment are neglect and financial exploitation. This is a form of psychological abuse in that the victim is treated like an object rather than as a human being in need of care. Physical abuse may occur if it will hasten financial remuneration from the victim.

Domineering, or bullying offenders blame and attack their victims as an expression of power and control. This group of offenders can be extremely harmful to older people since they are not empathetic or supportive of any one's needs but their own. They perpetrate serious psychological and physical mistreatment, some life-threatening; some engage in sexual abuse. They will justify their abusive behavior with rationalizations as to why the victim deserved it or charm their interrogators into believing the victims are disturbed and unreliable sources of information.

Sadistic offenders derive feelings of power by humiliating, terrifying, and harming others. They are often sociopaths, lacking guilt, shame, or remorse for their behavior. Signs of physical abuse such as bites, marks, burns, and scars left in sensitive areas are signs of sadistic abuse. When confronted by authorities or relatives, they may sweet-talk or attempt to control those who are trying to stop the abuse.

Although studies are continuously demonstrating the origins/causes of elder abuse, little is known about how to effectively treat the victims. Moreover, there is paucity of evaluation criteria testing interventions. In instances of domestic violence, the primary focus of intervention needs to be the victim's safety. Holding abusers accountable is the second goal. For these interventions to occur, often a collaborative, coordinated effort is required, i.e. combining social services and law enforcement agencies.

State and local jurisdictions have focused on mandatory reporting as a means to enhance understanding of the nature and scope of the problem. In 2001, the first National Summit on Elder Abuse, sponsored by the Administration on Aging, was convened. It was basically a call to action with the task of recommending a national policy agenda for protecting frail elderly victims. Ten essential priorities were identified:

- Support for a National Elder Abuse Act
- Support for a National Education and Awareness Effort
- Improvement of the Legal Landscape by Strengthening Elder Abuse Laws
- Development and Implementation of a National Elder Abuse Training Curriculum
- Creation and Development of Age-Appropriate Specialized Mental Health Services
- General Accounting Office Evaluation Study of Federal Programs Effectiveness
- Increased Awareness with the Justice System
- Establishment of a National Elder Abuse Research and Program Innovation Institute
- Investment in National Resource Center on Adult Protective Services (APS)
- Seek Presidential Executive Order to Encourage the Above

The Action Agenda urged stronger collaborative efforts and investment in training to ensure the safety of frail and vulnerable elderly. The federal government has a crucial responsibility to help state and local authorities to develop the infrastructure to ensure safety of elder abuse victims. Currently, however, child abuse and domestic violence have cornered the meager resources available and elder abuse remains a lower policy and financial priority. There is negligence in prioritizing this devastating abuse, steadily reducing funding of social service block grants for training of personnel, and failing to provide adequate training of specialists with expertise in adult learning techniques. State and local staffs, in addition to their other duties, are called upon to develop training curricula even though they may lack expertise on curriculum development and adult learning skills. They may also be called upon to act as trainers on a wide variety of highly specialized subjects such as indicators of physical and/or mental illness.

What's the Good News?

The National Center on Elder Abuse has compiled a Training Resource Inventory (2002) which is a collection of instructional resources that focus on educating elder rights advocates, service providers, mandatory reporters, seniors, community watchdogs, and the public. The idea for this resource is the result of the first National Policy Summit Meeting on Elder Abuse Prevention hosted by the National Center on Elder Abuse (NCEA) in 2001. The inventory is an extensive source on elder abuse, aging, and adult protective service networks. The Inventory is arranged by topics and each profile identifies trainees, topics to be addressed, and the contact person for the educational module. The National Center on Elder Abuse has also compiled a National Directory (2001) of state, regional, and local elder abuse coalitions. Each of the elder abuse prevention groups has been recognized as being effective in organizing efforts to prevent elder abuse on all levels. Each description includes contact information, program mission and description, goals, services, activities and accomplishments, training audiences, and funding sources. It is an invaluable source for information, ideas, and sharing strategies among service providers.

Elder Abuse Training Strategies

Law enforcement and criminal justice professionals need to be key players in every community's effort to prevent and address elder abuse, neglect, and exploitation. But in order for law enforcement and criminal justice professionals to coordinate their efforts, the elder abuse network needs to partner with them to develop appropriate training and technical assistance. Given the converging social and economic issues of the 21st century, adult training will require new approaches to ensure training programs are reality-based and relevant to today's adult learner. This is especially significant when those adult learners are in professions that are directly impacted by these converging trends (i.e., law enforcement, social services, and academia).

Adult learners arrive at the training seminars with their own perceptions, assumptions, biases, and expectations about the program rationale, objectives to be achieved, and even the ability of the trainer to help facilitate the process. A successful training program is participatory, experiental, and interactive. A needs assessment is recommended so that training is tailored to meet organizational/adult learner needs. Adults are relevancy and practically oriented. Therefore, training strategies and materials specific to a discipline or job role need to be customized in order to reflect conditions specific to the adult learner. Adult learners are more successful in an environment where their life experiences and maturity are recognized, respected, and incorporated into the learning process (Kirby Resource Group 2003).

Work with adult learners has demonstrated that the willingness to develop new skills exists when the following situations prevail:

- learners understand why they should learn something new
- the trainer understands, reflects, and respects learners' prior knowledge and experience and treats them as co-facilitators with valuable insights and suggestions
- the training directly and positively impacts on their everyday life or tasks
- the training provides measurable solutions

Trainers and Trainees

All training should be conducted by a multidisciplinary team led by an experienced trainer preferably from the same profession as the adult learners. When police are trained by a team led by a police officer, the training assures legitimacy, enhances learners' motivation, and attracts a larger audience. The training module should be designed and sponsored by an arm of the police department, i.e., behavioral science division. When a respected organization or department within the police department sponsors the training, participants assume that the training will be relevant to their concerns. Train-the-trainer is effective when knowledgeable facilitators also have demonstrated training skills specifically focused on adult educational methodology. In the case of law enforcement, it has been demonstrated that in order to maximize credibility of the trainer, it is mandatory that he/she have concrete law enforcement experience with elder abuse. Only an officer who has experience in the field can readily address and integrate the theoretical and practical issues of the training.

Trainers need to have an understanding of how the police approach their work with older persons, and must make explicit how this orientation fits with responding to elder abuse, neglect, and exploitation. As a result, this may mean that elder abuse is incorporated into a larger framework that better fits the police agenda, i.e., community policing, community relations, or the cycle of family violence. Trainers and trainees need to agree on how they will use the training to benefit victims or make their jobs work. It is also pertinent that law enforcement professionals understand that older adults in the community are not clients; they are victims. Law enforcement personnel are not responsible for long-term social service care; they are on the scene to address an incident of which an older adult is a participant, probably as a victim. Their role is to address the criminality of the episode and not to adjudicate right from wrong. If trainees balk and say that this is not police work, they need to be reminded that as professionals they entered into their line of work because they wished to make a difference in their community. Today, the majority of police officers' work may, in fact, be social service calls. Although each discipline views the plight of elder abuse victims through a different professional lens, there will always be some ground that they can agree on and again be referred to the question: How do we use what we are learning to benefit the older adult and/or make our jobs work?

Training Topics

Training efforts will need to address:

- Diagnosis and recognition of elder abuse, neglect, and exploitation. The ability to recognize a probable elder abuse situation is the major behavioral objective of this training goal.

- Investigation and documentation of abuse and neglect. This training component will address: What to look for? What needs to be investigated? What documents will be required in support of the investigation? How do we document accurately? Who will need to be interviewed? What to look for and document when the allegation concerns emotional or psychological abuse?

- Culturally competent communication skills. Trainers will need to incorporate knowledge, skills, and attitude objectives relevant to the normal aging process as well as older adult physical and mental vulnerabilities relevant to specific ethnic and cultural groups.

Training Strategies

The workshop is an appropriate educational format for use with law enforcement personnel. The workshop is a short-term intensive learning experience that provides participants an opportunity to share knowledge and experiences, and develop and practice new capabilities under the leadership of a facilitator (Sork 1984).

There are many advantages to the workshop format:

1. It is short-term and therefore feasible for people to arrange for participation.

2. It is transportable. It can be lodged in most locations, can be duplicated, and can be offered at several locations at the same time.

3. Due to the short-term nature of the workshop format, participants can begin to apply their new capabilities almost immediately.

4. Removing participants from their work environments for the duration of a program isolates them from distractions and enables them to concentrate on the workshop objectives.

5. Motivation and interest tend to remain high because learning is concentrated into a reasonable timeframe (Sork 1984).

As a specialized educational strategy, the workshop can be considered successful when it promotes change in the ability of the participants to perform in new ways and apply the new competences in their work environment. In order for professionals embarking on the development of new competencies and change in performance to maximize their learning experiences, they need to be involved in the development of the learning model. Failure to illicit their input may result in their inability to transfer new learning to their work environments because there may be no relationship between the workshop's objectives and methods and the characteristics and realities found in the work environment. The workshop facilitator needs to foster open and voluntary communication in the learning environment in order to encourage a free exchange of ideas, opinions, and feelings. This is a significant key to workshop learning. Participants gain a broader personal and professional perspective of aging related issues relevant to their work environment while instructors, in learning about professionals' day-to-day realities of working with aged individuals, can test the appropriateness of program content and objectives.

In New York City, almost 12% of the population is 65 and over, and there are neighborhoods in which the older population approaches 20%, which already mirrors the expected proportions in the United States by the year 2030. With birth rates decreasing and human longevity and urbanization increasing around the world, policymakers view New York as a frontier for economic, health, and social policy innovations to meet the challenge of population aging in an urban context. As a group, the older citizens of New York City need special services from the police, both in protection and crisis intervention. In order to provide the greatest service, the Department of Behavioral Science of the New York City Police Department has developed an extensive curriculum and training program focusing on bringing a social service perspective to policing relevant to the elderly of New York City.

The curriculum, totaling 150 hours of instruction, encompasses four major areas of study for Police Recruits:

- Track One—effective communication and cultural competence
- Track Two—Ethics and Mental Health
- Track Three—Crisis Intervention
- Track Four—The Service Role

A major component of Tracks three and four focuses on the elderly as victims of abuse, neglect, and exploitation. The course gives officers the knowledge base, skills, and attitudes appropriate to provide assessment, intervention, and psychological first aid for victims of crisis. The Behavioral Science curriculum employs various interactive methodologies as part of the training such as: role play, socio drama, forum and interactive theater techniques, simulation and reflective team exercises. The interdisciplinary theater workshops are facilitated improvisations and socio dramas conducted by actor trainers utilizing reflective team exercises in which the adult learner's performance is evaluated and critiqued. Crime statistics and empirical research do not adequately reflect the monumental affront, fear, and degradation impacted on the lives of abused elderly. Monetary loss may cause economic hardship; physical injury may cripple or kill the victim; psychological damage may result in self isolation or self-imprisonment. All of these forms of abuse result in hopelessness and frustration. It is important for the police officer, as a human service provider, to be cognizant of these issues so that his/her conduct enhances attention and respect for the special needs of this vulnerable target population.

A clearly structured modified interview schedule follows (New York City Police Department Behavioral Science Curriculm 2002) that can be used in preparing "actors" for a role play involving a police officer and an older abuse victim.

Interviewing an Older Abuse Victim:

1. Interview the victim away from the suspected abuser and, if possible, other people.

2. If you need to have another person assist in communicating, conduct the dialogue in the victim's presence and look for signs of corroboration from the victim (i.e., nodding in agreement).

3. Do not discuss the victim if he/she is not in the room. Do not refer to the victim as a third party.

4. Realize that the victim may have physical/mental disabilities and try to accommodate them. For example, the older victim may be hearing impaired. Therefore, speak distinctly and face them in case they are reading your lips.

5. Tell the victim what he/she can expect during the interview.

6. Allow the victim to describe the incident in his/her own words.

7. Practice being a responsive listener who actually listens without bringing pressure to bear on the interview process.

8. Ask both open ended and closed questions clearly without infantilizing the victim. Ask questions that will provide further exploration and elaboration but do not editorialize.

9. Acknowledge the victim's anxiety and try to discern its cause. For example, you may say, "You seem anxious. Are you concerned that someone will find out that you have spoken to me? Who?"

10. Even if the victim appears to be somewhat confused, do not discount the information. Realize that the victim may be fearful or nervous, not necessarily suffering from forms of dementia. Do not diagnose psychosocial ailments without corroboration with another social service/healthcare professional.

11. Accept and use the victim's terminology and descriptions for acts, body parts, etc.

12. Do not argue with the victim.

13. Do not discount a complaint because the victim is unwilling to cooperate. Victims are often protective of their abusers, particularly if the abuser is a close family member, i.e. adult child. A victim's decision to prosecute may protect him/her from further abuse and may lead to counseling rather than a jail sentence for the perpetrator.

14. Assess the dangerousness of the situation. If a threat to the victim is present, arrange for protection with Adult Protective Services.

15. Conclude the interview with appropriate closure so that the victim feels comfortable enough to leave. You need to always leave the victim more psychologically secure than he/she was when you arrived. Ensure that the victim is capable (physically, mentally, environmentally) to contact the police again if necessary.

Resources

The following resources may be helpful in developing new training materials for Law Enforcement personnel:

National Center on Elder Abuse (NCEA Washington). Several relevant publications, including "Elder Abuse Video Resources: A Guide for Training and Public Education."
Clearinghouse on Abuse and Neglect of the Elderly (CAN E). CANE, College of Human Resources, University of Delaware, Newark, DE.
Commission on Legal Problems of the Elderly, American Bar Association, Washington, DC.

References

Burston, G.R. 1975. Granny battering. *British Medical Journal*, 3: 529.

Comijs, H.C., A.M. Pot, J.H. Smit.1998. Elder abuse in the community: prevalence and consequences. *Journal of the American Geriatric Society*, 46, 885-888.

Gross, E.A. 1999. Telemarketing fraud. Unpublished doctoral dissertation, Department of Educational Counseling, University of Southern California, Los Angeles.

Lachs, M.S., and C. Williams. 1997. Risk factors for reported elder abuse and neglect: A nine-year observational cohort study. *The Gerontologist,* 37, 469-474.

Kirby Resource Group 2003. Greenville, SC

Moon, A. Summer 2000. Perceptions of elder abuse among various cultural groups: Similarities and differences. *Generations* 75-80.

National Center on Elder Abuse Training Resource Inventory 2002. National Association of State Units on Aging, Washington, DC

National Center for Elder Abuse (1998). National Elder Abuse Incidence Study. Washington, DC at www.aoa.gov/abuse/report default.htm.

National Directory 2001. National Center on Elder Abuse, Administration on Aging.

New York City Police Department. 2002. *Behavioral Science Curriculum*, Tracks 1-4.

Otto, J.M. 2002. *Survey of State Adult Protective Services Responses to Financial Exploitation of Vulnerable Adults.* National Center on Elder Abuse, Washington, D.C.

Paveza, G.J., D. Cohen, C. Eisdorfer. 1992. Severe family violence and Alzheimer's disease: Prevalence and risk factors. *The Gerontologist,* 32, 493-497.

Quinn, M.J. and S.K.Tomita. 1998. *Elder abuse and neglect: Causes, diagnosis, and intervention strategies,* (2nd ed.), New York: Springer Publishing.

Ramsey-Klawsnik, H. 2000. Elder abuse offenders: A typology. *Generations*, 17-22.

Reis, M. and D. Nahmiash. 1998. Validation of the indicators of abuse (IOA) screen. *The Gerontologist,* 38, 471-480.

Sork, T.J. 1984. Designing and implementing effective workshops. Jossey-Bass, Inc.: San Francisco.

The Public Policy and Aging Report Winter. 2002. Volume 12 (2), p.4

Wilber, K.H. and D.P. McNeilly. 2001. Elder abuse and victimization. In J.E. Birren and K.W. Schaie, eds. *Handbook of the Psychology of Aging*, (5ᵗʰ ed.) 569-591. San Diego: CA: Academic Press.

Wisconsin Coalition Against Domestic Violence (WCADV) 1998. *Family violence in later life power and control wheel.* Madison, Wisconsin. Handout.

Wolf, R.S. and K. Pillemer. 1989. *Helping elderly victims: The reality of elder abuse.* New York: Columbia University Press.

Wolf, R.S. 2000. The nature and scope of elder abuse. *Generations* XXIV, 11, Summer, 6-12.

Editorial Commentary

ഔരൂ

Terry Tirrito

In the past few years, local police departments have agreed to work cooperatively with senior citizens to prevent victimization of the elderly (Cantrell 1994). The Triad concept began when members of the American Association of Retired Persons (AARP), the International Association of Chiefs of Police (IACP), and the National Sheriffs' Association (NSA) met to consider methods to combat elder abuse. The SALT (Seniors and Lawmen Together) is the organization that the Triad usually creates when law enforcement personnel ask older persons, as well as people who work with them, to serve on advisory boards. The SALT generally conducts a needs assessment regarding criminal activity. In describing the operation of the program, Cantrell wrote,

> ...volunteers may staff reception desks in law enforcement agencies, present programs to senior organizations, conduct informal house security surveys, and become leaders in new or rejuvenated neighborhood watch groups. They may also provide information and support to crime victims, call citizens concerning civil warrants, or assist law enforcement agencies.

In some areas, the Triad creates senior shopping programs where stores provide vans to transport older persons in regularly scheduled shopping trips. Triads have conducted workshops in which older persons are taught how to safely carry money and well as carjacking prevention.

Other cooperative models include fiduciary abuse specialist teams (FAST). Representatives from law enforcement, adult protective services, the long-term-care ombudsman program, the office of the public guardian, the district attorney, the city attorney, health and mental health providers, and volunteers who are experts in banking, real estate, insurance, mortgages, tax, and estate planning are variously involved in these teams. It has been these types of teams who have been able to identify and build criminal cases against perpetrators (Nerenberg 1996).

References

Cantrell, B. 1994, February. Triad: Reducing criminal victimization of the elderly, *FBI Law Enforcement Bulletin,* 19-23.

Nerenberg, L. 1996. *Financial abuse of the elderly.* San Francisco: San Francisco Consortium for Elder Abuse Prevention.

10

GERICARE SPECIALIST:©
AN EDUCATIONAL RESPONSE
TO THE ELDER
HOME CARE CRISIS

ℰᴑℭᴙ

Jane M. Cardea,
Jane F. McGarrahan &
Bernice C. Brennan

The availability, desirability, and cost of current long-term and home care services for the frail or mentally/physically challenged elderly "beg the question" for the creation of cost-effective solutions to this growing health care problem. The need to strengthen direct, home-based, long-term care services to these compromised elders and to expand the services needed by families who desire to care for their elder member(s) at home is one of the greatest challenges facing our health care and social service systems. The burgeoning numbers of elderly and the need for additional long term care services present a unique opportunity for creative responses to these serious socio-economic crises.

As early as 1994, the Labor, Health, and Human Services Education Appropriations Bill recognized the needs for both additional long-term care services for the elderly and the expansion of labor opportunities for the economically disadvantaged or unemployed individuals through the development of innovative community-based solutions:

> The rapid growth in the number of elderly Americans has led to increased demands on the institutions, agencies, and personnel that care for people needing long-term care. Many areas of the country, for example, are experiencing severe shortages in the number of qualified nursing assistants and aides available to care for those suffering from physical limitations or cognitive disorders. The lack of training, benefits, and career opportunities for those in entry-level positions has encouraged high turnover. In light of current efforts to improve health care delivery and control spiraling costs. [Individuals are encouraged to explore] the feasibility of offering low-income individuals intensive training to serve as professional long-term care providers. Apart from providing much needed services in the community, such a program would offer educational and employment opportunities in an expanding field (p. 11).

Both the home health care needs of the elderly and new employment opportunities for the under unemployed are met through the proposed Gericare Specialist© program. This effort provides intensive training for a new type of health care worker to serve as a specialized long-term homecare provider.

An integrated curriculum designed for the training of a new entry-level, paraprofessional category of elder home health care provider responds to some of the significant overwhelming challenges in our society. Comprehensive, twenty-four hour, in-home care provided by a bonded paraprofessional on an on-going basis to an elder person who is unable to manage independent living but desires to remain in his or her home is not only a reasonable expectation by our society but an expectation that can be achieved. Marginally-employable individuals, particularly disenfranchised homemakers and minority or economically-disadvantaged women, are readily available and ideally suited candidates for this new position in the health care industry.

The proposed strategy calls for a 12-week program of classroom, laboratory, and clinical instruction that emphasizes knowledge, skills, values, and attitudes necessary to meet the specialized day-to-day health and social needs of the defined elder population. The new health care team member's licensure or certification includes certification as a nursing assistant with additional training in four areas of import to in-home elder care: communication, assessment, personal care, and home management skills. These new paraprofessionals will provide companion and caregiver services that complement the existing range of episodic formal and informal health and social support services and greatly expand the current role and responsibilities of the geriatric home care aide.

Background Information

Reductions in mortality rates and protocols to manage disease have increased the life expectancy for both men and women (Bengston and Murray 1993; Stanley and Beare 1999). Currently, 13% of our nation's population is over 65 years of age, and by the year 2030 it is estimated that 20% and possibly 25% of the US population will be over 65 and close to 10% of the entire population will be over 80 years of age (U.S. House of Representatives 1998). Today, home care is the fastest growing area of health and social service care and approximately 80% of all home care clients are elderly (Haupt 1998; Mezey 1996). The older segment of our elder population, those who are 85 years of age or older, is the group most in need of personal and health care services: this group has been growing at a more rapid rate than the total senior citizen population and the expectation is that this group will continue to expand over the next few decades (Brody et al 1983).

As the elderly population continues to grow, their unique social and economic problems become more pronounced. Many face serious financial loss along with threats to personal security and autonomy as they seek assistance for their health care through unsubsidized assisted living or expensive private home care. Those seeking assistance through established systems will find that the delivery of long-term home care services are often uncoordinated and fragmented (AARP 1991), and only 36% of all qualified persons needing long-term care receive these services (Short and Leon 1990). Further, as older patients are leaving the hospital more quickly and in more acute illness states than in the past (Fischer and Eustis 1988), many of the major federal programs designed to cover medical services for these individuals are not meeting their diverse needs or those of their family members who desire home care for their dependent elders (Bliezner and Ally 1990; Dellman-Jenkins, Hofer, and Chebra 1992).

Medically-Frail, Physically/
Mentally Challenged Older Adults

With age, natural degenerative processes are most frequently expressed in the elder population as chronic conditions or dependence (Cicerelli 1990; Kutner et al 1992). For example, Cox and Parsons (1994) cite a 1991 report by the American Association of Retired Persons:

> The degree of dependency and duration of the dependent status increase greatly with the onset of physical incapacity, which typically results from a chronic condition. Over 15% of people ages 65-69 and 49% of those 85 or older require help with one or more activities of daily living (p. 189)

Although science and technology have contributed to extending the life expectancy of most Westerners, these resources have not provided a comparable extension of the quality of life for the elderly (Hunter 1992). Even though the varieties of home care services for the elder population are increasing and the traditional services offered by health care institutions are remaining in place or are expanding, the current needs of many Americans who require or qualify for long-term care services, especially home care services, remain unmet (Gelfand 1993; Silverstone and Burack-Weiss 1983; Philadelphia Corporation for Aging 1986; U.S. Senate 1972). In addition, the narrow regulatory definitions qualifying an elder person for available long-term care services and the few constraints on standards of care for those who offer these services limit both the access and the quality of desirable home care services (Gelfand 1993; Leader 1991).

Poverty Rates and Under-or Unemployment

The issues of employability and wage compensation become particularly important when the purchasing power of today's wages are compared with a similar index of less than 15 years ago and information about employment and poverty rates is reviewed for a similar period of time. For example, "inflation has eroded the minimum wage to 73.7% of its January 1981 level ... this puts its [purchasing power] at its second lowest level in two decades ... the stagnant minimum wage means a loss of purchasing power and a lower standard of living for [many] workers and their families" (Partnership for Hope 1995a, 2). The median wage for former welfare recipients in 1999 was $7.15/ hour (Weil 2002, September). In a study of poverty estimates conducted by the U.S. Census Bureau for the years 1990 to 1992, "62.4 million Americans, over one-quarter of the U.S. residents, lived in poverty for at least two months of those two years. Approximately 13% [or 8 million] of these individuals were elderly. Of all adults in this poverty group, 58% lacked a high school diploma and 77% were not in the labor force" (Capps 1994).

Currently, a network of informal caregivers, primarily family members and women, pick up the slack between the high demand for long-term home care services and the availability of care facilities or trained personnel to meet these needs (Brubaker 1990; Epstein and Koenig 1990; Mahoney and Shippee-Rice 1994; Rankin 1990; Riordan and Saltzer 1992; Scharlach 1994). Many of these caregivers are displaced homemakers or women from disadvantaged and/or minority populations (Crown, Ahlburg, and Mac-Adam 1995). Because these informal caregivers are not usually highly-skilled or trained, and because wages for providing in-home care is usually based on what a family can afford to pay, these women are not well compensated. Interestingly, when home care services are compensated, wages are often low or at minimal wage level, employee benefits are few or nonexistent, much of the work is part-time, few opportunities for career advancement are available, and staff turnover is high (Feldman, Sapienza, and Kane 1990; Filinson 1994; Surpin 1988; Weil 2002). Were these low-paid individuals to become better educated with a body of information and skills that were state regulated, not only would they be able to provide better and more standardized health care but they also would have a marketable service that would lift them from the pool of unskilled and poorly compensated labor.

Trainees

The primary target populations for the training program are unemployed and marginally employable individuals who recognize the need for further training and who are willing to commit to an educational program that will assist them in becoming career motivated adults. Many would be the "more mature woman" whose inclusion in this type of program is supported in the literature by Richman (1989) who wrote "older-adult peer caregivers may in some ways be best suited to care for their frail and impaired contemporaries because they are most empathic and understanding" (p. 580). Dychtwald (1990) also noted that the elderly are more likely to accept the provision of personal care and home management services from older adults than their younger counterparts.

Candidate Characteristics

Selection of eligible candidates is accomplished by a written and verbal application process which assesses each person's potential ability to function at a defined level of autonomy and dependability. Criteria for program admission might include 1) effective communication and interpersonal skills; 2) readiness and willingness to learn; 3) integrity and responsibility for the management of personal and expected professional obligations; 4) educational background, life experiences, and personal achievements; 5) familiarity, genuine interest, and compassion for the needs of older adults; 6) mature judgment; 7) physical fitness commensurate with expected duties; and 8) felony, credit, and background check clearances.

Graduate Characteristics

At the completion of the 12-week training program, graduates can successfully:

- Implement interventions for medically-frail or physically/mentally challenged older adults which promote the elder person's independence in managing activities of daily living within the home for as long as possible.

- Use acquired knowledge of the aging process, national and community resources, ethical issues, legal mandates, and nutrition to 1) sustain and/or enhance the functional and psycho-social abilities of the older adult for as long as possible; 2) advocate for client's and family rights; 3) monitor environmental safety; 4) supervise the selection, storage, preparation, and presentation of palatable and nutritional foods; and 5) provide additional personal care and home management activities needed by service consumers.

- Accept responsibility for coordinating the activities of others providing client services (i.e., health care, financial, residence and/or grounds maintenance).

- Understand the rights, responsibilities, and professional parameters of the certified nursing assistant's role and participate in continuing education programs to retain currency of knowledge, practice, and state certification.

Educational Program

The proposed curriculum is based on knowledge obtained from 1) a literature review; 2) personal communications with a variety of experts familiar with the needs and concerns of the frail older adult and current resources available to them; and 3) the pooled experiential and educational expertise of the authors. Designed to complement and enhance the basic knowledge and clinical experiences acquired during the nursing assistant module of our curriculum, the proposed program prepares the adult learner for a self-directed, autonomous position as a new paraprofessional home care service provider for the elderly.

The integrated curriculum adopts a health promotion perspective as a central focus of all instructional activities. Two pivotal principles about adult learners were used as guidelines for program design, content delivery, and performance evaluation (Atherton 2002; Bloom 1964; Boyle 1981; Bransford and Vye 1989; Mezey 1996; Foshay 1990; Ornstein 1993; Redman 1993; Saylor, Alexander, and Lewis 1981; and Taba 1962). The first principle is that adult learners are most successful when they have a strong desire to learn and they can directly and immediately apply what they have learned to other situations. This belief guided decisions about logically sequencing program content and learning experiences and identifying critical selection criteria for potential trainees. For example, information presented in the classroom proceeds from a level of introductory content to a more advanced level of competence and mastery where laboratory and clinical experiences are used for the immediate reinforcement of presented knowledge and skill application. The purposeful inclusion of life experiences into classroom discussions by instructor and trainees is seen as another vehicle for all participants to align the relevance of curricular content with the reality of the long-term caregiving environment.

The second principle is that adult learners are most successful when they experience satisfaction from what they have learned. This belief guided the selection of learning and performance assessment strategies. For example, multiple learning activities in the classroom (i.e., discussion, role play, computer simulation, video/film presentations) and a variety of formative evaluation activities are listed throughout the curriculum to foster trainees' successful program completion, to improve the instructional delivery of program content, to revise the sequencing of presented information and practice experiences when indicated, and to promote an interactive learning environment among all participants. Finally, classroom activities on topics of values clarification, problem solving skills, and life task accomplishments or self-fulfillment are grounded in a moral health care tradition of caring, concern, and service to human beings, regardless of their ethnic or cultural background or their vulnerability to illness and impairment.

Educational Program Sequence: Preparation

Prior to program enrollment, applicants must first pass routine felony, background, and credit checks and obtain all necessary immunizations. Because the processes of felony and background checks are conducted differently in each state and required immunizations or malpractice insurance coverage for trainees may vary from state to state, individuals administering this curriculum must become familiar with all state-mandated screening processes, health requirements, and relevant insurance regulations. The work history of many applicants will be marginal; therefore, those responsible for enlisting participants might consider providing needed forms, reviewing required information on these forms, and providing a list of addresses and telephone numbers of nearby agencies offering the required services at minimal cost. This assistance at the pre-enrollment stage of the program will insure a better rate of applicant return.

It is anticipated that many of the program applicants will be marginally-employable and/or ethnically-diverse adult women. In addition, many applicants may be single parents with school-age children. Thus, ancillary support services such as child care and transportation assistance should be made available, and consideration ought to be given to offering the program during daytime school hours.[1] Finally, remediation activities should be provided in reading, writing, and math skills for anyone in need of this type

---

1.   The curriculum is designed as a five day/week, six hours/day, across 12 weeks for a total of 360 hours of instruction

of assistance, as a basic component of any recruitment plan. Applicants might also need to be encouraged to learn to drive and get a license.

Educational Program Sequence: Phase I

The proposed curriculum initially provides an "educational bridge" to ease the trainee's transition back into an academic environment. Educational experiences begin with a brief one or two day program orientation where CPR certification is accomplished and an overview of the new health care provider role is discussed. Next, a state-approved nursing assistant curriculum, involving basic nursing knowledge and skills, is introduced during morning hours[2]. Gericare Specialist© content and learning strategies provided during afternoon sessions are designed to supplement morning experiences with related information pertinent to elder home care. For example, once information about basic infection control or environmental cleanliness and aesthetics is taught in the morning, afternoon instruction and learning experiences could include 1) elder personal care and hygiene needs; 2) home safety; 3) table setting; 4) food preparation and presentation; and 5) elder home service plans. In addition, students are educated about talking and working with other health care professionals with rehearsals in the classroom and skills laboratory on telephone etiquette, professional versus personal conversations, and dress. Following completion of mandated contact and instructional hours for nursing assistant certification, the curriculum design shifts to a full day focus on elder care needs and services.

PowerPoint presentations and handouts are suggested as routine forms of classroom instruction to facilitate trainees' concentration on instructor's

---

2.   States mandate specific curriculum content and classroom contact hours for nursing assistant certification, and these curriculum modules are readily available upon request. Approved programs customarily involve approximately 120 hours of instructional time, and certification involves successful completion of the state-approved program plus successful completion of a written and laboratory skills performance examination. Individuals who participate in a state-approved instructor preparation program and successfully complete all requirements are usually able to offer a nursing assistant program at any site provided the necessary equipment, resources, and clinical experiences are available.

clarification or amplification of textbook materials. Small group activities, role play, classroom discussion, video/film presentations, computer-assisted simulations, story telling, and one-on-one student to student or instructor to student case study reviews and analyses are used to encourage the active classroom participation of each trainee. Peer support and study groups also are encouraged to assist trainees with the new lifestyle demands of being an adult learner and to facilitate the successful completion of the curriculum.

Instructor supervision and encouragement of student performance in the laboratory and clinical area begin with familiar skills, i.e., hand washing, bed making, basic social and communication skills, and personal hygiene and sequentially expand to other less familiar or unfamiliar skills, i.e., sterile dressing changes, tube feedings, and therapeutic communication. The rationale for each skill is first presented in the classroom, practiced immediately within the classroom or laboratory area, and finally performed in the clinical setting. Practice sessions are monitored by the instructor with trainees witnessing their successes or failures through self-observation and self-evaluation, group feedback, and instructor evaluation. Evaluations sometimes surprise trainees when they find they need assistance with what they believe are familiar and accomplished skills (i.e., hand washing one's own hands and helping another adult effectively wash their hands is not exactly the same skill). Trainees should be encouraged to progress at a comfortable rate of successful skill completion, with laboratory equipment and computer-assisted instructional modules available outside of class time for remediation and confidence building. Trainees' education also will be enhanced through the availability of laboratory monitors for equipment management and tutors for remedial instruction. Throughout the program, trainees should be encouraged to utilize any service they need to assure mastery of clinical skills.

Educational Program Sequence: Phase II

Phase II of the educational program begins with the trainee's receipt of the nursing assistant certificate. Using Eliopoulos' (1999) recommendations for the comprehensive assessment of an elder person's capability to successfully manage independent home living, the listed categories (i.e., activities of daily living and independent activities of daily living) were incorporated into four curricular modules of emphasis: communication, assessment, personal care, and home management. Unit objectives, lesson content, suggested learning activities, and optional evaluation strategies are provided as an organizing framework for each module. The provided information within each module using this suggested framework is known to be incomplete (i.e., the purposeful sequencing of knowledge and skills acquisition from a level of introduction to a level of role competence is not specified) as its purpose is to serve as a stimulus for further thought, discussion, and comprehensive curriculum development.

Educational Program Sequence: Evaluation

Formative and summative evaluation processes are designed to systematically identify acceptable benchmarks and successful teaching/learning strategies, provide an early warning system of program difficulties, and establish written documentation of trainee outcomes. Each criterion-referenced evaluation method must be clearly aligned with program, module, and unit objectives and distributed to the trainee well in advance of any assessment period. Throughout the presented curriculum framework, optional formative evaluation activities are provided to assess program accomplishments and to offer immediate feedback to instructor or trainee[3]. Traditional formative evaluation methods include individual and classroom conversations between trainee and instructor, graded classroom and clinical papers, unit examinations, and quizzes.

Summative evaluation activities are completed at the end of training or educational program experiences and conducted to assess areas such as course/program relevance, teaching effectiveness, clinical agency appropriateness for meeting course goals and objectives, and student preparedness for the defined role. Traditional summative evaluation methods of student performance include final examinations, laboratory skills demonstrations, and clinical performance assessments. Final evaluations of teaching effectiveness by trainees and instructor(s) ought to include items such as course materials, instructor availability and presentation style, pace of presented information, and appropriateness of testing methods using directed responses (i.e., Likert scale items) as well as open-

---

3. Quizzes and examinations were not listed as formative or summative evaluation strategies for any module, as it is assumed that these assessment activities are routinely incorporated as evaluation measures throughout the curriculum.

ended responses (i.e., "List three program strengths") on developed questionnaires. Laboratory assessment forms usually address categories such as equipment availability and currency, adequacy of space, and convenience of laboratory and library hours of operation for additional out-of-class practice, remediation, or study. Clinical agency/facility assessment documents address areas such as space for pre- and/or post-clinical conferencing, adequacy of practicum opportunities, availability for personnel for guidance and mentoring, and availability of cafeteria and parking facilities.

Information from these end-of-program or summative assessment activities are reported as aggregate data and shared with instructor(s) and program administrator(s) as quality control and program improvement mechanisms. In addition, this information may be shared with alumni and prospective students as a recruitment strategy or copied to external funding agencies as a fundraising or image enhancement activity. Immediate program outcomes (i.e., program graduation and instructor contract renewal) as well as trended outcomes across several program presentations (i.e., clinical agency contract renewal and equipment renovation or modernization) must be analyzed in a routine, systematic, and publicized manner to obtain comprehensive, valid, and reliable interpretations.

The first summative review that follows multiple, on-going evaluation processes should be conducted at the conclusion of Phase I of the educational program. At this point in the program, trainees will have completed all requirements for state certification as nursing assistants. A trainee self-evaluation plus written instructor review of trainee accomplishments and areas of concern may provide the impetus for those with marginal performance to strive for greater achievements or to leave the program and seek immediate employment as a nursing assistant. For others who continue in the program, affirmation of their early success may serve as an additional incentive in their quest to accomplish a higher level of professional recognition, better wages, and greater opportunities for career advancement in the health care industry.

Summary

The dilemma facing the long-term care industry today is succinctly outlined in an excerpt from a report by the Philadelphia Corporation on Aging (1996, May):

The city's elderly encounter many of the same health care issues that confront other older Americans- shortages of primary doctors who are knowledgeable and committed to serving older consumers, limited coverage of long-term care services, financial barriers like Medicare premiums and costs of services not covered by Medicare or Medicaid, limited emphasis on preventive care and health promotion, and the limited capacity [of the industry] to respond to the needs of special subgroups (i.e., the developmentally disabled, cultural minorities, and non-English speaking consumers (p.18-19).

The creation of a new, licensed or certified, paraprofessional role within the health care and social services systems is one proposed solution to the current and projected inadequate resources available for long-term in-home elder care. This solution offers a reasonable alternative to offset the spiraling costs of elder institutional care and an answer to reduce the growing numbers of marginally-employed and unemployed citizens. The organization of a preliminary framework identifying curricular content, learning experiences, and evaluation strategies across four modules is provided as a beginning realization of this vision. This information should serve as a catalyst for national discussion to refine and expand presented information and to develop appropriate certification or licensure processes for state adoption and implementation of the Gericare Specialist© role. Finally, much of the provided information could be applied to other populations of home care recipients (i.e., the pediatric population). Parallel discussions of educational and licensure or certification processes for a new care provider role serving these populations using our framework as a curricular model is encouraged.

Orientation

OBJECTIVE	SUGGESTED CONTENT	SAMPLE LEARNING ACTIVITIES	SAMPLE EVALUATION STRATEGIES
Understand education program expectations	Overview of 12 week program: • Curriculum • Professional Expectations: Attendance, Dress, Personal Hygiene, Documentation • Client/Family Rights • Performance Evaluation	Program syllabus Student Notebook: • Program policies and procedures • Module handouts • Class notes and reflections Case Presentations: Acceptable and unacceptable trainee behaviors Classmate Interview: "What Do You Case Presentations: Violations of Client/Family Rights	Adherence to program expectations Classroom/Clinical Preparation
Describe the role and scope of practice for the Gericare Specialist©	Gericare Specialist© Role in Health Care System: • Current Health Care Team Members Serving the Elderly • Inter-relationships and Interactions with Other Elder Health Care Providers	Panel Discussion: Opportunities for Gericare Specialists© Classroom Discussion: Legal and ethical issues	Reaction Paper: Responsibilities to self, client, family members, and other health care providers Employer/client/family satisfaction surveys

OBJECTIVE	SUGGESTED CONTENT	SAMPLE LEARNING ACTIVITIES	SAMPLE EVALUATION STRATEGIES
		Internet Activity: Access a website of two other health care providers (i.e., nurses, doctors. Social workers) for class discussion	
		Guest Speakers: Elder "Quality of Life": • Elders • Healthcare employers • AARP representative • Family caregivers of compromised elders	
	Job Description: • Title • Competencies and General Skills	Laboratory/Clinical Skills Checklist Classroom discussion: Personal Growth Contract	Successful completion of Skills Checklist CNA certification
	CPR Certification: Content and Skills	Laboratory Demonstration: • CPR on adult and child • CPR as single and team rescuer • CPR certification	
	Career Advancement Skills • Resume Preparation • Interviewing skills		Program Graduation Resume content and appearance Employment

Communication

OBJECTIVE	SUGGESTED CONTENT	SAMPLE LEARNING ACTIVITIES	SAMPLE EVALUATION STRATEGIES
Define important terms in the communication process Recognize basic strategies for effective communication	Glossary of Terms: • Verbal and Nonverbal Communication (Give examples of common non-verbal communication i.e., peace sign, salutes, waves, various cultural gestures, and clenched fist) • Roles in Communication (i.e., message, messenger, message receiver) • Effective Communication Strategies (i.e., sitting face to face, eliminating distractions, being in good lighting, speaking slowly and clearly, avoiding age-inappropriate jargon, being sensitive to person's cultural history)	Classroom/Laboratory Exercises: • Dyads: Practice effective and ineffective communication using verbal and nonverbal messages • Triads: Change roles of messenger, message recipient, and evaluator across all 3 participants to practice and evaluate effective communication processes Handout: Nonverbal communication	Clinical Performance Evaluations Classmate Evaluations of Communication Processes

OBJECTIVE	SUGGESTED CONTENT	SAMPLE LEARNING ACTIVITIES	SAMPLE EVALUATION STRATEGIES
	• Feedback Loop • Client Privacy and Confidentiality		
Normal Cognitive Aging Describe normal cognitive changes in the aging adult.	Normal Cognitive Changes in Elderly Slower Elder Learning Curve	Communication Notebook: Identify items or areas that need particular attention. Classroom/Laboratory Exercises: Health Education/Health Promotion Videos: Active, healthy, older adults • Dyad Discussion: - What changes will "slowing down" bring to my life? - How might my day to day activities be affected by slowing down? • Classroom Reports of Discussions:	Reaction Paper: When does one become old? Reaction Paper: What are my feelings about "slowing down"?

OBJECTIVE	SUGGESTED CONTENT	SAMPLE LEARNING ACTIVITIES	SAMPLE EVALUATION STRATEGIES
		Current Media Review: (Tabulate information about the elderly presented over 7 days for 2 of the following media: TV, radio, movies, magazines, newspaper): • What do the media tell us about aging? • What do you expect for yourself as you age?	
Communication Skills: Apply effective basic communication skills with the elderly	Elder Applications for Effective Communication: • Use simple sentences and repeat statements often Sensitive to person's generational ideas of "appropriate and inappropriate" interactions	Classroom/Laboratory Exercises: Triads: Practice ineffective skills between two classmates with one being a well elder; the third participant is the evaluator - How many of the tips can be violated - What are the most frequent violations • Triads: Practice effective skills with a compromised elder • Triads: Practice effective skills with a well and compromised elder with the evaluator using a skills checklist	Communication Skills Checklists Clinical Performance Evaluations Triad Evaluator Feedback Paper: Written videotape analysis of self and partner feelings and communication patterns (i.e., effective and ineffective)

OBJECTIVE	SUGGESTED CONTENT	SAMPLE LEARNING ACTIVITIES	SAMPLE EVALUATION STRATEGIES
Apply effective listening skills with the elderly.	Listening Skills: • Listening to feelings beneath the words • Listening to body language • Listening without interrupting Feelings and Nonverbal Communications	• Videotape Review and Analysis: Review a brief dialog between self as care provider and compromised elder -Describe personal feelings and reactions to experience -Use a checklist to evaluate effective and ineffective communication patterns • Classroom and Laboratory Exercises: Listing Feeling Words: Provide a list of feeling words: -Identify those feelings personally experienced -Relate these feelings to an elder person • Muting Video or TV Clip: Turn off the volume and have students assess what is being conveyed being sure to list cues Handouts: Feelings and Feeling Words	Reaction Paper: "What I Learned about Sound and Nonverbal Messages as Communication Enhancers and Detractors" Clinical Performance Evaluations Classroom/Laboratory Participation

OBJECTIVE	SUGGESTED CONTENT	SAMPLE LEARNING ACTIVITIES	SAMPLE EVALUATION STRATEGIES
		Classroom and Laboratory Exercises: Pictures of Well and Compromised Elderly: React to the feelings conveyed in pictures and obtain student responses to each picture... discuss commonalities and differences across responses • Picture Faces: Show pictures of faces and have students identify on paper the feeling most frequently associated with the presented image: • Discuss how nonverbal communications convey feelings Triads: Communicator attempts to convey a randomly-selected, emotionally laden message without using words; the listener attempts to interpret the message; the evaluator observes the communication skills of both and the success o f the effort.	Classroom/Laboratory Participation Clinical Performance Evaluations

OBJECTIVE	SUGGESTED CONTENT	SAMPLE LEARNING ACTIVITIES	SAMPLE EVALUATION STRATEGIES
Physical Changes As Impediments to Communication Identify physical changes that frequently occur and distort sensory processes of communication	Hearing Losses Visual problems Sensory decrease Language Problems (including aphasia and general decline in use of language)	Laboratory Exercise: General Experience of Loss: For one afternoon students will wear glasses that are petroleum jelly smeared or cellophane covered, ears blocked with cotton or padded earmuffs, and hands covered with gloves or mittens: • Discuss feelings experienced during this experience with classmates (Identify responses as those from "normal" and "compromised" positions • List day to day activities that will be impeded by sensory loss Experiencing Loss of Speech: Handout on language problems with definitions and examples Students participate in requesting and completing one routine activity of daily living without speech Students watch a brief video while experiencing at least 1 physical change impeding communication and report back on the experienced difficulties	Reaction Paper: "Personal Responses to Sensory Losses" Laboratory Demonstrations and Class Participation Clinical Evaluations

OBJECTIVE	SUGGESTED CONTENT	SAMPLE LEARNING ACTIVITIES	SAMPLE EVALUATION STRATEGIES
Cognitive Compromises in Communication From Diseases Common in the Elderly: Recognize the basic types of dementia or cognitive loss that impede communication	Dementias: Signs, symptoms, and progression • Multi-infarct • Alzheimer's type • Others (Diabetes, Parkinson's, Binswangers) Relating to Persons with Cognitive Loss from Disease • Sundowning (understanding the problem, home management, and when professional intervention necessary)	Classroom/Laboratory Exercise: Develop "progression -lines" for Alzheimer's and Multi-infarct dementias Field Trip: Visit a facility for persons with dementia and have a conversation with one of the compromised residents Students document responses to experience and compare experiences Internet Assignment: Obtain at least 1 website resource for care and communication of elder patients with Dementia Case Studies and Small Group Discussion: Persons with various types of dementia • Identify the probable type and effective and ineffective communication strategies • What can I expect from a person with dementia?	Reaction paper: 1) What is the Best Way For Me To Communicate with a Person with Dementia? 2) "What Should I Avoid When Communicating with a Person with Dementia? Paper: Case Study Report from Clinical Practicum Clinical Performance evaluations Oral Presentations and Class Discussion: Case Studies

OBJECTIVE	SUGGESTED CONTENT	SAMPLE LEARNING ACTIVITIES	SAMPLE EVALUATION STRATEGIES
Adapt basic communication skills for those elders who are cognitively and/or physically compromised	Hearing Loss: • Signs/Symptoms (diminished hearing, diminished acuity) • Aids for hearing (hearing aids, volume assisted phones, head sets for amplification) • Problems related to hearing loss (dangers, misinterpretation, difficulty communicating with others) Vision Loss and Frequent Eye Disorders: • Signs/Symptoms • Aids (glasses, drops, surgery) • Problems related to visual loss (poor "distance" judgement, difficulty with small print or lengthy text) Environmental Assistance for Losses: • Colors, sound, light • Letter boards or paper and pencil for those who cannot speak	Role Play and Class Discussion: Students participate in role play of hearing loss and visual impairment using an assistive device Team Assignment: House floor plans provided with instructions to make environment "more friendly" for a cognitively impaired elder (rationale for choices to be included)	Class Participation Clinical Evaluations Oral Presentations and Class Discussion : Team solutions and rationale to floor plan adjustments

OBJECTIVE	SUGGESTED CONTENT	SAMPLE LEARNING ACTIVITIES	SAMPLE EVALUATION STRATEGIES
Recognize and accommodate psychological issues in the elderly impaired person.	Depression • Prevalence signs/symptoms • Elder Suicide • Caregiver Responses Anxiety • Manifestations and Management (Home management and when professional intervention necessary) Dependence vs. Independence Resources for Elder Psychological Issues: (senior centers, mental health agencies, psychologists, psychiatrists)	Case Studies: Assess for signs of psychological impairment and propose appropriate intervention strategies Small Group Discussion: Describe the impact of depression/anxiety on the life of an elderly person. Handouts: Emotional problems common among the elderly. Guest Speaker: Geriatric Psychologist discussion on mental health issues of the elderly	Clinical Performance Evaluations Reaction Paper: "What To Do When My Client is Depressed or Anxious

OBJECTIVE	SUGGESTED CONTENT	SAMPLE LEARNING ACTIVITIES	SAMPLE EVALUATION STRATEGIES
Understand possible behavior problems that can occur in a compromised elder Demonstrate awareness of effective interventions for elder behavior problems	Sundowning Reversal of Sleep-wake Cycle Catastrophizing Paraphrenia Physical Aggression Withdrawal Wandering	Video Tapes Instruction: Understanding and managing problematic behaviors in the elderly Class Discussion and Role Play: Case examples of problem elder behaviors and management Handouts: On communicating with elders experiencing behavior problems Field Trip: Visit a facility that has a specialty unit for behavioral disturbances of the elderly and observe staff interactions with clients	Reaction Paper: "Identify Interventions that Would be Easy and Difficult for You to Adopt in the Home Management of Elder Behavior Problems" Pre-post Clinical Conference Reaction Paper: "Describe Observed Examples of Effective Communication and Management of Elder Problem Behaviors and Application to the Home Setting"

Assessment

OBJECTIVE	SUGGESTED CONTENT	SAMPLE LEARNING ACTIVITIES	SAMPLE EVALUATION STRATEGIES
Elder Needs: Describe activities of daily living (ADLs) and instru-mental activities of daily living (IADLs) needed by elder persons living at home	Facts and Fiction: Elder Home Needs Functional ADLs*: Feeding, Bathing, Dressing, Continence, Toileting, Ambulation Instrumental ADLs*: Transportation, Shopping, Meal Preparation, Telephone Use, Housekeeping, Laundry *Stanley and Beare (1999). p. 79	Case Presentations: Identification of ADLs and IADLs Journal Reflection: Personal assessment of own achievements based on Maslow's Hierarchy of Needs	Quizzes and Case Exemplars: ADLs and IADLs Laboratory Demonstrations Clinical Performance Evaluations: Formative and Summative
Use assessment of client's activities of daily living to establish status on Maslow's Hierarchy of Needs	Physical Self-Maintenance Scale* * Lawton and Brody, 1969	Film and Class Discussion: "On Golden Pond"	Comprehensive Service Plans
Develop a thorough service plan with prioritized inter-ventions based on Maslow's Hierarchy of Needs	Maslow's Hierarchy of Needs	Laboratory/Clinical Demonstration: Providing basic care to healthy and minimally-compromised elders	Pre-post Clinical Conference

OBJECTIVE	SUGGESTED CONTENT	SAMPLE LEARNING ACTIVITIES	SAMPLE EVALUATION STRATEGIES
Recognize the multiple factors influencing self and other's perceptions of the elderly	Normal and Abnormal Aging Processes of the Elderly:	Small Group Discussion: Describe personal changes that have occurred across lifespan	Journal Reflection: Personal attitudes and beliefs regarding the elderly
Identify the impact of aging on one's ability to sustain basic needs as defined by Maslow's Hierarchy of Needs	Social/Emotional Physical Memory and Judgment Changes Time and Energy Management Ageism: Definition and Cultural Manifestations	Small Group Discussion and Oral Presentation: Changes Over a 20 Year Period: (4, 24, 44, 64, 84) Small Group and Class Discussion: Positive and negative class reactions to well and compromised elder neighbors Clinical Simulation and Community Exercise: For 3 hours re- experience being elderly and use a "Buddy" system to: • Prepare and cook a hot meal • Use the telephone • Use a cane, walker, or wheelchair and walk at least 3 city blocks, crossing the street at least twice • Access public transportation and shop in different stores (i.e., grocery, clothing, special interest shops) Class Discussion: Re-experiencing being elderly in the community	Group Presentation Reaction Paper: "The Experience of Being Elderly"

OBJECTIVE	SUGGESTED CONTENT	SAMPLE LEARNING ACTIVITIES	SAMPLE EVALUATION STRATEGIES
Identify scope of required and potential care services needed by client and family member(s) for continued home maintenance	Model Template: Comprehensive Service Care Assessment: • Physical and social/emotional health • Religious and political beliefs/ practices • Family values, customs, and traditions • Cultural and ethnic influences • Agency and Internet Resources	Case Examples Class Discussions Handouts and PowerPoint Presentation Develop service care plan for assigned elder clients Develop a comprehensive service care plan for 1 well and 1 compromised elder client	Service plans are relevant for assigned clients with completeness of plan increasing as trainee progresses in curriculum Service plan readily available for use by Gericare Specialist© instructor, client, family members, and other health care service providers
Describe the importance of family in sustaining or sabotaging elder health	Family Roles (i.e. martyr, clown) and Values (i.e., religious or political beliefs, customs and traditions, "Living Will") Genogram Family Development: Tasks and Tools or Resources Across the Life Cycle	Personal Assessment: Own role(s) in family of origin or adoption and marriage (if appropriate) Class or Small group discussion: Elder family tasks and tools	Genogram of current nuclear family Clinical Decision-making and Clinical Evaluations

OBJECTIVE	SUGGESTED CONTENT	SAMPLE LEARNING ACTIVITIES	SAMPLE EVALUATION STRATEGIES
	Actions/Behaviors of Healthy Families	Clinical Exemplars: Healthy Families and Healthy Elders	Clinical Performance
		Case Study Presentations and Class Discussion: Healthy and unhealthy family behaviors	Paper: Personal Assessment of Healthy Family Behaviors
Client Orientation: Collect baseline information which is assessed and documented on a routine schedule or as indicated by sudden change	"Mini Mental Exams* (i.e., time, place, person) * PEPP (2001,Summer)	Laboratory Demonstrations: Practice mini-mental assessments on classmates in laboratory	Mini-Mental Exams are complete, accurate, and routinely conducted on clients
	Mobility, Gait, and Speech Patterns	Clinical Application: Complete a mini-mental exam on 1 well and 1 compromised elder with class discussion of findings and interpretations	
	Social Appropriateness: Group and Personal Interactions		

OBJECTIVE	SUGGESTED CONTENT	SAMPLE LEARNING ACTIVITIES	SAMPLE EVALUATION STRATEGIES
Community Assessment: Complete a comprehensive, individualized community assessment	Techniques of Therapeutic Client Interviewing Areas for Possible Inclusion: • Senior Centers, Respite and Day Care Facilities • Nearby Services: Pharmacies, Health Care Agencies • Emergency Numbers: Fire, Police, • Utility Companies: Water, Heat/Air Conditioning, Electric • Community Services: Senior Hotlines, Shelters, Drug/Alcohol Treatment Facility • Churches • Educational and Recreational Resources	Determine Community Resources: Review telephone book listings of local, state, and federal services/resources Practice Interview Techniques: With peers in laboratory and complete an interview on a well and compromised elder client Collect and Organize Community Information: An Elder Home Care Resource Manual • Types /kinds of resources/services • Costs of services • Access numbers, hours of operation, and contact person • Referral processes • Resource/Service address Create a Family Member List for Clients: Access, availability, and telephone number(s) of all family member resources	Emergency numbers and contact persons available by all client telephones Resource manual for clients readily available, stored in an "easy access" location, and includes: • Emergency numbers (fire, police, utilities) • Government and religious services • Community-based elder services (hotlines, shelters, drug/alcohol treatment centers

Personal Care

OBJECTIVE	SUGGESTED CONTENT	SAMPLE LEARNING ACTIVITIES	SAMPLE EVALUATION STRATEGIES
Personal Hygiene Maintain independence in tasks of personal hygiene for as long as possible	Personal Hygiene Tasks and Important Areas of Assessment: • Bathing/Showering: Skin Integrity and Body Odor • Hand Washing: Cracks, Abrasions, Sores, Discoloration • Foot Care: Circulation/Edema • Teeth/Denture Care: Breath Odor, Gum or Tooth Disease • Hair/Wig and Shaving Care: Scalp Diseases, Lice • Dressing and Clothing Selection/Cleanliness: Clothing Appropriate for Proposed Activities and Weather, Garment Odor and Condition	Role Playing, Laboratory, and Clinical Experiences: • Recognize "Good Practices" and demonstrate all skills for well and compromised clients • Organizes necessary equipment for easy access Maintain client privacy, dignity, and safety when undressed • Demonstrate complete bed bath, sponge and tub bath, and showering • Demonstrate transferring clients to bath/shower from wheelchair • Demonstrate proper oral hygiene and shampooing practices	Laboratory Demonstrations of Safe Practice Successful Completion of Skills Check List Clinical Performance evaluations

OBJECTIVE	SUGGESTED CONTENT	SAMPLE LEARNING ACTIVITIES	SAMPLE EVALUATION STRATEGIES
	Proper Body Mechanics and Bed Positioning: • Proper Lifting Techniques (Review) • Body Range of Motion Exercises (Active and Passive) • Pillow Positioning in Bed and Chairs	Laboratory/Clinical Demonstration: Practice turning, lifting, and ROM techniques on peers in laboratory and on clients	Laboratory Demonstrations Clinical Performance
Toileting: Describe age-related changes in bladder and bowel function Increase awareness of dietary influence on bladder and bowel function	Normal and Abnormal Changes in the Elderly Types of Incontinence: Stress, Urge, Overflow, and Functional Factors Influencing Incontinence and Constipation: • Fluid Retainers: salt, medications (esp. Prednisone) • Fluid Releasers: caffeine, cranberry juice • Stress, Infection, Surgery/Anesthesia	Maintain and calculate I/O chart on self for 24 hours Lecture, Handouts, Class/Small Group Discussion Dietary Adjustments: Assistance in incontinence/constipation correction Field Trip: (Grocery Store and Own Home): Review food product labels for salt, fat, sugar, and water content (include at least 1 canned soup, 1 frozen vegetable, 1 frozen dinner, 1 dry cereal, and 1 dessert)	Training program interventions: bowel and bladder control

OBJECTIVE	SUGGESTED CONTENT	SAMPLE LEARNING ACTIVITIES	SAMPLE EVALUATION STRATEGIES
	Procedures to re-establish bowel or bladder routine • Proper use and care of urinals and bedpans • Meal Plans (Time schedules, food portions and preferences, dietary changes)		Sample meal and care plans developed to reduce: Bladder incontinence Bowel incontinence Constipation
Identify risk factors for incontinence/constipation	**DRIP** Mnemonic: **D**elirium or **D**ementia **R**etention **I**ncontinence **P**harmacology* *Eliopoulos (1999) **DIAPERS** **D**elirium or **D**ementia **I**nfection **A**tropic Vaginitis **P**hysiologic or **P**harmacologic Causes **E**ndocrine Conditions **R**estricted Mobility **S**tool impaction		

OBJECTIVE	SUGGESTED CONTENT	SAMPLE LEARNING ACTIVITIES	SAMPLE EVALUATION STRATEGIES
Food Preparation and Eating/Drinking Habits: Identify how foods/fluids, personal preferences, and eating habits contribute to physical, social, and psychological elder health	Food Selection/Preferences Meal Preparation, Portions, and Presentation Table Setting and Table Etiquette	Create a 7 day menu plan for the following diets : • Well Elderly • Diabetic, 1000 calories/day • Low salt/low fat • Low cholesterol • Few or No Teeth	Meal plans are accurate, utilize seasonal foods and client preferences, and remain within client budget
Recognize normal nutritional/dietary changes in the elderly	Food Properties: Vitamin & Mineral Deficiencies Protein/Fat/Carbohydrate Needs Water Requisites Physiologic Changes: Changes in Eye and Taste		Clinical Evaluations Client Satisfaction
Recognize factors that influence appetite in the elderly	Appetite Depressants: Medication Drug/Alcohol Intake Grief/Depression, Infectious Disease/Cancer High Carbohydrate/Sugar Intake Food Color, Odors & Appearance	Describe strategies to increase appetite and limit intake of harmful substances Use the Nutrition Screening Tool for Older Adults* to conduct a nutrition screening on an elder person *Nat'l Institute on Aging	

OBJECTIVE	SUGGESTED CONTENT	SAMPLE LEARNING ACTIVITIES	SAMPLE EVALUATION STRATEGIES
Medication Management: Administer prescribed and over-the-counter medications safely	Appetite Stimulants: Medication Exercise Family/Social Gatherings Other: Presence/Absence of Teeth Physiological Changes (i.e., Slow Food Digestion, Eye/Hand Control) Personal Preferences Five Rights of Medication Administration: right name, right time, right dose, right route, right medication Important Medication Issues: • Medication storage and disposal of out-dated medications	Laboratory Demonstration: • Safe administration of tablets (crushed and uncrushed), capsules, liquids, drops, suppositories, inhalers • Accurate medication calculations	Laboratory Demonstration: Safe Medication Administration Clinical Performance Evaluations

OBJECTIVE	SUGGESTED CONTENT	SAMPLE LEARNING ACTIVITIES	SAMPLE EVALUATION STRATEGIES
Recognize common drug reactions or administration errors in elder clients: • Aspirin with Coumadin or Heparin • Vitamin C and Penicillin derivatives • Over/Under Dosing • Use of Outdated Prescriptions	• Anticipated results • Potential side effects • Interactions with other medications, foods/substances • Over/Under Dosing Emergency Procedures Reporting Drug Misuse Professional Liability, Recording and Responsibilities	Case studies: Include examples of untoward effects Clinical Application: Weekly chart of routine medications and time of administration	
Pain Management: Differentiate between symptoms of acute and chronic pain	PQRST Mnemonic*: Provocation/Palliation Quality Region Severity Timing *Wold (1999) FACES Rating Scale for Pain Intensity*	Journal Entry: Personal experiences with pain management (include both positive and negative experiences)	Clinical Decision-making Pre-post Clinical Conference

OBJECTIVE	SUGGESTED CONTENT	SAMPLE LEARNING ACTIVITIES	SAMPLE EVALUATION STRATEGIES
Provide safe and cost effective pain relief	Types of Pain Medication OTC (Over the Counter) or Prescription • Analgesic or Narcotic: anticipated response, side effects, interactions with other medications • Recognize contraindications (i.e., shallow/difficult breathing, recent antacid ingestion, interaction potential with other medications/alcohol) Complementary Therapies (i.e., massage, imagery, breath control, water)	5 Rights of Medication Administration (Review) Field Trip: Count the number of pain management products available in a local grocery or supermarket and pharmacy/drug store Identify 10 common medications taken for pain by the elderly and: • Provide a list of projected monthly costs for each medication • Provide a list of likely PRN doses and time of day for administration Discuss alternatives to medication management of pain and associate selected alternatives with common experiences of pain (i.e., lower light and less visual/auditory stimulation for headaches)	

OBJECTIVE	SUGGESTED CONTENT	SAMPLE LEARNING ACTIVITIES	SAMPLE EVALUATION STRATEGIES
First Aid and Sentinel Events: Identify common life-threatening crises for the elderly	Common Elder Crises: • Stroke (CVA) and impending symptoms (TIA) • Pulmonary Edema • Septicemia • Seizures • GI Bleeding • Drug Toxicities	Managed Risk Contract* *Brennan, 1997	Risk Management Contract completed, as necessary, for assigned clients Ability to prioritize activities in case of elder crisis or accident
Respond effectively to common elder accidents	Common Elder Accidents: • Falls • Hypothermia • Heat Exhaustion/ Cold Exposure • Burns • Bleeding: Abrasions, punctures, • Lacerations, and cuts • Poisoning: Ingested, bites	Sterile/Unsterile Dressing Changes Hot/Cold Applications Pressure Applications	Laboratory Demonstrations Clinical Performance

OBJECTIVE	SUGGESTED CONTENT	SAMPLE LEARNING ACTIVITIES	SAMPLE EVALUATION STRATEGIES
	Eight Steps in Emergency Action* *Foundation for Hospice And Homecare, 1990 Sentinel Events: • Suicide/Homicide • Rape • Malnutrition • Unexplained Absence Beyond 24 hrs. • Elder Abuse	Case exemplars: Elder Emergencies Class Discussion: Responsibilities in Sentinel Events to: • Self • Client • Family • Agency	
Infection Control Identify appropriate health promotion and disease prevention activities to abate infectious diseases in the elderly and protect self	Infectious Disease Transmission: Routes, Vehicles, and Vectors of Common Infectious Diseases Infectious Disease Information: • Respiratory Diseases: Flu, pneumonia, TBA • GI Distress: Diarrhea, Nausea and Vomiting	Class Discussion: Identify common routes of infectious disease transmission in the elderly Review personal and client immunization records for currency Film: CDC recommendations for standard precautions: • Hand washing • Eye, mouth, clothing protection	Clinical applications of CDC recommendations (Standard Precautions) Demonstrate appropriate disinfecting procedures in skills laboratory and clinical setting

OBJECTIVE	SUGGESTED CONTENT	SAMPLE LEARNING ACTIVITIES	SAMPLE EVALUATION STRATEGIES
Safely dispose of waste materials	Infectious Disease Management: • Cleaning Agents: Alcohol, H_2O_2, Bleach, Vinegar • Isolation Techniques Disposal Techniques: • Body Wastes • Contaminated Articles • Disposable Equipment	Laboratory Demonstration: Proper wearing of protective equipment (mask, gown, eye wear) Laboratory Demonstration: Proper "bagging" technique and disposal of body wastes	Return Laboratory Demonstration Clinical Performance

Home Management

OBJECTIVE	SUGGESTED CONTENT	SAMPLE LEARNING ACTIVITIES	SAMPLE EVALUATION STRATEGIES
Food Purchase, Storage, Preparation, and Presentation: Identify strategies that preserve the nutritional value and food palatability for the elderly	Fresh vs. Canned or Frozen Foods Cooking Methods (Baking, Boiling/Steaming, Micro-Waving, Fresh)	Contrast menu costs, cooking methods, seasonal availability, and preferences between fresh, frozen, and canned foods for 1 week for 1 well and 1 compromised elder	Submitted Weekly Meal Plans Clinical Performance Evaluations

OBJECTIVE	SUGGESTED CONTENT	SAMPLE LEARNING ACTIVITIES	SAMPLE EVALUATION STRATEGIES
Observe food purchasing strategies of elderly	Coupons and Other Purchasing Practices	Field Trip: Visit a local grocery store • Compare elder practices with other adults • Identify ease of product reach and aisle access for wheelchair/motor cart • List number of products available for diarrhea and constipation management	Reaction Paper: "What I Learned About Elder Products in the Grocery Store"
Safe Environment: Identify key factors in design of a safe elder home environment	Fall Prevention: • Scatter rug removal • Grab bars instillation • Spill clean up • Clothing and shoe storage in appropriate places; • Hazardous electrical cord removal Fire Safety: • Limit number of electrical devices plugged into common plug or extension cord	"Safe Home" Evaluation: Own and elder residence Fall-Risk Prevention Assessment Case presentations and role playing: Safe and unsafe home/neighborhood environments Smoke Detector Inventory: Own home and client homes	Paper: Safe Home Evaluation Studies (accurate and comprehensive) Clinical Performance evaluations

OBJECTIVE	SUGGESTED CONTENT	SAMPLE LEARNING ACTIVITIES	SAMPLE EVALUATION STRATEGIES
	Appliances turned off after use (i.e., stove, washer/dryer); smoke detectors installed at all house levels and batteries changed 2xs/yr (Halloween and Easter) Utility Maintenance: • Water, sewage, and electricity maintained in working order • Air conditioning and heating systems operational and cleaned periodically Emergency Preparedness: • Emergency alerting devices & informal alert system* (i.e., neighbors, postal workers) • Escape routes established from all floor levels • Emergency telephone numbers easily accessible	Class Discussion: Location(s) and procedure(s) in own and elder's home for: • Shutoff controls for gas, water and electricity • Location of emergency numbers for family, utility services, and community resources (i.e., fire, police, EMT) Emergency Preparedness: • Identify situation, needs, and resources • Prioritize activities for elder client and self	

OBJECTIVE	SUGGESTED CONTENT	SAMPLE LEARNING ACTIVITIES	SAMPLE EVALUATION STRATEGIES
Demonstrate safe utilization of assistive/adaptive devices	• Bio-terrorist/natural disaster considerations • Mobility Devices: Wheelchairs, walkers, canes, scooters, crutches • Overhead bed trapeze • Assistive/Adaptive Devices: Household utensils (i.e., eating, dressing, sewing) Patient Bill of Rights Reviewed	Laboratory Demonstrations: Ambulate within area on wheelchair/scooter Field Trip: Maneuver throughout own home with cane, walker, and crutches Case Presentations of Bill of Rights Violations	
Recognize signs of actual and potential elder abuse/neglect	Common Precursors of Elder Abuse/Neglect: • Alcohol/Drug Abuse • Marital or Financial Problems • Lack of Social Support Systems • Elder Incontinence or Confusion • Marked change in Functional Status		

Additional home managment topics necessary for curricular development: housekeeping skills, environmental infection control, transportation and travel considerations, time and financial managwment issues.

References

Allen-Burge, R., A.B. Stevens and L.D. Burgio. 1999. Effective behavioral interventions for decreasing dementia-related challenging behaviors in nursing homes. *International Journal of Geriatric Psychiatry*, 14, 213-232.

American Association of Retired Persons. 1991. *Aging America: Trends and protection, A report to the U.S. Senate Special Commission on Aging*. Washington, D.C.: U.S. Government Printing Office.

Atherton, J.S. 2002. *Learning and teaching: Knowles' andragogy*. Retrieved January 28, 2003 from dmu.ac.uk~jamesa/learning/know lesa.htm.

Bengston, V.L. and T.M. Murray. 1993. "Justice" across generations: Sociological perspectives on the life course and reciprocities over time. In L.E. Cohen, ed. *Justice across generations: What does it mean?* Washington, D.C.: Public Policy Institute of the American Association of Retired Persons.

Bliezner, R.and J.M.Ally. 1990. Family caregiving for the family. *Family Relations*, 39, 97-102.

Bloom, B.S., B.M. Bertram and D.R. Krathwohl. 1964. *Taxonomy of educational objectives*. New York: David McKay.

Boyle, E. 1981. *Planning better programs*. New York: McGraw Hill.

Bransford, J.D. and N.J. Vye. 1989. A perspective on cognitive research and its implications for instruction. In L.B. Resnick and L.E. Kloper, eds. *1989 Yearbook: Current cognitive research:* 173-205. Alexandria, VA: The Virginia Association for Supervision and Curriculum Development.

Breish, S.L. 1999, October. Communicating with the elderly depends on listening skills. *The American Academy of Orthopaedic Surgeons Bulletin*. Retrieved February 28, 2003 from http://www.aaos.org/wordhtml/bulletin/oct99/commun4.htm.

Brennan, B. 1997, September/October. Community resource assessment and documentation are the keys to an efficient parish nurse program. *Healing Ministry*, 4(5): 37-39.

Brennan, B. 1997. Newcomer to Philadelphia appreciative of SPARC program. *SPARC second quarter report: Together we can prevent stroke*. Harrisburgh, PA: KePRO.

Brody, E.M., P.T. Johnsen, M.C. Fulcomer and A.M. Lang. 1983. Women's changing roles and help to elderly patients: Attitudes of three generations of women. *Journal of Gerontology, 38, 597-606.*

Brubaker, T.H. 1990. *Family relations in later life.* Beverly Hills, CA: Sage.

Burgio, L.D., R. Allen-Burge, D.L. Roth, M.S. Bourgeois, K. Dijkstra, J. Gerstle, E. Jackson and L. Namkester. 2001. Come talk with me: Improving communication between nursing assistants and nursing home residents during caring routines. *The Gerontologist, 41*, 449-460.

Capps, R. 1994, February. *Health and poverty in San Antonio: A profile of needs and services.* San Antonio, Texas: Partnership for Hope.

Cicerelli, V.G. 1990. Family support in relation to health problems of the elderly. In T.H. Brubaker, ed. *Family relationships in later life:* 212-228. Beverly Hills, CA: Sage.

Cox, E.O. and R.J. Parsons. 1994. *Empowerment-oriented social work practice with the elderly.* Pacific Grove, CA: Brooks/Cole.

Crown, W.H., D.A. Ahlburg and M. MacAdam. 1995. The demographic and employment characteristics of home care aides: A comparison of nursing home aides, hospital aides, and other workers. *The Gerontologist, 35*(2), 162-170.

Dellman-Jenkins, M., K.V. Hofer and J. Chebra. 1992. Eldercare in the 1990s: Challenges and supports for educating families. *Educational Gerontology, 18*(8), 775-784.

Eliopoulos, C. 1999. *Manual of Gerontologic Nursing.* (2nd ed.): 109-111. Philadelphia, PA: Mosby.

Epstein, B.A. and V. Koening. 1990, Fall. Education for elderly care giving. *Journal of Extension.* Retrieved February 16, 2003 from http://www.joe.org/joe/1990fall/a1.html.

Family Liason Office 2003. *Caring for elderly parents.* Retrieved February 27, 2003 from http://www.state.gov/m/dghr/flo/rsrcs/pubs/2048.htm.

Feldman, P., A. Sapienza and N. Kline. 1990. *Who cares for them? Workers, worklife problems, and reforms in the home care industry.* New York: Greenwood Press.

Filinson, R. 1994. An evaluation of a gerontological training program for nursing assistants. *The Gerontologist, 34*(6), 839-841.

Fisher, L.R. and N.N. Eustis. 1988. DRGs and family care for the elderly. *The Gerontologist, 28, 383-389.*

Flarey, D.L. (n.d.). *Legal and ethical issues in case management: Course materials.* Nashville, TN: Heritage Professional Education.

Foshay, A.W. 1990, Autumn. The curriculum matrix: Transcendence and mathematics. *Curriculum,* 36-46.

Foundation for Hospice and Homecare. 1990. *A model curriculum and teaching guide for the instruction of the homemaker-home health aide.* Washington, DC.

Fodor, J.T. and G.T. Dalis. 1974. *Health instruction: Theory and application.* (2nd ed.). Philadelphia, PA: Lea and Febiger

Gelfand, D.E. 1993. *The aging network.* New York: Springer.

Grieve, D. 2001. *A handbook for adjunct/part-time faculty and teachers of adults.* (4th ed.). Washington, DC: Library of Congress.

Haught, B.J. 1998. An overview of home health and hospice care patients: 1996 National Home Health and Hospice Survey. *Advance data from vital statistics and health statistics, #297.* Hyattsville, MD: National Center for Health Statistics.

Hunter, S. 1992. Adult daycare: Promoting quality of life for the elderly. *Journal of Gerontological Nursing,* 12(2), 17-20.

Kutner, N.G., M.G. Ory, M.G., D.I. Baker, K.B. Schechtmen, M.C. Hornbrook and C.D. Mulrow. 1992. Measuring the quality of life of the elderly in health promotion clinical trials. *Public Health Reports* 107(5), 530-539.

Lawton, M.P. and E.M. Brody. 1999. Assessment of older people: Self-maintaining and instrumental activities of daily living. *The Gerontologist, 9,* 179-186.

Leader, S. 1991. *Medicare's home health benefit: Eligibility, utilization, and expenditures.* Washington, DC: Public Policy Institute, American Association of Retired Persons.

Maloney, D. and R. Shippee-Rice. 1994. Training family caregivers of older adults: A program model for community nurses. *Journal of Community Health Nursing. 11(2), 71-77.*

Mezey, M. 1996. Challenges in providing care for persons with complex chronic illness. In R.H. Binstock, L.E. Cluff, and O. von Merix, eds. *The future of long-term care:* 119-142. Baltimore, MD: Johns Hopkins University Press.

National Screening Initiative. 1991. *Determine your nutritional health.* Washington, DC: National Council on Aging.

Ornstein, A. and F. Hemkins. 1993. *Curriculum design: Curriculum foundation, principles, and theory:* 232-262. (2nd ed.). Boston: Allyn and Bacon.

Pace University 1998, October. Tipsheet: *Overcoming communication breakdowns with the elderly.* Retrieved February 19, 2003 from http://appserve.pace.edu/newsboard/wwwboard/1998/messages/10.ht ml.

PEEP (n.d.). Personal Hygiene and Assistance with Tasks of Daily Living. In *PEPP Program Literature.* Doylestown, PA.

Philadelphia Corporation for Aging. 1996, May. *Older Philadelphians: Needs, services, and future directions.* Philadelphia, PA, Author.

Rankin, E. 1990. Caregiver stress and the elderly: a familial perspective. *Journal of Gerontological Social Work.* 15(1/2), 57-72.

Richman, J. 1989. Unfinished business may make poor caregivers. *The Gerontologist,* 29, 579.

Riordan, R. and S. Saltzer. 1992. Burnout prevention among health care providers working with the terminally ill: A literature review. *Omega,* 25(1), 17-24.

Saylor, J.G., W.M. Alexander and A.J. Lewis. 1981. *Planning for better teaching and learning.* New York: Rinehart.

Scharlach, A.1984. Caregiving and employment: Competing or complimentary roles? *The Gerontologist, 34(3), 378-385.*

Short, P. and J. Leon. 1990. Use of home and community services by persons ages 65 and older with functional disabilities. *National medical expenditure survey research findings 5.* Rockville, MD: Agency for Health Care Policy and Research, U.S. Public Health Service.

Silverstione, B. and A. Buracck-Weiss. 1983. *Social work practice with the frail elderly and their families.* Springfiled, IL: Charles C. Thomas.

Squire, A. 2002. *Health and wellbeing for older people.* Barlbiere Tindall, Edinburg: England.

Stanley, M. and P.G. Beare. 1995. Health protection from a body systems approach. *Gerontological Nursing: A Health Promotion/Protection Approach.* 91-190. Philadelphia, PA: F.A. *Davis.*

Surpin, R. 1988. The current status of the paraprofessional in home care. *Caring,* 7(4), 4-9.

Taba, H. 1962. *Curriculum development: Theory and practice.* New York: Harcourt.

Tynan, C. and J. Cardea. 1987, October. Home health hazard assessment. *Gerontological Nursing,* 13(10, 25-27.

U.S. Census Bureau. 1990. *Census population and housing.* U.S. Census Bureau, Washington, D.C.: U.S. Government Printing Office.

U.S. House of representatives. 1994. *Report 103-156, U.S. Departments of Labor, Health and Human Services, Education, and related agencies appropriations bill:* 11. Washington, D.C.: U.S. Government Printing Office.

U.S. House of Representatives 1998. *Developments in aging: A report of the special commission on aging.* The 101st Congress, Washington, D.C.: U.S. Government Printing Office.

U.S. Senate Special Committee. 1992. *Developments in aging, 1986: Part I.* Washington, D.C.: U.S. Government Printing Office.

Weil, A. 2002, September. Ten things everyone should know about welfare reform. *Family focus on welfare reform: II.* Minneapolis, MN: National Council on Family Relations.

Wold, G. H. 1999. *Cognition and perception: Basic gerontologic nursing.* (2nd ed.). Philadelphia: Mosby.

Helpful Web Site Addresses:

Aging:	
Administration on Aging (AOA)	
Directory of Websites	www.aoa.gov/aoa/stats/profile
	www.aoa.gov/aoa/stats/statlink.html
Quick Index	www.aoa.dhhs.gov/research.html
Practitioner Resource	www.aoa.dhhs.gov/practice/default.htm
National Institute on Aging	www.aoa.dhhs.gov
International Year for Older Persons 1999	www.un.org/esa/socdev/iyop/index.html
National Council on Aging	www.ncoa.org
National Center for Health Statistics	www.cdc.gov/nchswww/default.htm
Physical Activity and Health: A Report of the Surgeon General	www.cdc.gov/nocdphp
Statistical Information on Older Persons	www.aoa.dhhs.gov/aoa/stats/statpage.html
Alzheimer's Disease:	
Alzheimer's Association	www.alz.org
Alzheimer's Disease Education and Referral Center	www.alzheimers.org

Arthritis:	
Arthritis Foundation	www.arthritis.org
American College of Rheumatology	www.rheumatology.org
Osteoarthritis Research Society	www.hypercon.com/evolve/oars.htm
Elder Care Services	www.longtermcarelink.net/state_programs3.html
Eyes:	
American Society of Cataract and Refractive Surgery	www.ascrs.org
National Eye Institute	www.nei.nih.gov
Health Insurance Consumer Guide	www.hiaa.org
Law for Seniors	www.seniorlaw.com
Nutrition:	
Nutrition Screening Initiative	www.aafp.org/nsi/index.html

Editorial Commentary

℘℃ℜ

Nieli Langer & Terry Territo

Games are experiential activities that have gained acceptance across the disciplines, abilities, and at all levels of education. A game is an activity carried out by individuals who may cooperate or compete in seeking to achieve specific objectives and who follow particular rules and operate within particular parameters. An instructional game is designed to elicit specific learning outcomes. Games set the stage for a mock world with specific rules that apply and guide the players. Participants are competing against one another or are working together to defeat a common barrier. An effective instructional game has a clear ending established by a specific occurrence or set or rules. When the self-esteem of learners is low or fragile, games may be used to reinforce a new skill. The greatest appeal of games as a training technique is their interactivity. The opportunity for each player to learn by doing and have fun makes games an invaluable method of instruction in the instructor's menu of instructional strategies. The most critical component of games is the debriefing period following the activity. The instructor/facilitator should be prepared with a list of questions to guide participants in discovering what they have learned through the process. It is through the debriefing that the game experience is examined and turned to learning. Participants should have the opportunity to express and analyze their emotions. Games help adult students grasp the total course content and test their individual attitudes, behavioral styles, and performance expertise (Horn 1977).

The field of aging education has, in recent years, been fortunate to have aging/education professionals create and disseminate games that are valuable educational strategies to be used in varied venues. These games may be an asset, too, in the training of home care employees.

References

Families and Aging: Dilemmas and Decisions Extension Business Office, Oregon State University, Ballard Hall 125, Corvallis, Oregon 97331-3604; 541-737-4131. This game provides greater understanding of family dynamics and gives participants a better basis for working more effectively with families.

Sex and Aging: A Game of Awareness and Interaction (same as above). The game provides participants a non-threatening way to discuss sensitive topics relevant to older adults' emotional and sexual needs.

Ensuring Quality Care for Residents and Caregivers. Aging Concerns, 835 Marylhurst Circle, West Linn, Oregon 97068. The game provides participants real-life situations faced by care providers such as the resident who wrongly accuses the provider of stealing money or the family who constantly complains about the care given to their relative.

Horn, R. 1977. *The Guide to Simulations/Games for Education and Training.* Cranford, New Jersey: Didactic Systems, Inc.

EPILOGUE

ಐಲಾ

Nieli Langer & Terry Tirrito

As people mature, they have learning needs that differ from those of children and adolescents. Adult learners take responsibility for their learning, are clear about what they want to learn, and are concerned with the practical applications and implications of learning. Only in adulthood does the individual respond to the challenge of critical reflection of their assumptions, ideologies, and beliefs. Although learners must decide on their own to engage in critical reflection, the potential to provide learner-centered instruction remains with the instructor.

Although instructors perceive adults as being different, these perceptions do not automatically translate into differences in approaches to teaching. Learners' goals and the material to be covered are some of the decisions instructors address before targeting the educational strategies used to realize learning objectives. The instructor who is knowledgeable and motivated, uses a variety of techniques, adapts to meet diverse needs, and emphasizes relevance of class material will be successful.

In order to help all current and future instructors, the editors offer the following guidelines:

Ten Commandments for Educators

1. Thou shalt never try to make another human being exactly like yourself; one is enough.

2. Thou shalt never judge a person's need, or refuse your consideration, solely because of the trouble he causes.

3. Thou shalt not blame heredity nor the environment in general; people can surmount their environments.

4. Thou shalt never give a person up as hopeless or cast him out.

5. Thou shalt try to help everyone become, on the one hand, sensitive and compassionate, and also tough-minded.

6. Thou shalt not steal from any person his rightful responsibilities for determining his own conduct and the consequences thereof.

7. Thou shalt honor anyone engaged in the pursuit of learning and serve well and extend the discipline of knowledge and skill about learning which is our common heritage.

8. Thou shalt have no universal remedies or expect miracles.

9. Thou shalt cherish a sense of humor which may save you from becoming shocked, depressed, or complacent.

10. Thou shalt remember the sacredness and dignity of the calling, and, at the same time, "thou shalt not take thyself too damned seriously."

From *How Adults Learn* by J.R. Kidd © 1973, 1959 by J.R. Kidd. Published by Cambridge The Adult Education Company. Used by permission of Pearson Education, Inc.

EDITORS AND CONTRIBUTORS

Bernice C. Brennan, Ph.D.
Holy Family University
Philadelphia, Pennsylvania

Jane M. Cardea, Ph.D.
Holy Family University
Philadelphia, Pennsylvania

Gil Choi, Ph.D.
College of Social Work
University of South Carolina
Columbia, South Carolina

Julie Miller-Cribbs, Ph.D.
College of Social Work
University of South Carolina
Columbia, South Carolina

Tan Kirby Davis
Consultant, Kirby Resource
    Group
Greenville, South Carolina

Kenneth J. Doka, Ph.D.
College of New Rochelle
New Rochelle, New York

Nina Dubler Katz, M.S.
Consultant
New Rochelle, New York

Nieli Langer, Ph.D.
College of New Rochelle
New Rochelle, New York

Melissa B. Littlefield, Ph.D.
University of Maryland
School of Social Work

Baltimore, Maryland

Jane F. McGarrahan, Ph.D.
St. Michael's Home for the Sisters
Of the Blessed Sacrament
Philadelphia, Pennsylvania

Vicki Murdock, Ph.D.
College of Social Work
University of South Carolina
Columbia, South Carolina

Larry P. Ortiz, Ph.D.
University of Maryland
School of Social Work
Baltimore, Maryland

Terry Tirrito, Ph.D.
College of Social Work
University of South Carolina
Columbia, South Carolina

INDEX